LAW LAW LAW

on the

Internet

The Best Legal Web Sites and More

By Erik J. Heels and
Richard P. Klau

American Bar Association
Law Practice Management Section

Cover design by Lisa Scalise.

Library of Congress Catalog Card Number 98-70596
ISBN 1-57073-553-0

02 01 00 99 98   5 4 3 2 1

Discounts are available for books ordered in bulk. Special consideration is given to state bars, CLE programs, and other bar-related organizations. Inquire at Book Publishing, American Bar Association, 750 N. Lake Shore Drive, Chicago, Illinois 60611.

Contents

About the Authors

Erik and Rick have been working together since 1994 when their "Online" column (now in its 5th year) debuted in the ABA's *Student Lawyer* magazine. In 1996, they pooled their writing and consulting efforts into Red Street Consulting. Most recently, they reviewed all 4,000 law firm Web sites and published reviews of the top 5 percent on the Red Street Web site (http://www.redstreet.com/). Combined, they have more than twenty years of Internet experience. Erik is the Director of Marketing for the Northeast Region of Verio Inc., a national Internet service provider. Rick is the Vice President of Marketing and Development for Trial-Net Inc., which specializes in litigation management intranets.

Erik Heels is a legal technologist and a patent lawyer. From 1992 to 1995, Erik wrote seven editions of his book *The Legal List: Law-Related Resources on the Internet and Elsewhere,* the last two of which were published by Lawyers Cooperative Publishing. He writes the "nothing.but.net" column for the ABA's *Law Practice Management* magazine (http://www.abanet.org/lpm/magazine/nbn/) and regularly speaks about issues related to law and technology. He earned his B.S. in Electrical Engineering from MIT and his J.D. from the University of Maine School of Law. Erik and his wife, Pirjo, live in the Boston area; they have two sons, Samuel and Benjamin, and are expecting their third child in May.

Rick Klau is a graduate of the University of Richmond School of Law. While in law school, Rick founded the *Richmond Journal of Law & Technology* (http://www.richmond.edu/~jolt/), the first student-edited law journal in the world to publish exclusively online (on the Web, LEXIS-NEXIS, and WESTLAW). He is a regular presenter at tradeshows, CLE seminars, and bar association meetings around the country on topics relating to the

Internet and the legal profession. Rick co-authors "Online" with Erik Heels, a monthly column for the American Bar Association's *Student Lawyer* magazine (http://www.abanet.org/lsd/stulawyer/). Rick and his wife, Robin, live in the Boston area where they are celebrating their first year of marriage and their first home.

Erik's Acknowledgments

THIS BOOK WOULD NOT HAVE BEEN possible without the help of many people.

Paula Tsurutani is no longer with the ABA, but she prodded me for over a year to do this book. Beverly Loder was instrumental in getting this book from proposal to print in record time.

Reviewers Jeff Flax, Tim Johnson, and Greg Siskind provided feedback on early drafts and helped shape this book into what it is. The list of meta sites at the beginning of each chapter was Jeff's idea. And Greg reminded us that face-to-face communication is one of the *five* generally accepted ways of communicating with clients today.

And, of course, there's Burgess Allison. Burgess encouraged me to get involved with the Law Practice Management Section several years ago, and I haven't looked back. I am honored to share the pages of *Law Practice Management* magazine with Burgess. In fact, it was my March 1997 "nothing.but.net" column (**http://www.abanet.org/lpm/magazine/nbn/nbn972 .html**)—about how lawlawlaw.com was the only good domain name left— that provided the inspiration for the name of this book. Thanks to Burgess also for reviewing this book and for providing keen insight about which jokes worked and which didn't.

A special thanks to the many lawyers, programmers, and other Web enthusiasts who have published useful information on the Web. Some of these early adopters who were listed in my first book, *The Legal List,* are not, unfortunately, listed here. Because the number of law-related organizations on the Web has grown so rapidly over the past couple of years, it is no longer possible to include all of them in one book. But this book, a compilation with commentary on selected law-related sites, would not have been possible without the hard work of Web enthusiasts who dragged their law firms, publishers, and organizations—sometimes kicking and screaming—onto the Web.

Last, but not least, thanks to my loving and growing family: my wife, Pirjo, and my two boys, Samuel and Benjamin. And I know that Sam will appreciate getting more time on the computer for playing his Arthur and Berenstein Bears CDs!

Thanks, and see you on the Net!

Erik J. Heels
Marlboro, MA

Rick's Acknowledgments

THERE ARE TOO MANY PEOPLE to thank in this space, but several need particular recognition.

Beverly Loder's persistence over the last year in encouraging us to write this book proved invaluable. At several junctures, it appeared that circumstances would intervene and the project would get derailed. Thanks to Beverly's attention, that didn't happen, and for that I'm grateful.

It's always hard to critique your own work, which is why the input from our reviewers Jeff Flax, Tim Johnson, and Greg Siskind was so helpful. Several components of the final product are direct results of their comments.

In many ways, this book is the culmination of a journey that started in my first year of law school. I'm convinced that were it not for the support of Dean Joe Harbaugh at the University of Richmond, I would have not accomplished half of what I did at the University of Richmond. His constant encouragement, and at times wildly optimistic expectations, set a high standard for me that I continue to strive to attain.

On a personal note, none of this would have happened without the support of my parents, who urged me to follow my dreams and not look back. Finally, I am incredibly lucky for the love and support of my wife, Robin, who allowed me to write this on countless nights and weekends right after we returned from our honeymoon. She makes this all worthwhile.

Rick Klau
Maynard, MA

Foreword

OH NO, YOU SAY, ANOTHER INTERNET BOOK! Ah, but those of you who have become converts to using the Internet's information resources and exploiting its marketing power know that the ABA Section of Law Practice Management is in the forefront of publishers on Internet books to assist the practicing lawyer. From the granddaddy of them all, G. Burgess Allison's *The Lawyer's Guide to the Internet,* to *The Lawyer's Guide to Marketing on the Internet* by Gregory Siskind and Timothy Moses, *The Lawyer's Guide to Creating Web Pages* by Kenneth Johnson, *The Internet Fact Finder for Lawyers: How to Find Anything on the Net,* by Joshua Blackman with David Jank, and Burgess Allison's *The Lawyer's Quick Guide to Microsoft Internet Explorer* and *The Lawyer's Quick Guide to Netscape Navigator,* LPM Publishing has brought you the most practical, user-friendly, how-to advice on making the Internet work for the practicing lawyer. As an added bonus, several of these books are supplemented with Web sites to keep them current in the fast-paced, ever-changing cyberworld.

For this book, Erik Heels and Rick Klau have weeded through the thickets of Web sites and other Internet resources to catalog and comment on the most important, most reliable, and most influential law-related sites. This book is not intended to be comprehensive, but to point you toward law-related providers who are making a difference. Mr. Heels, a patent lawyer whose best-seller, *The Legal List: Law-Related Resources on the Internet and Elsewhere,* has been through seven editions since 1992, is also the author of the "nothing.but.net" column in *Law Practice Management* magazine, and with Mr. Klau co-writes "Online," a syndicated column that first appeared in the ABA's *Student Lawyer* magazine. Mr. Klau also founded the *Richmond Journal of Law & Technology,* the first student-edited law journal in the world to publish exclusively online.

Law Law Law on the Internet brings you the best "meta sites," those catalog sites that are vital for legal research and directories that can lead you to other online resources; reviews of content-rich bar association sites; major vendors who publish work of substance (prefererably free) on the Internet; Federal and State agency publishers; full-text law journals; ABA-approved law schools; and (the heart of the book) the *National Law Journal*'s NLJ 250, the legal community's equivalent of the Fortune 500. Scattered alphabetically throughout the chapter are nontraditional, sidebar glossary entries that inform and entertain.

Because this book is a snapshot of what law firms and legal service providers are publishing, you can find out what your competitors are doing to service existing clients and attract new ones, recruit new lawyers, and inform the public. In addition to the NLJ 250, the authors provide a section on "The Best of the Rest" to recognize innovation by smaller firms.

LPM Publishing is pleased to make this highly informative and enjoyable resource available to you. We hope that it will make the Internet a more useful adjunct to your practice.

Robert J. Conroy
Judith L. Grubner
Co-Chairs, LPM Publishing

Preface

The Deal with this Book

In October 1995, only 40 percent of the *National Law Journal* 250[1] law firms had registered domain names, and only 10 percent of the NLJ 250 firms had Web sites.[2] A little more than two years later, the prediction that "It will soon be the rule, rather than the exception, that a law-related organization is on the Internet" has come true.[3] Today all but one of the NLJ 250 firms has registered a domain name, and 60 percent have Web sites.

Why is this important? Because it means that the Internet is finally ready for prime time. And it means that there is no reasonable way to include *all* of the law-related organizations on the Net in this book. So what's a perfectionist to do? The only rational choice is to make editorial decisions about who gets included in this book and who does not. So while earlier efforts focused on cataloging *all* of the law-related resources into one book, this book focuses on cataloging the best of all the law-related resources.

For example, in chapter 3, "Companies," we include major vendors, focusing on those that publish something of substance—preferably for free—on the Internet.[4] We also include smaller companies who, for one reason or another, are making a difference on the Internet. Companies

---

1. The *National Law Journal* 250 (NLJ 250) is an annual survey conducted by the New York Law Publishing Company. This is the 20th anniversary of the NLJ 250 survey, which is the legal community's equivalent of the Fortune 500.

2. According to *The Legal List, Law-Related Resources on the Internet and Elsewhere,* seventh edition, October 1995, Lawyers Cooperative Publishing, by Erik J. Heels.

3. Id. or ibid., we're not sure; or perhaps ego. The key to being a successful visionary is to make lots and lots of predictions in print and then reference only those that came true.

4. Trust us, if you build it, they *will* come. Content is still king. Presentation is queen. And experience—kind of like a knight. OK, so we're reaching here. Chess enthusiasts will appreciate the analogy. More on content, presentation, and experience in the section entitled "Three Elements of a Successful Web Site," page 18.

whose content focus is limited to a particular state are briefly mentioned in the reviews of each particular state. In chapter 5, "Law Firms," we include NLJ 250 law firms and small law firms that have made great strides in Internet publishing. We're open to suggestions about how to improve future editions of this book.

Our goal was to create a reference book that would help novices and net.veterans get the most out of their Internet experiences. For example, a new Internet user looking for tax law resources would get a good feel for the best of the Internet tax-related resources by looking in the index of practice areas in this book under "tax" for organizations whose practice areas include tax. Similarly, net.veterans looking to maximize their online experience—both as consumers and publishers of information—would enjoy our spirited reviews of all of the NLJ 250 law firm Web sites to see what is working and what is not.

Much has changed over the last two years. BBSs, Gopher, WAIS, and even Usenet are dead or dying. E-mail is becoming a more popular way to get the word out, and users are struggling with how to filter out the unwanted e-mail from the mix. The jury is still out on technologies such as PointCast, which delivers multimedia to users' desktops, but not by e-mail.[5] On the horizon are new developments such as Internet-based telephone and fax service, unified messaging, and video.

We have also seen consolidation in the Internet marketspace and the legal Internet marketspace. WorldCom has purchased UUNet and MCI, and Microsoft has purchased everything but the Justice Department. In the legal market, Counsel Connect was sold, bought, and consolidated with its former competitor, the New York Law Publishing Company (of Law Journal EXTRA! fame). Reed and Thomson continue to grow their two huge empires.

Finally, we hope that the information overload that is the Internet will still require somebody to weed through the millions of Web sites (and other Internet resources) to find the most important, most reliable, and most influential ones. And who better to help than the American Bar Association, whose mission is member services. We're pleased to play a small part in shaping the legal Internet community, and we hope to do so for years to come.

Thanks for reading!

---

5. And you never ever know what juries will do. Check out Matthew Bender's Web site review (page 95) to see what they're doing with PointCast.

CHAPTER**ONE**

About This Book,
the Net, and the Web

What's Here, What's Not, and Why

Right off the bat some of you will skim through the book looking for a listing of your favorite law firm Web site (perhaps your own), or a mention of the absolute best (but little-known) research site on the Web. They may not be here.

This book is not intended to be a comprehensive legal reference tool. Others have tried to do that, and in some cases they have succeeded. This book summarizes where things stand. The last three years have witnessed a tremendous upheaval in the way the legal profession views and uses technology, and we feel that the Internet is at the heart of that transformation. Up until now, no other book has really shown the effects of the revolution.

So what's here? Each of the eight chapters is organized as follows:

Overview
This section provides a brief summary of the chapter.

Best Meta Sites
We felt it would be helpful to tell you where to find the exhaustive list of resources related to the topic. In many cases, no one source will have everything you're looking for. If you use two or more sources in conjunction, you increase the odds that you'll find most (if not all) of what's out there.

In general, the two sites vital for legal research are FindLaw and Yahoo, in that order. FindLaw is one of those sites that lawyers just can't do without. Its singular mission—to catalog legal information on the Internet—means that it dominates what competition it does have. FindLaw's site navigation is intuitive, its organization is standard (a surprisingly rare trait among would-be catalog sites), and its graphics are light, meaning that the page will load quickly and give you what you need. Yahoo, on the other hand, because of its breadth, is a useful site when the research subject isn't necessarily legal.

Visionaries/Early Adopters/Middlers/Late Adopters/Luddites

When someone applies for a domain name, the Internet Network Information Center (InterNIC) catalogs the date of the application. As we assembled the information for this book, we realized that one of the interesting things to learn was when organizations registered a domain name. Though it's not an exact science, the adoption rate of the Internet in the legal profession can be broken down into five categories:

- **Visionaries:** Registered a domain name before 1993
- **Early Adopters:** Registered a domain name in 1993 or 1994
- **Middlers:** Registered a domain name in 1995
- **Late Adopters:** Registered a domain name in 1996 or 1997
- **Luddites:** As of this writing, still do not have a domain name

If you put the number of registrants on a bell curve (see page 6), you'd see that our categories are accurate. This produces some interesting results, such as the United States Postal Service getting listed as a visionary, and Yahoo getting listed as a middler. But take the listings for what they are: one measure of when organizations officially started their Internet journey.

Because we relied on the InterNIC record for this information, you'll notice that occasionally a firm's name is misspelled. This isn't because we misspelled it, or because the gremlins at the ABA typesetter wanted to play a joke. It's because whoever registered the domain name misspelled the firm's name when filling out the application. Needless to say, it matters how a firm (or a consultant) enters its information into the InterNIC's registered domain name database. Just as it matters how you choose to be listed (or not) in the local Yellow Pages. If your name is misspelled in the phone book, chances are you'll be harder to find.

Similarly, organizations sometimes get listed under the name of a parent company, a consultant, or an individual. In a handful of cases, we added "c/o" to the title of the listing to make the entry a little clearer. Again, you control how you are listed at the InterNIC, and it is important that the information you submit is accurate and guessable.

Reviews

What does it mean when there is no review? The answer to this depends on where you are in the book. In chapter 5, "Law Firms," we deal with a defined list—the NLJ 250. Consequently, the fact that a firm does not have a Web site is equally enlightening. For that reason, we included the firm's name but left the review section blank. When a review is not listed with the firm's name, you can assume that as of this writing there was no Web site to review.

For other chapters, the absence of an entry is not conclusive proof of the nonexistence of a Web site. Instead, it indicates that we chose not to include it due to limited space in the book. We think it's clear that the review for the State of Montana would mention that you can find all things Montana at that Web site. Where reviews are given, it's because the selected site stood out for one reason or another, because either the organization is well known (such as the White House) or the content is non-

▼▼▼▼▼

404

The problem of Web pages not being found (404 is the error message number returned by most servers for bogus filenames) is not limited to huge directories like Yahoo. The problem is everywhere. Files that are bookmarked or linked suddenly disappear. The 404 error message is about as useful as the DOS abort?-retry?-fail? error message. An old house can be charming, but an old Web site can be downright annoying. The solution to the 404 error message problem is for Web designers to make Web sites—old and new—more user friendly. When you enter an incorrect key sequence into a software program, it should react predictably and friendly. The same is true for Web sites. If you surf to http://www.yahoo.com/bogus-filename.html, you should expect to receive a helpful error message. Yahoo may not have conquered the problem of keeping its links current, but it has figured out

that Web sites can be user friendly. By programming their Web server software to return something intelligent (rather than simply "404"), Yahoo has incorporated user-interface techniques into the design of its Web site. Yes, Virginia, designing good Web sites does take more than a passing knowledge of HTML. Whenever you hear of a Web site that professes to be the final word on Web site design, append "bogus-filename.html" to the end of its URL. Sites that have failed the test include Microsoft (http://www.microsoft.com/bogus-filename.html), Netscape (http://www.netscape.com/bogus-filename.html), Killer Web Sites (http://www.killersites.com/bogus-filename.html), and Web Pages That Suck (http://www.webpagesthatsuck.com/bogus-filename.html). Sites that passed the test included Yahoo and Apple (http://www.apple.com/bogus-filename.html).

intuitive (such as the Department of Commerce, which is the parent organization of the U.S. Patent and Trademark Office).

As always, if you're looking for a site that is not listed, a good place to start your search is with one of the meta sites.

Practice Areas

A shrewd observer will look at some of the NLJ 250 firms' entries and point out that they must have more practice areas than those that are listed. In many cases, that person would be right. This book is intended to demonstrate what the legal profession is doing online, however, and if we use just that environment to learn about a firm (an increasingly common behavior in today's market), then the only thing we'll know about their practice areas is whatever is listed on their Web site. For example, if a law firm lists 100 practice areas on its Web site but includes substantive information about only a dozen of those, we have listed only the dozen.

Glossary

This book uses a nontraditional glossary. Listservs and sites that don't fit nicely into one of the chapters are included as entries in the glossary. Rather than stick the glossary at the end of the book, we decided to include glossary entries as running sidebars throughout the book. This way, when you look up a term in the glossary, you may discover an interesting Web site in the main listings. Similarly, when looking up an organization in the main listings, you may discover an interesting distraction from the sidebar glossary. Kind of like window shopping, or browsing. Or Web surfing!

The Dawn of the Internet

Where were you in 1969? A few brilliant scientists from the U.S. Department of Defense's Advanced Research Project Agency were designing and testing a highly fault-tolerant computer network called ARPANet.[1] One of the features of ARPANet is its ability to survive a nuclear war.[2] If a nuclear

---

1. Bill Gates and Steve Jobs were notably absent.
2. Nuclear survivability is an oft-cited and over-hyped feature of the original ARPANet. The real challenge was to design a network that was a distributed cooperative computing environment. No one machine had to know about all of the other machines connected to the network. Users of the network could concentrate on creating data and sending it along to their colleagues, and the computers kept track of the best way to send the data from one point to the next.

blast—or more likely, a backhoe—were to take out one segment of the network, the surviving segments would work together to redirect traffic around the problem.

Little did these scientists know that the experiment they began in 1969 would grow into what we now call the Internet. Yes, the Internet is nearly 30 years old, but most people heard about it only recently. And for good reason. To connect to the Internet, you need a client computer, computers that know where the other computers are,[3] hardware for sending data over phone lines,[4] and phone lines. For over two decades, all the equipment needed to connect to the Internet was prohibitively expensive. And the majority of the high-speed phone lines that connected one segment of the Internet to another was funded by the federal government, primarily the National Science Foundation.[5]

But in 1992, three things happened to bring the Internet to the masses. First, the price of computers and modems dropped significantly, while graphical user interfaces such as the Macintosh Operating System and Windows 3.0 continued to make computers easier to use. Second, the NSF's restrictions on commercial use of its "backbone" were relaxed,[6] and commercial providers began providing alternative backbones with no commercial use restrictions.[7] Third, and most important, we had a vice-presidential candidate who had *heard* of the Internet!

And just as good marketing propelled Windows onto the desktops of computer users everywhere,[8] press coverage of the Internet—starting with the 1992 presidential campaign—propelled the Internet and its TCP/IP standards onto computer networks at businesses worldwide.[9] Winston Churchill once said that democracy is not the perfect form of govern-

---

3. These computers are called "routers."

4. Modems for analog lines, CSU/DSUs for digital lines.

5. Whose NSFNet was the "Internet backbone" for many years.

6. In the 1980s, much of the Internet traffic passed over the National Science Foundation's (NSF) backbone network (NSFnet), which was funded by the government. The NSF promulgated the NSFnet Backbone Services Acceptable Use Policy (AUP), the full text of which is available at **ftp://nic.merit.edu/nfsnet/acceptable.use.policy**. Two "unacceptable uses" are enumerated: "Use for for-profit activities, unless covered by the General Principle or as a specifically acceptable use," and "Extensive use for private or personal business." Translation: some commercial use is more equal than other commercial use. At least they didn't use the phrase "information superhighway."

7. Several commercial Internet Service Providers (ISPs) were formed, and they joined together to form the Commercial Internet Exchange (CIX). The CIX's backbone Internet services were designed to be a commercial alternative to the NSFNet.

8. Not unlike how VHS won out over Sony's superior Beta format.

9. And yes, "worldwide" is one word, but the "World Wide Web" is written as three words. Gotta love standards!

ment, but it's the best that we've found so far. So too, with the TCP/IP protocols that underlie the Internet. More on TCP/IP later.

So what was the result of this proliferation of inexpensive, user-friendly computers, commercially enabled backbones, and Internet-clued politicians? The result was that in 1993 there were more stories about the Internet in the *New York Times* than in all previous years combined. That happened again in 1994, again in 1995, and yet again in 1996.

That said, 1995 is generally considered to be "the year of the Internet."[10] It was the year when people rushed to the Internet in search of fame and fortune. Here is, by year, the number of NLJ 250 law firms—the legal community's equivalent of the *Fortune* 500—who registered domain names over the last six years:

Year	Registrants
pre–1993	5
1993	9
1994	40
1995	127
1996	59
1997	9
post–1997	1 (we assume)

Those that registered their domain names in 1993 or 1994 can be fairly characterized as "early adopters."[11] Similarly, those that registered domain names in 1996 or 1997 can fairly be characterized as "late adopters."[12] And those that registered in 1995—well, we'll just call them "middlers." Why bother with labels? Because one calendar year is the equivalent of seven Net years, and a little time makes a huge difference. Those that were on the Net first are today reaping the benefits of being the first to be written about, linked to by other Web sites, and indexed by search engines and directories. This is not to say that there can be no benefit to a law firm (or to anybody else, for that matter) who gets on the Internet in 1996 or later. *Au contraire.* It's just that the job of getting noticed will be a bit more difficult for the late adopters.

---

10. In fact, *Newsweek* declared 1995 "The Year of the Internet." So it must be true.

11. Before then, you're a visionary. Davis Polk & Wardwell (dpw.com—07/89) and Heller, Ehrman, White & McAuliffe (hewm.com—01/90) were the first two. And who would have guessed it, but the U.S. Postal Service also qualifies as a visionary by this definition!

12. After that, you're a Luddite. Sorry.

Which is why, we hope, you are reading this book. This book is designed to help veterans and newcomers alike leverage the power of the Internet. It is designed to be a reference book that you'll return to again and again. It is also a useful snapshot of the state of the legal Internet community.[13]

That Darn Internet

This section offers a brief overview of how the Internet works—and how you can make it work for you.

The Internet is easier to demonstrate than to describe. But we'll give it a shot. A network is simply one or more computers connected by wires. An internet (lowercase "i") is one or more interconnected computer networks. The Internet (uppercase "I") is the worldwide network of interconnected networks. Computers connected to the Internet (or "on the Internet") can communicate with other Internet-connected computers because they operate according to standard protocols, the TCP/IP (Transmission Control Protocol/Internet Protocol) family of protocols.

All different types of computers (including those running the UNIX, Windows95, and Macintosh operating systems) can be configured with software that "speaks" the TCP/IP family of protocols. As such, all different types of computers can be connected to the Internet. All the computers connected to the Internet—and all the people using those computers—can share information with each other. The two most popular methods of sharing information—and the two methods on which this book will focus—are Internet e-mail and the World Wide Web.

Today, Internet e-mail is one of the five generally accepted ways of communicating with clients in a business environment. The other four are U.S. Postal Service (USPS) mail, the telephone, the fax machine, and (of course) face-to-face. The Internet's World Wide Web has proven to be both a power platform for publication and advertising and a means for supplementing other methods of business communication. So although the Internet has been around in one form or another since 1969, it is the World Wide Web that has changed the way we think about business. The question "Are you on the Internet?" used to mean "Do you have Internet e-mail?" Today, in many cases, it means "Do you have a Web site?"

---

13. And it gave us a chance to share our opinions. Some may argue that we have shared too much. For example, Point Communications (which was later acquired by Lycos) gained many friends by reviewing and publicizing the "top 5%" of the Web. We decided to review *all* of the NLJ 250 law firms. How else can you find the top 5 percent?

Four Tools to Use

This section is designed to explain in more detail some of the basic Internet terminology.

Most major new technological advances (telephone, electric light, radio, television) took about a decade to be adopted by a majority of U.S. households.[14] At the rate at which the World Wide Web is being adopted, it will accomplish the 50 percent milestone in half the time! So there is good reason for all of the hype in the popular press![15]

There are three Internet tools that you should learn how to use: e-mail, the Web, and FTP (File Transfer Protocol). There is nothing magic about these tools—they are simply computer programs (like Word-Perfect) that implement standard sets of rules called protocols. For example, using control-V for paste is a protocol on Macintosh computer systems. No matter what computer you use (whether a Macintosh, a Windows-based computer, or a UNIX-based computer) these tools should all work essentially the same way.[16]

E-mail and E-mail-Based Discussion Groups

E-mail is a tool that allows one user on the Internet to send a message to another user on the Internet. An e-mail message may contain text or pictures and sound encoded as text, but most often it is plain text. The various e-mail programs are the most widely used of the Internet tools, since the Internet is primarily used for communication between users.

The most popular Internet e-mail software is Eudora by Qualcomm. Eudora allows you to compose (and reply to) e-mail messages while you are offline, and then when you connect to the Internet, you can send and receive all of your e-mail at once. This is particularly helpful if you live in a remote area that requires you to make a long-distance phone call to connect to the Internet. Among Eudora's other useful features are its ability to store separate messages in separate "mailboxes" and provide the means for automatically storing messages in particular mailboxes through a process called filtering. For example, if you have subscribed to an e-mail-based discussion group, you may want to create a filter for each group that sends messages from that group into a particular mailbox.

---

14. Source: *Wired* 4/96, p. 70, which credits U.S. Bureau of the Census, *Historical Statistics,* and *Statistical Abstract 1990.*
   15. It also makes it easier to justify exclamation points!
   16. We know we said four tools. Be patient.

The good news is that Internet e-mail software is everywhere these days, and it's getting easier to use and more sophisticated all the time. While the Internet is worldwide, you pay only for the cost of your local access. Therefore, you can send e-mail to somebody in Finland just as easily (and inexpensively) as to somebody next door!

Internet e-mail will not replace USPS mail, the telephone, or the fax machine. It does not *supplant* old ways of communicating, it *supplements* them. One advantage of Internet e-mail is that it costs less than a telephone call or a letter (at least for those with unlimited flat-rate access). And, unlike a phone call, an Internet e-mail does not require that the recipient be immediately available to receive it. As such, Internet e-mail content tends to be more substantive than voicemail messages. Among the most useless voicemail messages I receive are those that say "Hi, it's Bob. Call me." If Bob had sent me an e-mail, I could have replied, quoting relevant portions of his e-mail back to him in my reply, at my convenience.

Here is an example of quoted e-mail reply.

```
Date: Sat, 21 Nov 1997 14:10:31 -0400
To: "Loder, Beverly" <bloder@staff.abanet.org>
From: "Erik J. Heels" <heels@redstreet.com>
Subject: Re: timelines
Cc: "Richard P. Klau" <rklau@redstreet.com>

Greetings Bev,
    At 1:48 PM -0400 11/20/97, Loder, Beverly wrote:

>Erik—
>Just a quick note to thank
>you and Rick for getting your
>latest draft in ahead of
>schedule—again! You guys are
>the best!
>See you at TechShow in
>Chicago!
>—Bev


    No problem. Glad to be of
service. Thanks for your kind
words.

Regards,
Erik
```

▼▼▼▼▼

555-1212 (http://www.555-1212.com/) Save money on directory assistance, and get more information to boot. The Web's version of 555-1212 will let you search the white and yellow pages nationwide, as well as access some other nifty features. Is there a number on your phone bill that you don't recognize? Go to 555-1212 and enter it in the "reverse look-up" field. If the phone number is listed, you'll get the name and address of the person who called.

But sometimes you just have to make a phone call, mail a package, or fax a signed document so you have a particular signature on file. Each method of communication has advantages and disadvantages. For those who haven't started using Internet e-mail, the bad news is that you will have to learn a new technology. The good news is that the new methods of communicating will supplement the way you use the older methods.

In addition to sending e-mail to an individual user, you can send e-mail to multiple users via mailing list software such as the *listserv* family of list servers. Lists of e-mail addresses managed by list server programs go by many different names, including listserv lists, mailing lists, and discussion groups. Whatever they might be called, they all work in pretty much the same way. The list server software maintains a list of e-mail addresses of users who have subscribed to a particular list. The software handles all subscription requests. It also delivers all messages to the list.

Listserv lists, like other Internet tools, are easier to demonstrate than to describe. For example, I subscribed to the Late Show News listserv list by sending the following message:

```
Date: Sat, 21 Nov 1997 14:10:31 -0400
To: listserv@american.edu
From: "Erik J. Heels" <heels@redstreet.com>
Subject: SUB LATE-SHOW-NEWS Erik J. Heels
Cc:

SUB LATE-SHOW-NEWS Erik J. Heels
```

Note that I included the same text in the subject and the body of the message. This particular list server software only requires that these commands be in the body of the message, but I prefer to also include it in the subject for two reasons. First, I save all of my outgoing mail, and if I ever need to find this message, I can (with Eudora) simply sort my outbox by subject and quickly find this message. Second, some list server software requires this information in the subject line (while ignoring the body of the message). By always following the same syntax, I can be sure that my subscription request will be properly processed.

Once you have subscribed to a few listserv lists and given your e-mail address to friends and family, you will soon find yourself buried with e-mail. So how do you cope with this information overload? One way is to simply have two Internet e-mail accounts, one for listserv list e-mail and one for everything else. Of course this means that you'll have to pay for more than one account. Another way is to use Eudora's ability to filter e-mail from listserv lists into separate mailboxes.

If you can connect to an Internet Service Provider (ISP) via a local phone call, and your ISP charges a flat rate for unlimited monthly usage, filtering is probably the way to go. You will have to wait for your listserv list e-mail to be downloaded from the mail server to your local computer, but at least you won't be paying for the connect time.

Many different kinds of list-management software packages exist.[17] It is not always possible to tell which list-management software package is running which list, because, for example, some ListProcessor-managed lists use the e-mail address of "listproc," others "listserver," and still others "listserv." Your best bet is to send the word "help" in the subject and the body of your message to the list server. Then save the instructions that you receive. You may even want to print out the help message. For example, to get help about the ABA's list server, send a message in the following form:

```
Date: Sat, 21 Nov 1997 14:10:31 -0400
To: listserv@abanet.org
From: "Erik J. Heels" <heels@redstreet.com>
Subject: help
Cc:

help
```

The World Wide Web

The World Wide Web (or often "WWW" or "the Web") has revolutionized the Internet to the point where "being on the Internet" is often considered the equivalent of "having a Web site." The Web uses the hypertext[18] model, where documents are connected to each other via links. HyperCard on the Macintosh or the help feature on Microsoft Windows are both examples of hypertext systems. So is a simple ATM machine.[19]

---

17. Including the original BITNET (an older network linking institutional and departmental computers at 550 participating Corporation for Research and Educational Networking (CREN) Members and Affiliates in the United States) LISTSERV software, ListProcessor (or "ListProc") by Anastasios Kotsikonas, Majordomo by Brent Chapman, PMDF Mailserv, and Mailbase (used in the United Kingdom).

18. Or, more properly, hyper*media,* since links can be more than just text.

19. ATM machines (which is redundant, since ATM stands for Automated Teller Machine, but everybody calls them ATM machines) use a hypertext model. An ATM screen is analogous to a Web page.

The Web was developed by CERN, the European Laboratory for Particle Physics.[20] A Web server is a computer set up to publish (or serve) documents to client computers. Each hypertext document on the Web can contain links, which often appear as underlined text or images. When you select a particular link, you can view documents, run other Internet programs, or connect with other Web servers. A set of Web pages is collectively referred to as a Web site, and the Web page that is the starting point for a Web site is called a home page.

To access the Web, you run a browser program that can read and retrieve documents. Netscape Navigator is the most popular Web browser, and there are versions for all major operating systems including UNIX, Windows95, and MacOS. Microsoft Internet Explorer is another browser that is available on multiple platforms. Web browsers can access information from FTP, Usenet news, Gopher, Web, and other servers. If you have not yet browsed the Web, you are missing out on one of the most amazing advances in computing technology in recent memory.

In 1993,[21] graphical-based software for accessing (or browsing) the World Wide Web was invented.[22] The World Wide Web transformed the Internet from a world where you had to "telnet"[23] to remote machines to run computer programs on the remote machine, and where you had to "FTP"[24] to remote machines to copy files to and from the remote machine, to a world where you could run programs and transfer files to and from remote machines by simply selecting hypertext links.

An added bonus of the World Wide Web is that Web servers (computers running World Wide Web server software) generally do not require a username and password, whereas telnet and FTP generally did require a username and password. Now combine the hypertext-based World Wide Web with graphics-based software for browsing the World Wide Web and you have graphics-based point-and-click access to Internet programs and data. The first popular World Wide Web browser was written by the Na-

---

20. We think it should be ELPP, but apparently the French have different words for everything!

21. The Web, which was originally text-based, was invented in June 1991. The first graphical Web browser, Mosaic, was invented in 1993. *See* **http://www.w3.org** for details.

22. Okay, so maybe there were *four* things that happened in 1992 to start the Internet era: cheap computers, commercial backbone, Internet-clued vice-presidential candidate, and a graphical Web.

23. Telnet is a protocol that allows a user who is logged in to one machine to log in to another machine, much like dialing up a remote computer bulletin board system (BBS).

24. FTP stands for File Transfer Protocol. FTP allows users to log in to a remote computer for the limited purpose of copying files to and from the remote computer. Copying files to the remote machine is called "uploading," while copying files from the remote machine is called "downloading."

tional Center for Supercomputing Applications (NCSA) at the University of Illinois Urbana–Champaign. That software was called NCSA Mosaic, or simply Mosaic. Mosaic became so popular that the terms "Mosaic" and "World Wide Web" were, for a period, used interchangeably.

FTP

File Transfer Protocol (FTP) is a tool that allows users on one computer (the client computer) to connect to another computer (the server computer) for the limited purpose of copying files from (and sometimes to) the server. A computer that is set up to accept incoming FTP requests from another computer is called an FTP server. FTP servers are used in conjunction with Web servers to provide a vehicle for transferring large files (such as software) that are too large to be transferred via Web servers. For example, if you are downloading a demonstration version of the latest Netscape Navigator, there is no need for you to "browse" (or view) the encoded text of the program in the window of your browser. By making the software available via FTP, Netscape has made the download process more efficient because FTP can eliminate the unnecessary step of viewing the file to be downloaded.

For users with only e-mail access, you can use any of several FTP by e-mail services, such as:

> ftpmail@oak.oakland.edu
> ftpmail@sunsite.unc.edu
> ftp-request@netcom.com

For a list of more Internet services that can be accessed via e-mail, see the "Accessing the Internet by E-Mail FAQ," available on the Internet at MIT's FTP archives (**ftp://rtfm .mit.edu/pub/usenet/news.answers/ internet-services/access-via-email**).

Paper

Once you are on the Internet, it is relatively easy to find out more about the Internet itself. Your Internet Service Provider most likely has

agent
A software program that can perform tasks for human users in their absence. Many agents are designed to search WWW servers for particular types of information. The "Eclipse" feature on LEXIS-NEXIS is a software agent.

Anarchist's Cookbook, The
The infamous book that angered Senator Diane Feinstein. It turns out that there are—get this—books on the Internet. Even more shocking, some of these books talk about Bad Things. In the wake of the Oklahoma City bombing, news surfaced that Timothy McVeigh might have found out how to build a bomb by downloading the information off the Internet. This led Senator Feinstein (no, we're not making this up) to hold hearings in the Senate to ban the publishing of bomb-making information on the Internet. When it was pointed out that this same information was available in libraries and even through the Government Printing Office, Senator Feinstein could not be reached for comment. Needless to say, bomb-making information can still be found on the Internet. The First Amendment lives on.

Internet-related information available online. But sometimes it is simply easier to have a book by your side, like this one![25] A short, concise, easy-to-read text is Brendan P. Kehoe's *Zen and the Art of the Internet: A Beginner's Guide to the Internet* (Prentice-Hall, Englewood Cliffs, NJ). Ed Krol's *The Whole Internet Users Guide and Catalog,* Second Edition (O'Reilly & Associates, Inc., Sebastopol, CA), is considered the bible of Internet references texts. It is comprehensive and is an Internet classic. The best book on "netiquette" (Internet etiquette) is Virginia Shea's *Netiquette* (Albion Books, San Francisco, CA). Finally, for a well-written, humorous, persuasive accounting of how lawyers can benefit now from the Internet, we suggest G. Burgess Allison's *The Lawyer's Guide to the Internet* (Law Practice Management Section, American Bar Association, Chicago, IL).

After you've gotten on the Internet, you might want to check out certain Request For Comment (RFC) documents that provide information to the Internet novice. The Internet Engineering Task Force (IETF) also uses RFCs to implement and document Internet standards (such as FTP, Telnet, HTTP, and HTML). Certain RFCs (called FYIs) are used for informational purposes. Others document Internet history. The RFCs are a goldmine of information and can be browsed at the InterNIC (**http://www.internic.net/ds/dspg0intdoc.html**).[26]

Four Reasons to Get on the Internet

Once used exclusively by the few (government, military, and research users), the Internet is now being used by the many (companies and consumers). As more people get on the Internet, fewer people will be able to ignore it. Today, it is wise for businesses to include USPS addresses, telephone numbers, fax numbers, and e-mail addresses on fax leaders, letterhead, business cards, and e-mail signature files. Your clients will want to contact you in more than one way.

You need to be on the Internet—from the perspective of both a server and surfer. You need to serve information (via a Web site) to market your services, serve existing clients, and recruit employees. You need to surf

---

25. Thus, paper is the fourth "tool to use."

26. To receive introductory information on the Internet via e-mail, send a message with **document-by-name rfc1594** in the body of the message to **mailserv@ds.internic.net.** You will receive RFC number 1594, "Answers to commonly asked 'New Internet User' Questions."

the Web to supplement traditional legal research. Consider these four reasons for getting on (as both a client and a server) the Net.

Reason 1: Clients and Potential Clients Are There

One of the reasons law firms are rushing to the Web is that clients and potential clients are there. With over ten million[27] America Online subscribers alone, the number of people with access to the Internet keeps increasing.

Reason 2: Colleagues (and Competitors) Are There

Another reason law firms are getting on the Internet is to communicate with (and compete with) colleagues. If a competitor has a Web site and your firm does not, then you have to consider the disadvantages of *not* getting on the Internet along with the advantages of getting on.

Two years ago, there were only a few law firms and government organizations on the Internet. Today, it is the rule rather than the exception that an organization has some sort of Internet presence.[28] The rules have changed. The bar has been raised. And, in fact, there is even an RFC that defines exactly what it means "to be on the Internet" because of this changing definition (**http://ds.internic.net/rfc/rfc1775.txt**).

In 1995, 10 percent of the firms listed in the NLJ 250 had some sort of Web presence, and 40 percent of them had a registered domain name. Today, 60 percent of them have their own Web site, and all but one have registered domain names!

Reason 3: Law-Related Information Is There

The Internet also supplements traditional (paper-based and electronic) legal research. Surfing the Web for information on a particular legal topic is one way to get quickly up to speed on an issue. On the Internet one can find primary law (cases, statutes, and treaties), secondary law (law review articles and the like), and tertiary law (discussion groups, unpublished manuscripts, and the like). As standards for citing to URLs (**http://www.richmond.edu/~jolt/about.html**) and for paragraph-based citation (**http://www.wisbar.org/bar/sbcite.html**) are adopted, more and more information will be published on the Web in the future.

---

27. According to Jupiter Communications, the number is 20 billion. For the uninitiated, Jupiter (**http://www.jup.com**) is an industry group that, in our opinion, consistently provides inflated figures when estimating various Net statistics.

28. As predicted by a True Visionary a couple of years ago.

Reason 4: Cost-Effective Communication, Publishing, and Marketing

Estimates of the number of individuals on the Internet vary widely, but it is safe to say there are probably 75 million users worldwide.[29] This makes the Internet the world's second-largest communication network, after the telephone network.

As a means of communication, the Internet can supplement the phone, fax, and paper mail. As a means of publication, the Internet provides ways to research, advertise, shop, and have fun. Functionally, the Internet is simply a medium for sending and receiving information. What can you do that involves sending and receiving information? The possibilities are endless: audio, video, interactivity, and whatever technologies come along next.

Three Target Audiences for Your Web Site

Not to put too fine a point on it, but we hear the question all the time: "Why should my firm be on the Internet?" Never mind that it's our opinion that in a couple years, this will be like asking "Why should our firm have a phone system?" The question gets to the heart of why this book is important. Too often, it's easy to dismiss those asking the question as Luddites—as if answering the question would be reinforcing the fact that they just didn't get it.

So why should someone bother with a Web site? What's in it for a firm? We submit that there are three reasons—in no particular order—for why your firm should be on the Internet.

Clients

Every once in a while, your clients want to feel like they matter to you. So you send them the occasional newsletter, answer some of their phone calls, and maybe even sponsor a seminar that they can attend to help them address an issue that confronts them in their business. Each of these steps costs money—especially the newsletters and the seminars—and your firm probably has a limit on the amount that can be spent on these activities.

---

29. According to Jupiter Communications, 20 billion users. But seriously, according to Network Wizards' semi-annual Internet domain name survey (**http://www.nw.com/zone/WWW/report.html**), there were over 19 million hosts (computers) connected to the Internet in July 1997. We estimate the current number to be 25 million computers, and with about three users per computer, we conclude that there are 75 million Internet users today.

Creating a Web site allows you to expand your client services. Whether it means publishing an archive of the articles the firm has written over the years, providing information about upcoming seminars, or just posting an e-mail directory so that clients can send e-mail to their lawyers, there are many ways of leveraging the Internet to make your clients feel closer to your firm.

Perhaps your existing clients aren't aware of some of the services your firm provides. If they stop by your site, they may realize that you can solve some other problems for them. Having a list of practice areas and specializations on the Web site just might result in several thousand dollars in billable hours.[30] At the extreme end of client service, some firms are setting up "extranets"[31] so that their clients can log in to the firm's network, check their bill, review documents, and even communicate securely with the lawyers on their case. Publishing an archive of articles is particularly useful, because a simple search engine allows clients to search all articles by keyword. Whatever you do with the Web site, the goal is to make the client feel like you have made an effort to keep them informed.

Potential Clients

A recent survey indicated that more than 90 percent of all *Fortune* 500 companies had Internet access within the company.[32] The percentage among small to mid-size companies with Internet access is growing, thanks to the decreasing cost of high-speed access and the increasing number of things one can do on the Internet. Easier access means that the number of people using the Internet as a supplement to their search for representation will also increase. The better the information about your firm on your Web site, the more likely it is that they will view you favorably when making their selection. As one example, Arent Fox partner Lew Rose stated in a September 22, 1997, article in the *Washington Post* that the Arent Fox Web site has brought in more than $500,000 in new business.[33]

Potential clients using the Internet to surf for firms will be looking for solid examples of your firm's expertise. Don't just provide explanations of your practice areas. Sit in your visitor's chair and try to figure out what would make them select you. Is it your high-profile clientele? The name

---

30. The folks in marketing call this "cross-selling." We call it good business.
31. See page 78.
32. We don't remember where we read this, but it seems to make sense.
33. Beth Berselli, "Firms Find Web Sites Attract Clients, Recruits, Prestige." *Washington Post*, September 22, 1997, p. F7.

recognition of your partners? Whatever it is, leverage it. And don't hide it three levels deep on your Web site. Lead the visitors through your site, and make the selection simple.

Potential Coworkers

Pop quiz: Who's the most wired demographic in the legal market? Answer: law students. Take advantage of this by giving them the details they want: how to get a job. Different law firms take different approaches to their recruiting information. Some reluctantly provide basic details, sending the message that the last thing they could possibly want is more resumes. More enlightened firms realize that their Web site can serve to screen applicants. Of course, you'll always get the I'll-send-3,000-resumes-and-hope-for-the-best law students,[34] but many will spend the time reading the information provided to determine whether or not this is the kind of program for them. Details like how many summer associates you hire, what kind of projects they'll work on in the summer, and whether or not they'll have a mentor for the program will all help law students gauge their interest.

Three Elements of a Successful Web Site

Evaluating a Web site's effectiveness is an admittedly subjective task. After all, some people apparently like the <blink> tag, and others think that adding a background music clip to a Web site makes it stand out. Personal preferences aside, there are a few basics that should help identify the good Web sites from the bad. While the majority of this book focuses on the first criterion—content—the others are equally important in evaluating the overall effectiveness of a site.

Content

Some clichés are actually good ones. One that's been around a while on the Net is "Content is king."[35] It isn't entirely true that content is all that

---

34. See **spam**, page 179.

35. Using a chess analogy, we've come up with two entirely new clichés: presentation is queen, experience is kind of like a knight. Think about it. In chess, the king can only move one square at a time. Boring, plain vanilla, but you'll lose the game without him. The queen can glide effortlessly from one end of the board to the other, livening up the bland black-and-white board. The knight—like a good nav bar—can be very powerful, jumping from where you don't want to be to where you do.

matters. Anyone who's spent time at a disorganized site with page after page of links knows this. Good content is the foundation on which first-rate Web sites are built, however. No formula exists for a law firm, a legal publisher, or a bar association to follow that ensures their content is "good." After all, what works for one may be useless for another. But a few guidelines are probably in order.

1. How recent is the information? Nothing is more irritating than seeing a good article about a topic you're interested in and then being unable to determine when it was published. We're lawyers! Publishing newsletters, articles, and other pieces of content without providing dates renders them useless.

2. Is the information relevant? Think about your audience. Sure, the lawyers in your firm probably want a six-paragraph biography about the last time they spoke before the local county bar association, but is this really important to people browsing your site (other than the lawyer's mother)? Keep in mind who will be visiting your site, and tailor your information to their interests.

3. Why should someone hire you? In most cases, a Web site serves some marketing purpose for the firm. What good is it if you don't give someone a reason to hire your firm? At the very least, describe your practice areas and include news articles describing your firm's expertise. Anything to highlight what sets you apart from other firms.

4. Where are you? It never ceases to amaze us that Web sites actually hide contact information. How many times have you ended up at a Web site, tried to find a phone number (or even an e-mail address), only to end up—eight clicks later—looking at a picture of someone's building? If someone has to go through that much effort to give you a call, they won't. And you'll lose that business.

Presentation

From our point of view, presentation[36] deals with how well the elements of the site are put together. Are the graphics professionally designed? Is the overall layout of the site consistent throughout? When a visitor shows up at your Web site, do they think "Lexus" or do they think "Yugo"? Too few firms equate developing a Web site with developing a firm's brochure. We place more emphasis on the Web site than on the brochure. After all, more people will see the Web site, and you'll always be able to

---

36. Which is queen, the most powerful piece on the chess board.

add more content. The brochure gets printed once, and then you use it until it's so woefully out of date that the named partners have changed.

It's gratifying to see that some law firms have moved on to second-generation Web sites. This means that they started somewhat conservatively then realized that they could do more. These firms typically tried to do the first version in house—or perhaps asked the partner's son-in-law to do it.[37] The results were generally mediocre, so firms turned to professional designers to help them in their next attempts. That said, some sites developed entirely in house demonstrate a solid appreciation of what goes into a good Web site. But these are the exception rather than the rule.

When designing your site, focus on how your site appears to someone unfamiliar with your firm. Is it easy to find the information you're looking for? Is the page cluttered with too many options? If you don't ask these questions at the beginning, you may find yourself answering them in front of a meeting of partners who have heard nothing but complaints from frustrated visitors.

Experience

As visitors finish their tour of your site, what impressions do they have? The "experience" of a Web site is linked to both the content and the presentation, but gets to the heart of whether or not a Web site is successful. Do visitors feel like they got to read information that they wanted to see, or were they forced to read information the firm wanted to reveal? Was the design intuitive, so they could always find what they were looking for, or did they have to guess what "Section Headings" meant? Was the site navigation intuitive? Were there interactive elements? A search engine?

Of the three categories, "experience" clearly falls into the "I'll know it when I see it" camp. Though there are some fundamentals in both content and presentation, experience is most definitely the one area where no formula exists. Good designers can capture the experience of a site with some simple graphics carried throughout the site. Clumsy designers can ruin years' worth of good articles by trying to do too much or simply botching the presentation of the site.

---

37. Not unlike the newsletters that resulted from first-generation desktop publishing software. Can you say *"way* too many fonts"?

Two Stories about the Power of the Net

Erik's Story

At the beginning of this chapter, we asked where you were in 1969 when the Internet was invented. Where were you in 1984? I first experienced the Internet at MIT in 1984, when the Internet was already 15 years old. Interestingly enough, *none* of the organizations listed in this book (including Stanford, Harvard, and Yale) were on the Internet in 1984.

A few years ago, I had the opportunity to ask my grandmother, who died last year at 93 years young, what the most amazing invention of her lifetime was. Many possible answers ran through my mind: the airplane, the artificial knee, the laptop computer, and the Internet. In the split second that it took her to reply, I realized just how much I had taken for granted when she said, "Electricity." She went on to explain that the old oil lamps were "a lot of work for not a lot of light." She said you had to trim the wick, keep them filled with oil, and clean the chimney.

I think that some lawyers would say that the Internet is a lot of work for not a lot of law, but as this book shows, things are changing. I've been working in the legal Internet community since 1992, when I first wrote *The Legal List* (see page 185). I have also had the good fortune of being able to choose to practice patent law or to pursue a career in the Internet space. Along the way, I have worked with many of the great leaders of the legal Internet community who are helping to provide meaningful Internet experiences for legal professionals.

This book is a testimony to the power of the Internet. Rick and I first met via e-mail in late 1993. We were introduced by a mutual friend at the Electronic Frontier Foundation who was familiar with what each of us was trying to do at our respective law schools. Rick and I worked together for over two years[38] before meeting face-to-face, and I've had the pleasure of working 9-to-5 with Rick after he graduated from law school.

After swearing that I'd never attempt a book like this again alone, I was able to convince Rick into co-authoring this book. This book is proof of the potential of the Internet. The Net may not be as powerful as electricity, but it's clearly been the most powerful invention of my time—so far.

---

38. As co-columnists for "Online," a syndicated column that first appeared in the ABA's *Student Lawyer* magazine. We just completed our fourth year writing "Online."

Rick's Story

As a sophomore in college, I wrote a column for my college newspaper about the Gulf War. I didn't want to rely on secondhand reports from newspapers and magazines and simply reprint what they were saying, but was unsure of how to gather my own information. A roommate had recently introduced me to the Internet,[39] so I was eager to find out what was at my disposal. It was 1990, and I was armed with an IBM PS/2 (10 megahertz, DOS 3.3, 20 MB hard drive) and a token-ring adapter.

I subscribed to a discussion group that focused on international politics,[40] and soon found myself exchanging e-mail with a student in Israel. When the Iraqis started their Scud missile attacks against Israel, I was able to get firsthand reports about their effect on the Israelis. The Internet had proven itself a viable communications tool.

When I started law school, I became fascinated by the issues surrounding the use of technology. A summer spent clerking at the Electronic Frontier Foundation (**http://www.eff.org**) reinforced this interest, and by my second year of law school, I was committed to finding a way to get more involved. Along with several classmates, I founded the Richmond Journal of Law & Technology (**http://www.richmond.edu/~jolt**), the first student-edited law journal in the world to publish exclusively online.[41] That first issue, which confronted the issues of trademarks and domain names as well as copyright on the Net, was well received. What we proved was that we could publish a high-quality publication at low cost and increase our audience at the same time.

Working with Erik throughout my law school career was another "proof of concept" for me. For a time we even considered *not* meeting so that we'd have a better story to tell. We did finally meet—more than two years after our first e-mail exchange—and have worked together ever since.

This book is the culmination of endless discussions since we first exchanged e-mail. We enjoy comparing notes on what we like, what we don't like, and what blows us away. This book summarized four years[42] of e-mail, office conversations, and presentations. Enjoy.

---

39. My college provided the networking tools if you had your own computer.

40. Back then, such broad groups were nevertheless fairly quiet groups, given the Internet's relative anonymity.

41. And not just on the Web—also on WESTLAW and LEXIS! (Footnote by Erik. Rick is too modest to tell the whole story.)

42. Seventeen years, according to Jupiter Communications.

One Final Thought about the Future of Electronic Publishing

Books, LEXIS, WESTLAW, and the Net

Much has been made about the fact that information on the Internet is not always reliable. While this is true, it is unfair to assume that this is because the information is on the Internet. Rather, information found online is just like information found elsewhere: The source of the information is the best indicator of how reliable (or unreliable) the information may be.

Case in point: The Securities and Exchange Commission (SEC) maintains an electronic database of all securities filings called EDGAR. Prior to 1995, the SEC did not make EDGAR available on the Internet. Nevertheless, a public interest group called Town Hall would access EDGAR on a regular basis and then make the same information available on the Net at Town Hall's Web site (http://www.townhall.org).[43]

This service started in 1994, and many on the Net came to use the Town Hall EDGAR site as a reliable source of SEC information. The problem was that the information, while authentic, was still not official. The information was not provided directly to the Internet by the SEC—there was a middleman. A large law firm in New York was one of the many groups that used the Town Hall information, mainly to confirm that filings on behalf of their clients had been received—seeing it on the Town Hall site provided an easy way to see that the filing had already been processed.

One afternoon, when confirming the filing, a librarian at the law firm accessed the Town Hall site and searched for filings from their client. No record of the filing existed. According to Town Hall, the filing had not been made. Panicked, the law firm called the SEC and was able to confirm that the filing had been received and processed. One of the lawyers at the law firm had a friend who worked at Town Hall and called to see what had happened. The friend explained that it was his job to manually update the information, and he had been sick the day before.

What this anecdote illustrates is that information on the Net is only as reliable as its source. Many in the legal profession take this for granted when considering other types of information, but have come to treat the Internet differently. In the Town Hall example, the hasty conclusion might be that the Net is unreliable for legal research. The more reasoned reply, however, is that the Net can be a good tool for legal research. It is just not the only tool, and it is not necessarily always the best tool.

---

43. See **Internet Town Hall**, page 127.

Compiling a Research Strategy: Using the Tools Available

Any good researcher knows that one needs dozens of tools to do a thorough job of researching a topic. Case law is marginally useful until the case law has been Shepardized. In writing an article, case law is incomplete if not accompanied by other law review articles. In researching new topics of law, it is possible that law review articles and case law are useless, and West's federal digest or American Law Reports (ALR) may be the most helpful tool.

As the amount of legal information on the Net increases, its value as a research tool increases. The more important question to ask is what kinds of information are most suited for Net research as opposed to more traditional research methods.

And we think the glass is half full. There's plenty of good stuff on the Net today. Much of it free. Much of it reliable. What follows is the best of the Web for legal professionals.

CHAPTER **TWO**

Bars and Bar Associations

Overview

At the most fundamental, a bar association is a service organization. Lawyers join bar associations to benefit from the services offered. These services range from discounts on popular services (car rentals, LEXIS-NEXIS research time, and insurance) to networking (committee meetings, luncheons, and awards banquets). In some states, the bar itself—the state organization that oversees the practice of law—publishes information on the Web. In other states, the bar association—the nongovernment agency that serves its members—has a Web site. Where membership in the state's bar is mandatory, the line between the bar and the bar association is blurry or nonexistent. As such, we sometimes refer to "the bar" when we mean "the bar association" and vice versa.

In either case, the most valuable bar associations are those that understand what their members need. Increasingly, the Internet is both a conduit between association and member as well as a benefit itself. Some bar associations publish member directories; others give their members access to threaded discussion lists. There are many ways to provide valuable services to members. The key is that the bar associations, to remain viable, must figure out what it is their members need and then provide it. Too few are doing this today, but we expect that more will recognize the value in doing so. This also requires lawyers to realize the benefit they'll receive in using the service, and many lawyers are still a year or two away from having that recognition.

Best Meta Sites

Yahoo! Bar Associations (http://www.yahoo.com/Business_and_Economy/ Companies/Law/Organizations/Bar_Associations/). Not subdivided by region, but listed alphabetically. Also includes a link to Women's Bar Associations.

FindLaw Organizations (http://www.findlaw.com/06associations/). Separates national, state, and foreign bar associations. Also lists other directories of bar associations that may help locate the right one.

Hieros Gamos: Associations (http://www.hg.org/bar.html). Probably the best collection of links to international bar associations (it is sponsored, of course, by Lex Mundi).

Early Adopters

American Bar Association (abanet.org)

Middlers

Arkansas Bar Association c/o Law Office Information Systems Inc.
    (arkbar.com)
Colorado Bar Association (cobar.org)
Hawaii State Bar Association (hsba.org)
Illinois State Bar Association (isba.org)
Indiana State Bar Association (inbar.org)
Kentucky Bar Association (kybar.org)
Maryland State Bar Association (msba.org)
Massachusetts Bar Association (massbar.org)
Minnesota State Bar Association (mnbar.org)
Missouri Bar (mobar.org)
New Hampshire Bar Association (nhbar.org)
New York State Bar Association (nysba.org)
North Carolina Bar c/o NCLegal, Inc. (barlinc.org)
Oregon State Bar (osbar.org)
Pennsylvania State Bar Association (pa-bar.org)
State Bar of California (calbar.org)
State Bar of Wisconsin (wisbar.org)
Tennessee Bar Association (tba.org)
Utah State Bar (utahbar.org)
Washington D.C. Bar (dcbar.org)
Washington State Bar Association c/o Northwest Lawyer, Inc. (wsba.org)

Late Adopters

Alabama State Bar (**alabar.org**)
Alaska Bar Association (**alaskabar.org**)
Bar Association of the District of Columbia (**badc.org**)
Connecticut Bar Association (**ctbar.org**)
Delaware State Bar Association (**dsba.org**)
Florida Bar Association (**flabar.org**)
Iowa State Bar Association (**iowabar.org**)
Kansas Bar Association (**ksbar.org**)
Louisiana State Bar Association (**lsba.org**)
Maine State Bar Association (**mainebar.org**)
Mississippi Bar (**msbar.org**)
Nebraska State Bar Association (**nebar.com**)
New Jersey State Bar Association (**njbar.com**)
Ohio State Bar Association (**ohiobar.com**)
Rhode Island Bar Association (**ribar.com**)
State Bar of Arizona (**azbar.org**)
State Bar of Georgia (**gabar.org**)
State Bar of Michigan (**michbar.org**)
State Bar of Montana (**montanabar.org**)
State Bar of New Mexico (**nmbar.org**)
State Bar of South Dakota (**sdbar.org**)
State Bar of Texas (**texasbar.com**)
Vermont Bar Association (**vtbar.org**)
Virginia Bar Association, The (**vba.org**)
Virginia State Bar (**vsb.org**)
West Virginia State Bar (**wvbar.org**)

Luddites

Idaho State Bar (none)
Nevada State Bar (none)
North Dakota Bar (none)
Oklahoma State Bar (none)
Wyoming State Bar (none)

▼▼▼▼▼

Apple
The once and future king of computers. Jobs-less Apple got stuck in a rut and missed the Internet boat. Now Jobs has Apple selling computers on the Internet, à la Dell. In our opinion, it all comes down to Apple's lawyers and the look-and-feel case. If only . . .

NATIONAL BAR ASSOCIATIONS

American Bar Association

- *cyberspace:* abanet.org

- *earth place:* Chicago, IL

- *born on:* 20 Dec 1994 (early adopter)

- *review:* We love this site! Could a bar association site *be* any more perfect? We especially enjoyed the pages of the Law Practice Management Section. Four thumbs up! (Did we gush enough?)

- *practice areas:* USA; *ABA Journal;* administrative law section; affordable housing and community development law, forum on; air and space law, forum on; American bar endowment; American Bar Insurance Plans Consultants, Inc. (ABI); antitrust law section; bar services; broadcast programming; business law; central and east European law initiative (CEELI); children and the law; citation issues; commission on opportunities for minorities in the profession; communications law, forum on; construction industry, forum on; continuing legal education, center for (CLE); criminal justice section; disability law, commission on mental and physical; dispute resolution; domestic violence, commission on; elderly, commission on legal problems of the; entertainment and sports industries, forum on; family law section; forums; franchising, forum on; general practice, solo and small firm section; government affairs office; government and public sector lawyers division; health law section; homelessness and poverty, commission on; impaired lawyers, commission on; individual rights and responsibilities; intellectual property law; international law section; international liaison office; judicial division; justice initiatives; labor and employment law, section of; law and national security, standing committee on; law practice management section; law student division; lawyer advertising, commission on; lawyer referral, standing committee on; lawyers' professional liability, standing committee on; legal assistants, standing committee on; legal education opportunities, council on (CLEO); legal education/admissions to the bar; legal services; legal technology resource center; litigation section; media relations and public affairs, division of; natural resources, energy and environmental law, section of; pro bono/lawyers public service responsibility, standing committee on; professional responsibility, center for; public contract law; public education, division for; public services;

public utility, communications and transportation law, section of; real property, probate and trust section; science and technology section; senior lawyers division; small firm resource center; solo and small firm practitioners, standing committee on; specialization, standing committee on; state and local government law; substance abuse, standing committee on; tax section; tort and insurance practice section; unmet legal needs of children, steering committee on; women in the profession, commission on; young lawyers division

STATE BARS AND BAR ASSOCIATIONS

Alabama State Bar

- *cyberspace:* alabar.org
- *earth place:* Montgomery, AL
- *born on:* 25 Feb 1996 (late adopter)
- *practice areas:* Alabama

Alaska Bar Association

- *cyberspace:* alaskabar.org
- *earth place:* Anchorage, AK
- *born on:* 11 Aug 1996 (late adopter)
- *practice areas:* Alaska

State Bar of Arizona

- *cyberspace:* azbar.org
- *earth place:* Phoenix, AZ
- *born on:* 13 May 1996 (late adopter)
- *review:* The only bar site with Native American audio effects. Includes Arizona court opinions.
- *practice areas:* Arizona

Arkansas Bar Association c/o Law Office Information Systems Inc.[1]

- *cyberspace:* arkbar.com
- *earth place:* Van Buren, AR

---

1. See page 2.

- *born on:* 27 Nov 1995 (middler)
- *review:* Wow! Law Office Information Systems Inc. bought the Arkansas Bar Association!
- *practice areas:* Arkansas

State Bar of California[2]

- *cyberspace:* calbar.org
- *earth place:* San Francisco, CA
- *born on:* 28 Aug 1995 (middler)
- *review:* A well-organized site with something for lawyers, those who want to be lawyers, and those who need lawyers. Consumers should check out "An Illustrated Guide to the Complaint Process." Includes a search engine interface on the home page, so no extra clicks are required if you want to search the site.
- *practice areas:* California; antitrust and trade regulation, business law section, criminal law section, environmental law section, estate planning, trust and probate law section, family law section, intellectual property law section, international law section, labor and employment law section, law practice management and technology section, legal services section, litigation section, public law section, real property law section, senior lawyers section, solo and small firm section, taxation section, workers' compensation law section

Colorado Bar Association

- *cyberspace:* cobar.org
- *earth place:* Denver, CO
- *born on:* 28 Oct 1995 (middler)
- *review:* Worth visiting just to see the nontraditional approach they've taken for their home page: a cartoon drawing of a lawyer's office. Includes Colorado court opinions.
- *practice areas:* Colorado; agricultural and rural law, business law, criminal law, environmental law, family law, health law, judiciary, litigation, mineral law, patent, trademark, and copyright, real estate law, solo/small firm, taxation law, trust and estate, water law, workers' compensation

---

2. Bert & Ernies Sports Bar & Grill, Inc. (**bert-n-ernies.com**) is another California bar.

Connecticut Bar Association

- *cyberspace:* ctbar.org
- *earth place:* Rocky Hill, CT
- *born on:* 05 Apr 1996 (late adopter)
- *review:* A simple structure with basic information easily accessible. Includes articles from the *Connecticut Lawyer*.
- *practice areas:* Connecticut

Delaware State Bar Association

- *cyberspace:* dsba.org
- *earth place:* Wilmington, DE
- *born on:* 22 Apr 1996 (late adopter)
- *practice areas:* Delaware

Bar Association of the District of Columbia

- *cyberspace:* badc.org
- *earth place:* Washington, DC
- *born on:* 05 Jun 1996 (late adopter)
- *practice areas:* District of Columbia

Washington D.C. Bar

- *cyberspace:* dcbar.org
- *earth place:* Washington, DC
- *born on:* 19 Apr 1995 (middler)
- *review:* Although the InterNIC shows this domain registered to the Washington D.C. Bar Association,[3] we're pretty sure it's registered to the Washington D.C. Bar. Which underscores the need of the legal profession to communicate what we're all about. See also **Virginia Bar Association.**
- *practice areas:* District of Columbia

---

3. See http://www.washingtonbar.org for that site.

Florida Bar Association[4]

- *cyberspace:* flabar.org
- *earth place:* Tallahassee, FL
- *born on:* 11 Mar 1996 (late adopter)
- *review:*
- *practice areas:* Florida

State Bar of Georgia

- *cyberspace:* gabar.org
- *earth place:* Atlanta, GA
- *born on:* 16 May 1996 (late adopter)
- *practice areas:* Georgia

Hawaii State Bar Association

- *cyberspace:* hsba.org
- *earth place:* Honolulu, HI
- *born on:* 29 Dec 1995 (middler)
- *practice areas:* Hawaii; real property and financial services

Idaho State Bar

- *cyberspace:* none
- *earth place:* ID
- *born on:* (Luddite)
- *review:* Missing in action.
- *practice areas:* Idaho

Illinois State Bar Association

- *cyberspace:* isba.org
- *earth place:* Springfield, IL
- *born on:* 11 Sep 1995 (middler)
- *review:* Includes Illinois Supreme Court decisions and a member-only discussion group. This is a good example of what information we have included for bar association Web sites. On the sections

---

4. Jungle Jims Bar and Grill (**http://jungle-jims.com**) is another Florida bar.

page, many sections are listed, but only a few have substantive information online. Those few are shown below.

- *practice areas:* Illinois; civil practice and procedure, family law, legal technology, real estate law, tort, law, trusts and estates, young lawyers division

Indiana State Bar Association

- *cyberspace:* inbar.org
- *earth place:* Indianapolis, IN
- *born on:* 28 Oct 1995 (middler)
- *practice areas:* Indiana

Iowa State Bar Association

- *cyberspace:* iowabar.org
- *earth place:* Des Moines, IA
- *born on:* 16 Aug 1996 (late adopter)
- *review:* Includes a judges-only section and Iowa court opinions. From the state that has perhaps the most restrictive regulations about lawyers advertising on the Web.
- *practice areas:* Iowa

Kansas Bar Association

- *cyberspace:* ksbar.org
- *earth place:* Topeka, KS
- *born on:* 26 May 1997 (late adopter)
- *review:* We'd tell you how good this site is, except that we can't get into it. Not only is the home page unreadable in Netscape (it showed up fine in Internet Explorer), but almost all of the substantive content is restricted to registered INK (Information Network of Kansas) subscribers.
- *practice areas:* Kansas

BBS
Bulletin Board System. A computer that is accessible via one or more dial-in modems. BBSs can also be connected to the Internet. There are many BBSs nationwide, most of which serve local markets. Some BBSs are law-related, and many offer Internet access of one sort or another. But for the most part, BBSs are a dying breed. For local BBSs in your area, see Yahoo's index of BBSs (http://www.yahoo .com/Computers_and_Internet/ Communications_and_Networking/ Bulletin_Boards/).

Kentucky Bar Association

- *cyberspace:* kybar.org
- *earth place:* Frankfort, KY
- *born on:* 03 Jun 1995 (middler)
- *review:* One of the first bar association Web sites. Includes information on how to contact legal service and pro bono programs for those who cannot afford a lawyer.
- *practice areas:* Kentucky

Louisiana State Bar Association

- *cyberspace:* lsba.org
- *earth place:* New Orleans, LA
- *born on:* 22 Apr 1997 (late adopter)
- *practice areas:* Louisiana

Maine State Bar Association

- *cyberspace:* mainebar.org
- *earth place:* Augusta, ME
- *born on:* 05 Mar 1996 (late adopter)
- *practice areas:* Maine

Maryland State Bar Association

- *cyberspace:* msba.org
- *earth place:* Baltimore, MD
- *born on:* 10 Oct 1995 (middler)
- *review:* Not to be confused with the Mississippi Bar (msbar.org).
- *practice areas:* Maryland

Massachusetts Bar Association

- *cyberspace:* massbar.org
- *earth place:* Boston, MA
- *born on:* 07 Jun 1995 (middler)
- *review:* Includes legislative information.
- *practice areas:* Massachusetts

State Bar of Michigan

- *cyberspace:* michbar.org
- *earth place:* Lansing, MI
- *born on:* 20 Feb 1996 (late adopter)
- *review:* Includes recent, but poorly organized, Michigan Supreme Court and Court of Appeals decisions.
- *practice areas:* Michigan; administrative law, alternative dispute resolution, American Indian law, animal law, antitrust, franchising and trade regulation, appellate practice, arts, communications, entertainment and sports, aviation law, business law, computer law, criminal law, environmental law, family law, general practice, health care law, intellectual property law, international law, judicial conference, juvenile law, labor and employment law, law practice management bylaws, law practice management, law student, legal administrator, legal assistants, litigation, negligence law, probate and estate planning, public corporation law, real property law, senior justice, senior lawyers, taxation, workers' compensation law, young lawyers

Minnesota State Bar Association

- *cyberspace:* mnbar.org
- *earth place:* Minneapolis, MN
- *born on:* 28 Dec 1995 (middler)
- *practice areas:* Minnesota

Mississippi Bar

- *cyberspace:* msbar.org
- *earth place:* Jackson, MS
- *born on:* 12 Apr 1996 (late adopter)

browser
The client software program used to access the World Wide Web. Netscape Navigator and Microsoft Internet Explorer are the most popular World Wide Web browsers.

Canter & Siegel
This couple actually managed to make the words "Green Card" the most despised subject heading in Internet history (followed closely by "Make Money Fast" and "Craig Shergold: Business Cards"). Lawrence Canter and Martha Siegel figured out how to "spam" newsgroups—so-called after the Monty Python sketch in which a diner serves nothing but spam. (People who ordered off the menu ended up repeating the word *spam* a lot, so the digerati thought that endless duplicates of the same e-mail was similar.) Their original note, claiming to help foreigners in a Green Card lottery, showed up in thousands of newsgroups. They would go on to spam many others, write a book, and then vanish. Mr. Canter was later disbarred from Tennessee, in part because of his actions with the Green Card Usenet post. See **spam**.

- *review:* Includes Web-ified version of publications designed for legal consumers. Not to be confused with the Maryland State Bar Association (**msba.org**).
- *practice areas:* Mississippi

Missouri Bar

- *cyberspace:* mobar.org
- *earth place:* Jefferson City, MO
- *born on:* 26 Dec 1995 (middler)
- *practice areas:* Missouri

State Bar of Montana

- *cyberspace:* montanabar.org
- *earth place:* Helena, MT
- *born on:* 09 Apr 1997 (late adopter)
- *review:* This underscores the difference between state bar Web sites (generally thin on content) and state bar association Web sites (generally content-rich).
- *practice areas:* Montana

Nebraska State Bar Association

- *cyberspace:* nebar.com
- *earth place:* Lincoln, NE
- *born on:* 11 Sep 1996 (late adopter)
- *review:* Includes Nebraska legislative information.
- *practice areas:* Nebraska

Nevada State Bar

- *cyberspace:* none
- *earth place:* NV
- *born on:* (Luddite)
- *review:* See http://www.dsi.org/statebar/nevada.htm. Nearly missing in action, this is one of the last organizations in this book not to have a registered domain name.
- *practice areas:* Nevada

New Hampshire Bar Association

- *cyberspace:* nhbar.org
- *earth place:* Concord, NH
- *born on:* 29 Nov 1995 (middler)
- *practice areas:* New Hampshire

New Jersey State Bar Association

- *cyberspace:* njbar.com
- *earth place:* New Brunswick, NJ
- *born on:* 21 Feb 1996 (late adopter)
- *practice areas:* New Jersey

State Bar of New Mexico

- *cyberspace:* nmbar.org
- *earth place:* Albuquerque, NM
- *born on:* 22 Jun 1997 (late adopter)
- *practice areas:* New Mexico

New York State Bar Association[5]

- *cyberspace:* nysba.org
- *earth place:* Albany, NY
- *born on:* 28 Oct 1995 (middler)
- *review:* A full-service, well-designed Web site.
- *practice areas:* New York; antitrust law, business law, commercial and federal litigation, corporate counsel, criminal justice, elder law, entertainment, arts and sports law, environmental law, family law, food, drug and cosmetic law, general practice, health law, intellectual property law, international law and practice, judicial, labor and employment law, municipal law, real property law, tax, torts, insurance and compensation law, trial lawyers, trusts and estates law, young lawyers

---

5. Bathtub Billy's Restaurant and Sports Bar (**http://www.bathtubbillys.com**) is another New York bar.

North Carolina Bar c/o NCLegal, Inc

- *cyberspace:* barlinc.org
- *earth place:* Raleigh, NC
- *born on:* 04 Sep 1995 (middler)
- *review:* A few too many links on the home page, but the site includes some very interesting content, including a list of those who passed the North Carolina bar exam. Also includes links to North Carolina Supreme Court decisions. Very helpful section pages.
- *practice areas:* North Carolina; bankruptcy, law, dispute resolution, elder law, environmental law, general practice, solo and small firm, health law, intellectual property law, litigation

North Dakota Bar

- *cyberspace:* none
- *earth place:* ND
- *born on:* (Luddite)
- *review:* Missing in action.
- *practice areas:* North Dakota

Ohio State Bar Association

- *cyberspace:* ohiobar.com
- *earth place:* Columbus, OH
- *born on:* 20 Mar 1996 (late adopter)
- *review:* A well-designed site with lots here for the public and for members (such as discussion forums and private mailboxes).
- *practice areas:* Ohio; administrative law, agricultural law, alternative dispute resolution, antitrust law, aviation law, banking, commercial and bankruptcy law, computer law, construction and government contracts, corporate counsel, corporation law, criminal justice, disability law, elder law, eminent domain, environmental law, estate planning, trust and probate law, family law, federal courts and practice, federal taxation, government lawyers, health care law, insurance law, intellectual property law, international law, judicial administration and legal reform, labor and employment law, law libraries and legal information services, law office automation and technology, lawyer's assistance, legal aid, legal education, legal ethics and professional conduct, litigation, local government law,

media law, natural resources law, negligence law, paralegal/legal assistants, public understanding of the law, public utilities law, real property law, school law, senior lawyers, solo, small firms and general practice, specialization, sports and entertainment law, taxation, traffic law, unauthorized practice of law, uniform state law, women in the profession, workers' compensation law, young lawyers

Oklahoma State Bar

- *cyberspace:* none
- *earth place:* OK
- *born on:* (Luddite)
- *review:* Missing in action.
- *practice areas:* Oklahoma

Oregon State Bar

- *cyberspace:* osbar.org
- *earth place:* Lake Osweg, OR
- *born on:* 08 Sep 1995 (middler)
- *practice areas:* Oregon

Pennsylvania State Bar Association

- *cyberspace:* pa-bar.org
- *earth place:* Harrisburg, PA
- *born on:* 12 Dec 1995 (middler)
- *review:* A content-rich site including court opinions, court rules, and CLE information. And there are plans for discussion groups, searchable ethics opinions, and more.
- *practice areas:* Pennsylvania; alternative dispute resolution committee, amicus curiae brief committee, corporate banking and business law, health care law committee, intellectual property committee, interdis-

CDA
Communications Decency Act. Passed by Congress and signed by President Clinton, the law was supposed to prevent "harmful" and "indecent" material from getting in the hands of minors. Joe McCarthy could have drafted a less blatantly unconstitutional law. Predictably, opponents called it unconstitutional and proponents called the opponents perverts. When it went to the Supreme Court, the Justices resoundingly rejected the law, rightly deciding that it was overly broad.

client
The user side of a client/server-based system. Clients receive information from servers. Unlike human clients, a client pays nothing for receiving this information.

ciplinary committee on medical and health-related issues, joint task force to ensure gender fairness in the courts, legal services for exceptional children committee, legal services to persons with disabilities committee, legal services to the public, professionalism committee, public utility law section, solo and small firm section, unauthorized practice of law committee

Rhode Island Bar Association

- *cyberspace:* ribar.com
- *earth place:* Providence, RI
- *born on:* 14 May 1996 (late adopter)
- *review:* Includes Rhode Island Supreme Court opinions.
- *practice areas:* Rhode Island

State Bar of South Dakota

- *cyberspace:* sdbar.org
- *earth place:* Pierre, SD
- *born on:* 02 Jul 1996 (late adopter)
- *review:* Includes South Dakota Supreme Court opinions.
- *practice areas:* South Dakota

Tennessee Bar Association

- *cyberspace:* tba.org
- *earth place:* Nashville, TN
- *born on:* 07 Mar 1995 (middler)
- *review:* The search engine (named "Page Finder") is helpful, although the interface takes some getting used to. This site's home page is a bit busy, and the major areas of the site have nonintuitive names (e.g.; "Polling Place" and "Opinion-Flash"), but once you figure out what's here, the site is very rich in content. For example, LawBytes is a consumer-oriented service that provides descriptions of the law in plain English. Lawyers will find Opinion-Flash (e-mail delivery of summaries of Tennessee appellate decisions and new Tennessee Supreme Court rules and orders) very useful.
- *practice areas:* Tennessee; antitrust and business regulation, commercial, bankruptcy and banking law, corporation and business law, criminal justice, dispute resolution, environmental law, family

law, general, solo, and small firm practitioners, health care law, labor and employment law, law office technology and management, litigation, real estate law, senior lawyers division, tax, probate and trust law

State Bar of Texas

- *cyberspace:* texasbar.com
- *earth place:* Austin, TX
- *born on:* 19 Nov 1996 (late adopter)
- *practice areas:* Texas

Utah State Bar

- *cyberspace:* utahbar.org
- *earth place:* Salt Lake City, UT
- *born on:* 22 Dec 1995 (middler)
- *review:* The large photographic image on the home page is a bit of a distraction, and it does not serve as a clickable image map. Includes a simple searchable member directory database.
- *practice areas:* Utah

Vermont Bar Association

- *cyberspace:* vtbar.org
- *earth place:* Montpelier, VT
- *born on:* 12 Apr 1996 (late adopter)
- *review:* This site has lots of corporate sponsors. We believe this is an example of a Web site designed under Microsoft's association initiative, where certain software and services are provided free of charge to bar associations in exchange for banner advertising and the like.
- *practice areas:* Vermont

Virginia Bar Association, The

- *cyberspace:* vba.org
- *earth place:* Richmond, VA
- *born on:* 27 Mar 1997 (late adopter)
- *practice areas:* Virginia

Virginia State Bar

- *cyberspace:* vsb.org
- *earth place:* Richmond, VA
- *born on:* 11 May 1996 (late adopter)
- *review:* Although the InterNIC shows this domain registered to the Virginia State Bar Association, we're pretty sure it's registered to the Virginia State Bar. Which underscores the need of the legal profession to communicate what we're all about. See also **Washington D.C. Bar.**
- *practice areas:* Virginia

Washington State Bar Association c/o Northwest Lawyer, Inc.[6]

- *cyberspace:* wsba.org
- *earth place:* Seattle, WA
- *born on:* 10 Nov 1995 (middler)
- *review:* This site's conservative use of graphics makes it perform very well. Includes a calendar of upcoming CLE seminars.
- *practice areas:* Washington

West Virginia State Bar

- *cyberspace:* wvbar.org
- *earth place:* Charleston, WV
- *born on:* 31 May 1996 (late adopter)
- *practice areas:* West Virginia

State Bar of Wisconsin

- *cyberspace:* wisbar.org
- *earth place:* Madison, WI
- *born on:* 08 Feb 1995 (middler)
- *review:* "Serving the members of the State Bar of Wisconsin and the Public" is the goal proclaimed by this Web site. A great goal and a

---

6. See page 2.

great Web site. The "What's New" section contains a summary of the ABA's backing of a vendor-neutral citation system as well as links to related documents. Includes the *Wisconsin Lawyer* magazine. Also includes Wisconsin Supreme Court Decisions and member-only areas. Its organization is at times nonintuitive, but overall this site is a great model for state bar associations considering getting on the Web.

- *practice areas:* Wisconsin; administrative and local government law, alternative dispute resolution, bankruptcy, insolvency and creditor's rights, business law, children and the law, construction and public contract law, criminal law, elder law, environmental law, family law, general practice, health law, Indian law, individual rights and responsibilities, intellectual property, international practice, labor and employment law, litigation, office management, real property, probate and trust law, sports and entertainment law, taxation

Wyoming State Bar

- *cyberspace:* none
- *earth place:* WY
- *born on:* (Luddite)
- *review:* Missing in action.
- *practice areas:* Wyoming

▼▼▼▼▼

Clipper Chip

A gift from former President Bush to President Clinton. The Clipper Chip is the presidential idea that Just Won't Die. The idea is that criminals will start using encryption to encode their communications, rendering the government unable to stop them. So in comes Clipper—the "friendly" encryption program that lets us citizens use cryptography—except when the government doesn't want us to. The FBI really wants it, the White House really wants it, and the civil liberties groups scream bloody murder every time it comes up for debate.

CHAPTER **THREE**

Companies

Overview
This chapter focuses on those organizations that provide substantive content online to the legal community. Companies that are online, yet provide little or no content, are likely omitted from this list. In short, we list companies that are making a difference in the Internet marketspace.

Best Meta Sites
BigBook (http://www.bigbook.com). BigBook is a nationwide directory that uses information from American Business Information. You can search by business name, business category, and geographic location. Phone numbers, maps, and addresses for each business are provided.

Yahoo! Companies (http://www.yahoo.com/Business/Companies/). More than 300,000 companies from around the world are listed here.

Visionaries
Legi-Slate, Inc. (legislate.com)
The Bureau of National Affairs, Inc. (bna.com)

Early Adopters
Copyright Clearance Center (copyright.com)
Counsel Connect Inc. (counsel.com)
Cyberlaw and Cyberlex (cyberlaw.com)
Law Offices of McAvoy and Kronemyer (lawyers.com)
Lawyers Cooperative Publishing (lcp.com)
Matthew Bender (bender.com)

New York Law Publishing, Inc. (ljextra.com)
Nolo Press (nolopress.com)

Middlers

FindLaw (findlaw.com)
Internet Lawyer c/o GoAhead Productions Inc. (internetlawyer.com)
Law Journal EXTRA! (ljx.com)
Law Office Information Systems Inc. (pita.com)
LawSource, Inc. (lawsource.com)
Lawyers Weekly, Inc. (lweekly.com)
Legal Communications (legalcom.com)
Martindale-Hubbell (martindale.com)
The Seamless Website (seamless.com)
West Publishing Corp. (wld.com)
Yahoo (yahoo.com)

Late Adopters

College Hill Internet Consultants (collegehill.com)
Court TV (courttv.com)
Educational Online Network, Inc. d.b.a. CLE Online (cleonline.com)
Glasser LegalWorks (legalwks.com)
Legal Recruitment Network (emplawyernet.com)
Reed Elsevier, Inc. (reed-elsevier.com)
Tennessee Commission on Continuing Legal Education and
    Specialization (cletn.com)
The Thomson Corporation (thomcorp.com)
Thomson & Thomson (saegis.com)
Timeline Publishing (versuslaw.com)

THE BIG TWO

Reed Elsevier, Inc.

- *cyberspace:* reed-elsevier.com

- *earth place:* Miamisburg, OH

- *born on:* 05 Jun 1996 (late adopter)

- *review:* Reed Elsevier, Inc., is the world's largest English-language
  publisher. Its holdings include Butterworths, LEXIS-NEXIS, and
  Martindale-Hubbell. In October 1997, Reed Elsevier and Wolters
  Kluwer announced their intent to merge. In a market dominated by

a few major players, we feel that it is essential to know—and keep track of—who owns whom so that legal consumers can know what information is reliable and what is not. Just like nobody ever got fired for buying IBM, nobody will ever get fired for relying on products from giants like Reed and Thomson.

The Thomson Corporation

- *cyberspace:* thomcorp.com
- *earth place:* Stamford, CT
- *born on:* 02 Jul 1996 (late adopter)
- *review:* The Thomson Corporation (TTC) is the world's second-largest English-language publisher. (Reed is the largest.) And legal publishing is only part of what they do. The Thomson Financial & Professional Publishing Group (TFPPG), one of four major units of TTC, publishes over 6,500 products. TFPPG is further divided into four groups: West Group (Bancroft Whitney, Banks-Baldwin Law Publishing Company, Clark Boardman Callaghan, Foundation Press, Information America, Lawyers Cooperative Publishing, The Rutter Group, West Publishing Company, WESTLAW), RIA Group (Carswell, Creative Solutions, Electronic Selection Systems, Practitioners Publishing Company, Research Institute of America, RIA Software, Warren Gorham & Lamont), Thomson Financial Services, and Thomson Technology Services Group.

THE BEST OF THE REST

College Hill Internet Consultants

- *cyberspace:* collegehill.com
- *earth place:* Providence, RI
- *born on:* 04 Jan 1996 (late adopter)
- *review:* The founders of College Hill are not lawyers, but they play lawyers on the Net. Well, not exactly. They are not holding themselves out as lawyers, far from it. But their success in the legal vertical Web consulting and design market is a clear indication of business acumen. Most nonlawyers who try to break into the legal vertical market often fall flat on their face. Not College Hill. They do first-class Web work for reasonable fees, and they provide value-added services—most notably their Internet Legal Practice News-

letter—to the legal Internet community. College Hill recently relocated to the Boston area, an area with a wealth of technical expertise. You know how after you buy a new car you notice more of that model on the road? Now that you've heard of College Hill, you are sure to notice their presence on the Net.

Copyright Clearance Center

- *cyberspace:* copyright.com
- *earth place:* Danvers, MA
- *born on:* 08 Jun 1994 (early adopter)
- *review:* A not-for-profit organization that provides its members a lawful way to copy documents from its collection of nearly two million titles. Although no free content appears on the site, there is a helpful FAQ about copyright law.
- *practice areas:* copyright

Counsel Connect Inc.

- *cyberspace:* counsel.com
- *earth place:* New York, NY
- *born on:* 30 Nov 1994 (early adopter)
- *review:* Counsel Connect (formerly LEXIS Counsel Connect) began in March 1993 as a proprietary online service for lawyers. The idea was that lawyers would benefit from a closed network where they would have access to e-mail, news from the *Wall Street Journal,* and discussion areas. Counsel Connect was originally founded by American Lawyer Media (an affiliate of Time Warner), but increased in popularity when they joined forces with LEXIS-NEXIS, and became LEXIS Counsel Connect. LEXIS and ALM are no longer partners in the venture, and today the service is known once again as Counsel Connect.

Counsel Connect today boasts of 40,000 members, and is the de facto online meeting area for lawyers. Access to Counsel Connect is via a secured Internet connection (in the past it had been via a proprietary dial-up connection). Counsel Connect is a useful service, as it provides lawyers with a trusted resource. Of particular help are the discussion areas, which provide lawyers and support staff with a central place to receive advice, tips, and suggestions from people who have been in similar circumstances. The key benefit that

Counsel Connect offers is that the audience is limited, which means that there is less risk of unknown individuals crowding out the conversation. Another positive aspect of Counsel Connect is its "QRFPs," or Quick Requests for Proposals. These are moderated by Counsel Connect's editors, and allow businesses and other organizations to find out which law firms are capable of doing the work needed. It is a win-win situation—the law firms get qualified leads, and the businesses get quality proposals in response to allow them to assess what the law firm is capable of doing.

Affiliated sites include CalLaw (**http://www.callaw.com/**), Illinois Law (**http://www.statelaw.com/**), and TexLaw (**http://www.texlaw.com/**) which publishes daily updates on California, Illinois, and Texas law, respectively. Practice directories are available on Counsel Connect's public site (**http://www.counselconnect.com/ practice_directories/**), and we assume these will soon be merged with those from Law Journal EXTRA!, since American Lawyer Media (whose products and services include *American Lawyer* magazine, various regional print publications, and Counsel Connect) and the New York Law Publishing Company (whose products and services include the *National Law Journal* and Law Journal EXTRA!) are owned by the same company—U.S. Equity Partners, L.P., as of October 1997. U.S. Equity Partners purchased American Lawyer Media in August 1997.

- *practice areas:* antitrust, commercial litigation, environmental regulation and litigation, ERISA and employee benefits, intellectual property, labor and employment, product liability and insurance defense, white-collar crime, and corporate compliance

Court TV

- *cyberspace:* courttv.com

- *earth place:* New York, NY

- *born on:* 02 Jul 1997 (late adopter)

- *review:* Started in July 1991 and now owned jointly by Liberty Media, NBC, and Time Warner, Court TV is a cable television station dedicated to

▼▼▼▼▼

Computer ESP
(http://www.uvision.com/)
We don't remember how we found this site, but we're glad we did. If you're in the market to buy computer equipment—hardware or software—then stop by Computer ESP. This is the best site for price-shopping computer accessories. In most cases you'll see prices from reputable online merchants that are 20 to 40 percent less than the retail prices you'll see at Computer City or CompUSA.

providing consumers with legal news and information. Its Web site is the best resource for consumers about current events in the legal field. Although there is not a great deal of primary or secondary law, per se, at the site, there is a collection of documents (such as transcripts and depositions) relating to court cases in the news. One of the best resources on the site is the Court TV Cradle-to-Grave Legal Survival Guide (http://www.courttv.com/legalhelp/lawguide/), excerpted from the book with the same name, which contains essays on a wide variety of legal topics affecting consumers, such as buying and selling a home, divorce, small business issues, wills, and workers' compensation.

- *practice areas:* buying and selling a car, buying and selling a home, child support, consumer issues, copyrights, criminal law files, divorce, driving, finding a lawyer, getting hurt, getting sick, having and owing money, how the courts are structured, insurance, lawyer's fees, legal resources, litigation alternatives, living wills, Medicare and Medigap, patents, paying taxes, pensions and retirement plans, power of attorney, prenuptial agreements, pursuing a civil lawsuit, renting, sexual harassment, small business issues, small claims court, social security, the law: what it is and where it comes from, traveling on airlines, workers' compensation, working

Cyberlaw and Cyberlex

- *cyberspace:* cyberlaw.com
- *earth place:* Sunnyvale, CA
- *born on:* 15 Jul 1994 (early adopter)
- *review:* This site offers articles and commentary on legal issues affecting computer technology. CyberLaw is maintained by California lawyer Jonathan Rosenoer.
- *practice areas:* computer technology, Internet

Educational Online Network, Inc. d.b.a CLE Online

- *cyberspace:* cleonline.com
- *earth place:* Round Rock, TX
- *born on:* 18 Jul 1996 (late adopter)
- *review:* They say that pioneers usually end up with arrows in their backs, and that the settlers make all the money. Maybe it's because we're Red Sox fans, but we hereby root for the pioneers. CLE Online is clearly a pioneer. They are one of the first companies to offer on-

line Continuing Legal Education (CLE) on the Internet. Of the 50 states, 38 (all but Alaska, Connecticut, Hawaii, Illinois, Maine, Maryland, Massachusetts, Michigan, Nebraska, New Jersey, New York, and South Dakota) have Mandatory CLE (MCLE), and others may join in that trend. Not all states approve online CLE, but stay tuned. Let's just say it's a growth market ideally suited for Internet-based products and services.

FindLaw

- *cyberspace:* findlaw.com
- *earth place:* Palo Alto, CA
- *born on:* 13 Dec 1995 (middler)
- *review:* Simply put, FindLaw is the Yahoo of the legal profession. And with more innovations than you can shake a stick at. Well, you could shake a stick at them, but what would be the point of that? Among their innovations are LawCrawler, a front-end interface to AltaVista that enables you to limit searches to law-related Internet sites. Also on FindLaw's site are law review articles and abstracts as well as plenty of Supreme Court opinions. FindLaw's founders have a wealth of legal and technical experience, and it shows.
- *practice areas:* administrative law, antitrust and trade regulation, banking law, bankruptcy law, civil rights, commercial law, communications law, constitutional law, contracts, corporation and enterprise law, criminal law, cyberspace law, dispute resolution and arbitration, education law, entertainment and sports law, environmental law, ethics and professional responsibility, family law, government benefits, government contracts, health law, immigration law, Indian law, injury and tort law, intellectual property, international law, international trade, judges and the judiciary, labor and employment law, law and economics, legal theory, litigation, probate, trusts and estates, property law and real estate, securities law, tax law

Glasser LegalWorks

- *cyberspace:* legalwks.com
- *earth place:* Little Falls, NJ
- *born on:* 13 Mar 1996 (late adopter)
- *review:* The founders of Glasser LegalWorks, Stephen A. Glasser and Lynn S. Glasser, are well-known leaders in the legal publishing

field. Glasser LegalWorks is dedicated to the delivery of timely, specialized information in a variety of formats.

Internet Lawyer c/o GoAhead Productions Inc.[1]

- *cyberspace:* internetlawyer.com
- *earth place:* Gainesville, FL
- *born on:* 09 Dec 1995 (middler)
- *review:* Would you buy a car without test-driving it? Probably not. With that in mind, the publishers of *The Internet Lawyer* newsletter recently added the bulk of their newsletter to their companion Web site. The site's increasing popularity is a sign of the times. Lawyers need good sites to help them weed through the Internet, and this is one of those sites.

Law Journal EXTRA!

- *cyberspace:* ljx.com
- *earth place:* New York, NY
- *born on:* 12 Jun 1995 (middler)
- *review:* Originally a proprietary online service, Law Journal EXTRA! (LJX) was the first online service to switch to an Internet-based delivery system. LJX seamlessly integrates print content from its parent's (The New York Law Publishing Company) other publications: the *National Law Journal,* the *New York Law Journal,* and *Law Technology Product News.* They also have companion sites covering continuing legal education (http://www.legalseminars.com/), legal research (http://www.legalresearcher.com/), job hunting (http://www.lawjobs.com/), and intellectual property law (the Intellectual Property Center, http://www.ipcenter.com/). The seminars site has a slick and intuitive calendar interface to Law Journal Seminars-Press's upcoming events. Click on a date on the calendar, and you're taken to detailed information about the courses offered on that date. The practice areas pages (including the Intellectual Property Center) contain memos from leaders in each field on a variety of legal topics. Each practice page also includes links to primary law sources on the Internet, which are updated daily, of course. In October 1997, U.S. Equity Partners, L.P. (a private equity fund sponsored by Wasserstein Perella—the same company that purchased American Lawyer Media from Time Warner Inc. in August 1997)

---

1. See page 2.

agreed to purchase the National Law Publishing Company from Boston Ventures and James Finkelstein. The nation's two largest legal periodical publishers are now owned by the same company and are run by James Finkelstein, president of The New York Law Publishing Company.

- *practice areas:* administrative law, admiralty law, antitrust law, arbitration and ADR, banking, bankruptcy, civil rights, commercial law, government contracts, franchising, communications law, computer law, constitutional law, corporate law, mergers and acquisitions, criminal law, employment and labor, energy/public utilities, environmental law, family law, federal practice, health law, immigration law, insurance law, intellectual property, copyright, patent, trademark, international law, international trade, Internet law, landlord/tenant, media law, sports and entertainment, New York practice, products liability, professional responsibility, real estate law, securities law, taxation, torts (negligence/malpractice), wills, trusts and estates, personal finance

Law Office Information Systems, Inc.

- *cyberspace:* pita.com

- *earth place:* Van Buren, AR

- *born on:* 16 Nov 1995 (middler)

- *review:* Law Office Information Systems, (LOIS) Inc., publishes state and federal law libraries on CD-ROM and the Internet. For example, for $960 per year, you have unlimited access to LOIS libraries for your state, your federal circuit, the U.S. Reports, and the U.S. Code. It's not as comprehensive as LEXIS-NEXIS or WESTLAW, but it may suit your needs.

- *practice areas:* case law, statutes, administrative codes, court rules, jury instructions, attorney general opinions

computer virus

Maine's criminal code (17-A MRSA Sec. 432) defines a "computer virus" as "any computer instruction, information, data or program that degrades the performance of a computer resource; damages or destroys a computer resource; or attaches itself to another computer resource and executes when the host computer program, data or instruction is executed or when some other event takes place in the host computer, resource, data or instruction." Let's see. Many law firms have resisted upgrading from Windows 3.1 to Windows95 (or from DOS to Windows 3.1) because Windows95 degrades the performance of their computers. In Maine, they could press charges against Microsoft on the grounds that Windows95 is a virus. Or against Apple because of MacOS 8.0. In fact, even screensavers fall into Maine's very broad definition of "computer virus"!

Law Offices of McAvoy and Kronemyer

- *cyberspace:* lawyers.com

- *earth place:* San Diego, CA

- *born on:* 07 Sep 1994 (early adopter)

- *review:* No Web site here, but "lawyers.com" is a darn valuable chunk of intellectual property, one that has been sitting idle for nearly the last three years! It is registered to the San Diego-based Law Offices of McAvoy and Kronemyer. And if you try to access **http://www.lawyers.com/**, you'll get the Web site of their Internet Service Provider, but that's fodder for another article, another day. If you use your imagination, I'm sure you could come up with a company or two that might want to be associated with lawyers on the Net. Any takers? We have an idea for how this domain name could be used. First, create a nonprofit organization dedicated to helping consumers nationwide find lawyers. Second, buy the domain name lawyers.com and dedicate that site to helping consumers find lawyers. Nonprofit organizations such as state and local bar associations and lawyer referral services would be listed for free on the lawyers .com site. Commercial services such as *Martindale-Hubbell* and *West Legal Directory* that provide free Web-based services should also be listed for free. Others could purchase advertising space on the site. Third, ask the major Web directory companies to donate the rights to the search term "lawyers" to the lawyers.com site. This way, whenever people search for lawyers at the major Web directories, they'd see the banner ad for lawyers.com. Since the lawyers.com organization would be a nonprofit organization, the Web directory companies may be able to take a tax deduction for donating various search terms. This model could easily be extended to include doctors, too. We can think of no single thing that the legal community could do for the Internet community other than creating a lawyers .com site that serves the legal needs of consumers. Such a venture would require incredible cooperation among law firms, bar associations, and legal vendors. Done right, it could improve the image of lawyers in the eyes of all Web surfers, who now only find things like lawyers jokes when they try to find lawyers.

LawSource, Inc.

- *cyberspace:* lawsource.com

- *earth place:* Oakland, CA

- *born on:* 18 Oct 1995 (middler)

- *review:* While FindLaw's directory is the most complete compilation of law-related Web sites, LawSource's American Law Sources On-line (ALSO!) is the most complete compilation of primary and secondary print law sources, with links to those that are accessible via the Net. Have you ever been frustrated looking for a particular state's legislation online only to find (hours later) that the information does not exist on the Web? If you had visited ALSO! first, you would have learned whether or not that state's laws are Net-ready. LawSource is the perfect complement to FindLaw. Both are located in the Bay Area. Hmm, can you say merger?

- *practice areas:* international, federal, state

Lawyers Cooperative Publishing

- *cyberspace:* lcp.com

- *earth place:* Rochester, NY

- *born on:* 25 Jun 1994 (early adopter)

- *review:* Now part of West Group (a Thomson Publishing company), this site features three content services: New York Slip Opinions, Massachusetts Advance Sheets, and *The Legal List*. The first two are subscription-based services that allow you to receive primary law from New York and Massachusetts on the Web. The third, *The Legal List,* is the eighth edition of the book originally written by Erik Heels, who wrote the first seven editions. (Erik sold the rights to *The Legal List* to Lawyers Cooperative Publishing in 1995 and completed the sixth and seventh editions for them that year.) The eighth edition departs significantly from the focus of the previous seven and is now primarily a print product focused on Internet legal research. Excerpts are available online.

Crypto
See **encryption.**

Cyberia-L
Cyberia (formerly "CyberLaw") is the veteran of law-related discussion lists. Maintained by William & Mary law professor Trotter Hardy, Cyberia counts among its subscribers lawyers, law professors, journalists, law students, and computer scientists. Cyberia is focused on emerging topics of law and technology and often breaks news to the legal profession ahead of more conventional news sources. Traffic is from moderate to heavy, with an average of twenty to thirty messages per day. If you are willing to handle the volume, you will find a wealth of information exchanged among Cyberia subscribers. To subscribe: Send e-mail to <listserv@listserv.aol.com>, with the command "subscribe Cyberia-l [Your Name]" where [Your Name] is your name. Omit the quotes.

Lawyers Weekly, Inc.

- *cyberspace:* lweekly.com
- *earth place:* Boston, MA
- *born on:* 16 Feb 1995 (middler)
- *review:* Lawyers Weekly Publications (whose periodicals include *Lawyers Weekly USA* and regional publications such as *Massachusetts Lawyers Weekly*) entered the world of Web-based publishing later than most of its competitors, but it was definitely worth the wait. Court opinions, legislative information, featured articles from their print publications. It's all here. And the site's organization makes it very easy to navigate.
- *practice areas:* Massachusetts, Michigan, Missouri, North Carolina, Ohio, Rhode Island, Virginia

Legal Communications

- *cyberspace:* legalcom.com
- *earth place:* Philadelphia, PA
- *born on:* 15 Sep 1995 (middler)
- *review:* Legal Communications, publishes the *Legal Intelligencer, Pennsylvania Law Weekly,* and *legal.online.* The newsletter *legal.online,* the first legal Internet newsletter, gets a bit lost in the structure of this site, which is too bad, since *legal.online* is an excellent newsletter. The content is here, but the presentation across publications is inconsistent.
- *practice areas:* Pennsylvania

Legal Recruitment Network

- *cyberspace:* emplawyernet.com
- *earth place:* Los Angeles, CA
- *born on:* 22 Apr 1996 (late adopter)
- *review:* A Web site dedicated to helping legal employers and employees find each other is probably the most boring Web site you could imagine, which makes EmplawyerNet's slick implementation all the more impressive. Employ, lawyers, Internet—EmplawyerNet. Get it? Even if you are not interested in hiring new associates or in seeking a new job, you should visit this site, register, and try it out. The level of customer service that EmplawyerNet provides is like that of an-

other great Web site, Amazon Books (http://www.amazon.com/). For example, EmplawyerNet integrates e-mail notification into its site for job seekers. Whenever a new listing appears that matches your interests, EmplawyerNet sends you an e-mail telling you about the listing. Similarly, Amazon sends you e-mail when your book order is confirmed, and again when it is shipped. Why is EmplawyerNet so good? Because its president, William Seaton, is a veteran of legal recruitment who understands the power of the Internet. It doesn't get much better than EmplawyerNet.

Legi-Slate, Inc.

- *cyberspace:* legislate.com
- *earth place:* Washington, DC
- *born on:* 03 Feb 1992 (visionary)
- *review:* LEGI-SLATE publishes congressional and regulatory information online. A subscription-based service, LEGI-SLATE also delivers selected materials via e-mail. Free services are also available, including LEGI-SLATE News, which includes daily updates on legislative and regulatory developments.
- *practice areas:* U.S. Congress, federal regulations, state legislation and regulations

Martindale-Hubbell

- *cyberspace:* martindale.com
- *earth place:* New Providence, NJ
- *born on:* 28 Sep 1995 (middler)
- *review:* Martindale-Hubbell, a division of Reed Elsevier, Inc., publishes the *Martindale-Hubbell Law Directory*—the premier directory of lawyers—in hardcopy, CD-ROM, and the Internet. The *Martindale-Hubbell Law Directory* (or often *Martindale-Hubbell*) is now in its 130th year, so it's got a pretty good head start on the competition. The Web-based version debuted on June 1, 1996, and includes almost all the fields that appear in the other formats. Lawyer ratings are a notable exception, in part because of the rules governing lawyer advertising on the Internet.
- *practice areas:* administrative law, admiralty and maritime, agricultural law, antitrust and trade regulations, appellate practice, banking and finance, bankruptcy, business law, civil rights, commercial

law, communications, constitutional law, construction law, contracts, corporate law, criminal law, education, elder law, employee benefits, energy, entertainment and sports, environmental law, family law, government contracts, government, health and hospital law, immigration, Indians and native populations, insurance, intellectual property, international law, investments, labor and employment, legal ethics, litigation, media law, mergers and acquisitions, military law, natural resources, personal injury and torts, probate, trusts and estate, products liability, professional liability, real estate, securities, taxation, technology and science, transportation, workers' compensation, zoning, planning and land use

Matthew Bender

- *cyberspace:* bender.com

- *earth place:* Albany, NY

- *born on:* 09 Dec 1994 (early adopter)

- *review:* In September 1997, Matthew Bender & Company, Inc., announced that it would make legal news and information available via the PointCast Business Network under the brand name Legal Insider. PointCast is a program that uses the Internet to deliver (or "push"—e-mail being the most established "push" technology) content directly to users' desktops. The Legal Insider edition of PointCast offers two legal-specific channels designed to provide updates on legal news, jury verdicts, and critical case information. The Legal Tool channel includes Shepard's Cite Tracker (case citation checking and validation), and Blue Sheet (jury verdict reports and analysis from around the country) with analysis and settlement information. The Legal News channel includes national legal headlines (daily updates on the national headlines provided by Law Journal EXTRA! and other sources) and state and local headlines (regional news stories from around the country provided by Cal-Law, LJX, the Blue Sheet and others). PointCast expects to release Legal Insider on their Web site (http://www.pointcast.com/products/insider/legal/) in the fourth quarter of 1997. Matthew Bender's Authority-On-Demand service allows you to purchase the information you need, when you need it, via their Web site with your credit card.

- *practice areas:* banking and commercial law, business law, California law, Collier bankruptcy law, employment law, environmental law, federal practice, Florida law and practice, immigration law, insurance law, intellectual property law, mid-Atlantic and Midwest law, New York law, personal injury law, real estate law, tax and estate planning law, Texas law, workers' compensation law

New York Law Publishing, Inc.

- *cyberspace:* ljextra.com
- *earth place:* New York, NY
- *born on:* 23 Aug 1994 (early adopter)
- *review:* See Law Journal EXTRA!

Nolo Press

- *cyberspace:* nolopress.com
- *earth place:* Berkeley, CA
- *born on:* 23 Aug 1994 (early adopter)
- *review:* Nolo Press has been in the business of providing self-help information to consumers since 1971. Nolo publishes books and software on consumer law subjects such as wills, small claims court, divorce, and debt problems. Its Web site was the first to provide law-related information to consumers. The Nolo site's claim to fame is probably its extensive collection of lawyer jokes, but it also contains articles (excerpted from its newsletter) about various self-help law topics. For example, the Nolo Press Self-Help Law Center also has information about small claims court (**http://www .nolo.com/ChunkCM/CM .index.html**). That page describes how small businesses can use small claims court to collect unpaid bills. At the end of the article, there are links to publications for sale by Nolo that offer more help in this area. The Nolo Press Self-Help Law Center is not very well

Cyberlaw
Claimed by some to be a practice area, Cyberlaw is actually the name of a newsletter published since 1993 by California attorney Jonathan Rosenoer. Yes, he has trademarked it.

cyberspace
The term "cyberspace" was first used by science fiction writer William Gibson in his book *Neuromancer,* the original cyberpunk novel (New York: Ace Science Fiction Books, 1984). Gibson defined the term as "the mass consensual hallucination in which humans all over the planet meet, converse, and exchange information." Are you hallucinating? We're not. But we're using the Internet.

organized, but the search engine can help to find your way. The Nolo Press Self-Help Law Center is an Internet classic and a must-see for consumers of legal information.

- *practice areas:* wills and estate planning, spouses and partners, parents and children, older Americans, real estate, small business, employment, patent, copyright and trademark, tax problems, debt and credit, consumer, legal research, courts and mediation

Tennessee Commission on Continuing Legal Education and Specialization

- *cyberspace:* cletn.com
- *earth place:* Nashville, TN
- *born on:* 17 Oct 1996 (late adopter)
- *review:* The Tennessee Commission on Continuing Legal Education and Specialization (TN CLE) was the first organization to propose and implement a standard for publishing accredited CLE course information on the Web, using public search engines (such as Alta-Vista and Infoseek) as the standard interface. The TN CLE solution has the potential to revolutionize the way lawyers search for CLE course information. (In the name of full disclosure, we should mention that Erik was involved in the development of this Web site.)

The Bureau of National Affairs, Inc.

- *cyberspace:* bna.com
- *earth place:* Washington, DC
- *born on:* 20 May 1992 (visionary)
- *review:* As publishers of newsletters, loose-leaf services, and other products, BNA provides a smattering of free content on its site—usually reprints of articles from its newsletters.
- *practice areas:* health care, business, labor relations, economics, taxation, environmental protection, safety, public policy, regulatory issues

The Seamless Website

- *cyberspace:* seamless.com
- *earth place:* San Francisco, CA
- *born on:* 21 Feb 1995 (middler)

- *review:* The most useful page on this site is the Commons, which is a topically organized page of links to other pages and sites on **seamless.com**. Each topical area also has a threaded discussion area. In other words, the Commons is a front-end to the Web sites and pages hosted at The Seamless Website. Good breadth of coverage, but not much depth.

- *practice areas:* business law and venture capital, civil litigation defense, computer generated evidence, consumer law and commercial class action, criminal law, cyberspace law, cyberspace social policy, estate planning, information law and intellectual property, insurance law, international law, Internet law, labor law, law office technology, law practice management, legal documents, personal injury, politics, real property, trade secrets

Thomson & Thomson

- *cyberspace:* saegis.com

- *earth place:* North Quincy, MA

- *born on:* 06 Mar 1997 (late adopter)

- *review:* SAEGIS is a service of Thomson & Thomson, a Thomson Publishing company specializing in trademark and copyright research. SAEGIS is a series of services designed to allow business users to track and select trademarks and servicemarks. For example, you can sign up for a service that will track whether other users are using your federally registered trademarks on the Internet. You can also search a derivative version of the InterNIC's registered domain name database (the "whois" database).

- *practice areas:* intellectual property, copyright, trademark

Timeline Publishing

- *cyberspace:* versuslaw.com

- *earth place:* Redmond, WA

- *born on:* 23 May 1996 (late adopter)

- *review:* Versuslaw's "V." service includes full text opinions from

dictionary
One very helpful Web site is a Web-based dictionary. The hypertext Webster interface (http://c.gp.cs.cmu.edu:5103/prog/webster), written by a graduate student at Carnegie-Mellon, provides a point-and-click client interface (for non-linemode browsers) for accessing the various Webster's dictionary services on the Internet. It's quick. It's simple. It does one thing. And it does it very well. All in all, rather nifty! For the record, here's the definition of "nifty" given by the hypertext Webster interface: nif·ty \nif-tē\ *adj* [origin unknown] : FINE, SWELL—**nifty n.**

federal and state appellate courts. It is a subscription-based service that is designed to be a low-cost alternative to WESTLAW and LEXIS-NEXIS. Prices range from $14.95 for a day of access to $595 for a year.

- *practice areas:* federal and state appellate courts

West Publishing Corp.

- *cyberspace:* wld.com

- *earth place:* St. Paul, MN

- *born on:* 24 May 1995 (middler)

- *review:* West Group is now a Thomson Publishing company. The *West Legal Directory* is their entry into the lawyer directory market and competes head-to-head with *Martindale-Hubbell's Law Directory*. Martindale-Hubbell has more name recognition among legal professionals, but West has done a good job marketing the *West Legal Directory* to consumers.

- *practice areas:* administrative, admiralty, agriculture, alternative dispute resolution, antitrust and trade regulation, banking and finance, bankruptcy, commercial, communications, computer and technology, constitutional, construction, corporations and business organizations, criminal, education, energy, entertainment and sports, environmental, family, general practice, government agencies, government contracts, health, immigration, insurance, intellectual property, international, labor and employment, legal ethics and professional responsibility, litigation, military, Native Americans, pension and benefits, personal injury and torts, probate, trusts and estates, product liability, professional malpractice, real property, securities, taxation, transportation, workers' compensation

Yahoo!

- *cyberspace:* yahoo.com

- *earth place:* Santa Clara, CA

- *born on:* 18 Jan 1995 (middler)

- *review:* Yahoo is the most popular Web site, with 682,963 other sites and pages linking to it. Need we say more? Their legal directories (http://www.yahoo.com/Government/Law/) are not the most comprehensive (and most legal professionals do *not* work for the government, OK?!), but they're not bad either.

* *practice areas:* arbitration and mediation, business law, cases, companies and firms, constitutional, consumer, continuing legal education, countries, criminal law and justice, disabilities, district attorneys, elder law, employment law, entertainment, environmental, events, federal, general information, health, immigration, indigenous peoples, institutes, intellectual property, international law, journals, judiciary and Supreme Court, law enforcement, law schools, lawyer jokes, legal ethics, legal research, lesbian, gay, and bisexual resources, newsletters, organizations, privacy, property, self-help, sexuality, software companies, tax, telecommunications, U.S. states, women's resources, Usenet

CHAPTER**FOUR**

Federal Law Stuff

Overview

It is said that President Clinton is awfully concerned about how historians will record his presidency. We're not sure that this will weigh heavily on the future Schlesingers of the world, but one thing you can say positively about the Clinton administration is that federal information has come of age on the Internet while President Clinton has been in office. (Note that we're not claiming that President Clinton invented the idea of publishing government information on the Internet. For the record, we're pretty sure Vice President Al Gore did.)

What does this mean? Think back to 1992. Were you on the Internet yet? If so, what were you doing? Chances are, you used e-mail. Maybe you would telnet into little-known databases and retrieve documents you needed. Maybe you dialed in to FedWorld (started in 1992) and downloaded information relevant to a case you were working on. It's probably safe to say, however, that you weren't relying much on the Internet for substantive information. This is understandable. After all, there wasn't much generally accessible information out there. Most of it was specialized—research data, educational documents, and so on.

Within a year of taking office, a content-rich site at http://whitehouse.gov was born. Visitors to the Virtual White House could find speeches, transcripts of the president's radio address, press conferences, and position papers. Access was easy, organization was good, and the traffic (by 1993 standards) was tremendous. Other agencies soon followed suit, and the C-SPAN crowd had another medium to feed their hunger for federal information.

Today, almost every federal agency has a Web site. More importantly, most of them are publishing much of their work-product online. For researchers, or practitioners looking for hard-to-find material, it has never been easier to obtain of the information one needs. This chapter identifies the Internet presences of the three branches of government, as well as selected agencies that provide law-related information.

Best Meta Sites

The Federal Web Locator (http://www.vcilp.org/Fed-Agency/fedwebloc.html). Sponsored and maintained by the Villanova Center for Information Law & Policy (VCILP), this site is probably the most comprehensive source for Web-based information provided by the U.S. federal government.

FindLaw: Federal government (http://www.findlaw.com/10fedgov/). A good complement to the Federal Web Locator.

American Law Sources On-line (http://www.lawsource.com/also/usa.cgi?us1). A lot of front-ends to primary federal law, ALSO supplements the links to federal Web sites that FindLaw and the VCILP sites provide.

Visionaries

Department of Education (ed.gov)
Department of Health and Human Services (dhhs.gov)
Department of Justice (usdoj.gov)
Department of Veterans Affairs (va.gov)
Environmental Protection Agency (epa.gov)
Federal Reserve Board (frb.gov)
House of Representatives (house.gov)
Library of Congress (loc.gov)
Occupational Safety and Health Administration (osha.gov)
U.S. Information Agency (usia.gov)
U.S. Postal Service (usps.gov)

Early Adopters

Administrative Office of the U.S. Courts (uscourts.gov)
Department of Agriculture (usda.gov)
Department of Commerce (doc.gov)
Department of Commerce (fedworld.gov)
Department of Housing and Urban Development (hud.gov)
Department of Labor (doleta.gov)
Department of State (state.gov)
Department of the Interior (doi.gov)

Department of Transportation (**dot.gov**)
Department of Treasury (**ustreas.gov**)
Federal Deposit Insurance Corporation (**fdic.gov**)
Federal Trade Commission (**ftc.gov**)
Government Printing Office (**gpo.gov**)
National Archives and Records Administration (**nara.gov**)
National Transportation Safety Board (**ntsb.gov**)
Senate (**senate.gov**)
Small Business Administration (**sba.gov**)
White House (**whitehouse.gov**)

Middlers

Central Intelligence Agency (**odci.gov**)
Federal Communications Commission (**fcc.gov**)
Legal Services Corporation (**lsc.gov**)
Nuclear Regulatory Commission (**nrc.gov**)
Securities and Exchange Commission (**sec.gov**)

Late Adopters

Equal Employment Opportunity Commission (**eeoc.gov**)
National Labor Relations Board (**nlrb.gov**)
Office of Special Counsel (**osc.gov**)
Supreme Court of the United States (**supreme-court.gov**)

JUDICIAL BRANCH

Administrative Office of the U.S. Courts

- *cyberspace:* uscourts.gov

- *earth place:* Washington, DC

- *born on:* 13 Sep 1993 (**early adopter**)

- *review:* This page is maintained by the Administrative Office of the U.S. Courts on behalf of the U.S. Courts. This site functions as a clearinghouse for information from and about the judicial branch of the U.S. government. Students and laypersons will learn a lot from the "Understanding the Federal Courts" section, but there really isn't any substantive information here. If you're in search of actual court decisions, you'd be better off going to Villanova's Federal Court Locator.

Supreme Court of the United States

- *cyberspace:* supreme-court.gov
- *earth place:* Washington, DC
- *born on:* 30 May 1997 (late adopter)
- *review:* At least it's registered. Currently nothing is located here.

LEGISLATIVE BRANCH

House of Representatives

- *cyberspace:* house.gov
- *earth place:* Washington, DC
- *born on:* 02 Nov 1989 (visionary)
- *review:* If you're looking for the upcoming committee schedule, or you want to know what's coming up on the House floor, you'll find the information here. If you're looking for the actual text of bills, you ought to head over to Thomas, maintained by the Library of Congress. Some forward-looking representatives have taken advantage of the fact that they get Web space on this server to promote committees they're involved in, or provide ways for their constituents to get in touch with them.

Senate

- *cyberspace:* senate.gov
- *earth place:* Washington, DC
- *born on:* 12 May 1993 (early adopter)
- *review:* More or less a mirror of the House of Representatives site. All senators have Web sites (we checked—Jesse Helms is online at http://www.senate.gov/~helms/), and much of the information to be found here is general background information. You'll find some detailed committee information, and links are provided to the GPO for more documents.

Library of Congress

- *cyberspace:* loc.gov
- *earth place:* Washington, DC
- *born on:* 03 Oct 1990 (visionary)

- *review:* As it should be, this is one of the best Web sites within the U.S. government. If you think of the Web as an efficient way to cat-alog information, it's logical that the country's library uses it as an outstanding archive of some remarkable data. Not only is the LOC home to Thomas, the online archive of legislative activity, but it is also home to dozens of exhibits on American history. Kudos to the Library of Congress staff who have produced a marvelous resource.

Government Printing Office

- *cyberspace:* gpo.gov
- *earth place:* Washington, DC
- *born on:* 28 Oct 1993 (early adopter)
- *review:* It'll take more than one visit to absorb the information available here. Over the past few years, the GPO has coordinated with many other government agencies to make the GPO the central repository for government documents. Not only does this mean that we have—believe it or not—a standard for the publication of government data on the Internet, but we have a fantastic place to go regardless of what kind of record you're looking for.

EXECUTIVE BRANCH

White House

- *cyberspace:* whitehouse.gov
- *earth place:* Washington, DC
- *born on:* 17 Oct 1994 (early adopter)
- *review:* Press releases, executive announcements, federal statistics—you name it, you'll find it at the White House Web site. Consider-ing its age (it first went online in 1994), this site continues to be a fantastically helpful resource.
- *note:* A parody of the official White House site can be found at www.whitehouse.net. But with the official site boasting (at one time) a sound clip of Socks the Cat meowing, is this a case of art imitating life? Our favorite link from the home page is the one that says "Why?: Because we like you." That one also explains the motiva-tion of the authors of this site. And if you think this site is bad, be glad we didn't include whitehouse.com!

Central Intelligence Agency

- *cyberspace:* odci.gov
- *earth place:* Washington, DC
- *born on:* 07 Apr 1995 (middler)

Department of Agriculture

- *cyberspace:* usda.gov
- *earth place:* Ft. Collins, CO
- *born on:* 14 Mar 1994 (early adopter)

Department of Commerce

- *cyberspace:* doc.gov
- *earth place:* Washington, DC
- *born on:* 20 Apr 1993 (early adopter)
- *review:* Among government agencies, the Department of Commerce was clearly an early adopter. Between its Small Business information, the Bureau of Export Administration, and the U.S. Patent and Trademark Office (**http://www.uspto.gov/**), the Department of Commerce produces volumes of information of interest to lawyers. The organization could be better, but they concentrate on the content, which isn't really a bad thing.

Department of Commerce

- *cyberspace:* fedworld.gov
- *earth place:* Springfield, VA
- *born on:* 09 Sep 1993 (early adopter)
- *review:* One of the great things about doing this book is revisiting a site we haven't seen in a while. Such is the case with FedWorld— one of the original "supersites" on the Internet that aggregated government information. FedWorld began in 1992, and was a dial-up service that provided access to information housed at the National Technological Information Service (NTIS), and acted as a gateway to more than 100 federal bulletin boards. Today, FedWorld is an integrated Web site that consolidates access to government databases, provides a common search interface, and serves as an archive for useful documents. Substantively, you'll find international trade documents (rules, regulations, forms), FAA documents, the entire EPA Clean Air Act database, IRS documents, and many more.

Department of Education

- *cyberspace:* ed.gov
- *earth place:* Washington, DC
- *born on:* 22 Dec 1992 (visionary)

Department of Health and Human Services

- *cyberspace:* dhhs.gov
- *earth place:* Washington, DC
- *born on:* 06 Oct 1992 (visionary)

Department of Housing and Urban Development

- *cyberspace:* hud.gov
- *earth place:* Washington, DC
- *born on:* 08 Apr 1994 (early adopter)

Department of Justice

- *cyberspace:* usdoj.gov
- *earth place:* Rockville, MD
- *born on:* 25 Aug 1992 (visionary)

Department of Labor

- *cyberspace:* doleta.gov
- *earth place:* Washington, DC
- *born on:* 28 Sep 1994 (early adopter)

Department of State

- *cyberspace:* state.gov
- *earth place:* Washington, DC
- *born on:* 03 May 1994 (early adopter)

Department of the Interior

- *cyberspace:* doi.gov
- *earth place:* Washington, DC
- *born on:* 01 Sep 1993 (early adopter)

DNS

Software is used to translate domain names into Internet Protocol (IP) addresses. This software is called the Domain Name System (DNS) software. (The folks who named this stuff were big fans of descriptive—but not necessarily creative—names.) So if you are browsing the Web and you see an error message like "Netscape is unable to locate the server. The server does not have a DNS entry," it means that the translation from domain name to IP address failed for one reason or another. Most likely it failed because the address you used was invalid, or because some Web server was overloaded or temporarily off-line.

Department of Transportation
- *cyberspace:* dot.gov
- *earth place:* Washington, DC
- *born on:* 21 Jan 1993 (early adopter)

Department of Treasury
- *cyberspace:* ustreas.gov
- *earth place:* Washington, DC
- *born on:* 11 Jan 1994 (early adopter)

Department of Veterans Affairs
- *cyberspace:* va.gov
- *earth place:* Silver Spring, MD
- *born on:* 31 Aug 1989 (visionary)

Environmental Protection Agency
- *cyberspace:* epa.gov
- *earth place:* Research Triangle Park, NC
- *born on:* 19 Oct 1989 (visionary)

Equal Employment Opportunity Commission
- *cyberspace:* eeoc.gov
- *earth place:* Washington, DC
- *born on:* 05 Dec 1996 (late adopter)

Federal Communications Commission
- *cyberspace:* fcc.gov
- *earth place:* Washington, DC
- *born on:* 29 Aug 1995 (middler)
- *review:* If you practice in the communications field, you probably can't afford to miss the FCC's Web site. One of the most active of government Web sites, the FCC site contains speeches, daily digests of all FCC activity, information about the Telecom Act of 1996, and up-to-date documents relating to auctions that the FCC presides over.

Federal Deposit Insurance Corporation

- *cyberspace:* fdic.gov
- *earth place:* Arlington, VA
- *born on:* 14 Jan 1994 (early adopter)

Federal Reserve Board

- *cyberspace:* frb.gov
- *earth place:* Washington, DC
- *born on:* 28 Jul 1988 (visionary)

Federal Trade Commission

- *cyberspace:* ftc.gov
- *earth place:* Washington, DC
- *born on:* 19 Feb 1993 (early adopter)

National Archives and Records Administration

- *cyberspace:* nara.gov
- *earth place:* College Park, MD
- *born on:* 29 Sep 1993 (early adopter)
- *review:* This site is worth visiting if only for the images and files relating to Elvis's visit to meet with President Nixon. When an aide drafted a memo for H. R. Haldeman suggesting that it would be good for the president to meet with "some bright young people," Haldeman scrawled dryly in the margin, "You must be kidding." Seriously, though, the historical records relating to the three branches of government are bound to be helpful for anyone doing research on an historical subject.

domain name
A domain name is the part of your Internet address that uniquely identifies your organization. The ABA's domain name is abanet.org. The domain name system was created so that humans (that's us) could easily remember various Internet addresses. It is like using speed-dialing on your phone rather than memorizing various phone numbers. The analogy to phone numbers is a good one, because each domain name has a numerical counterpart (a series of numbers like 123.23.123.123) that represents a unique address (called an Internet Protocol address) for the computer providing your Internet services. There are exceptions, but this is the general rule.

National Labor Relations Board

- *cyberspace:* nlrb.gov
- *earth place:* Washington, DC
- *born on:* 13 Jan 1996 (late adopter)
- *review:* While decisions available on the site only go back a year or so (currently, the oldest volume of decisions available is 321, which goes back to July 1996), all decisions published by the NLRB since then are online. The library of decisions is searchable, and if you browse the opinions by volume, you only have the opportunity to view the decision as an Adobe Acrobat PDF file; if you use the search engine, you get the option of viewing a PDF file or as plain text. Interestingly, all decisions are links to GPO, where the full text of the decisions are archived.

National Transportation Safety Board

- *cyberspace:* ntsb.gov
- *earth place:* Washington, DC
- *born on:* 10 Nov 1994 (early adopter)

Nuclear Regulatory Commission

- *cyberspace:* nrc.gov
- *earth place:* Rockville, MD
- *born on:* 20 Jul 1995 (middler)

Occupational Safety and Health Administration

- *cyberspace:* osha.gov
- *earth place:* Washington, DC
- *born on:* 20 Mar 1991 (visionary)

Office of Special Counsel

- *cyberspace:* osc.gov
- *earth place:* Washington, DC
- *born on:* 12 Sep 1996 (late adopter)

Securities and Exchange Commission

- *cyberspace:* sec.gov
- *earth place:* Alexandria, VA
- *born on:* 31 Aug 1995 (middler)

Small Business Administration

- *cyberspace:* sba.gov
- *earth place:* Washington, DC
- *born on:* 11 Jan 1994 (early adopter)

U.S. Information Agency

- *cyberspace:* usia.gov
- *earth place:* Washington, DC
- *born on:* 30 Nov 1992 (visionary)

U.S. Postal Service

- *cyberspace:* usps.gov
- *earth place:* Raleigh, NC
- *born on:* 28 Aug 1991 (visionary)
- *review:* While not a legal site per se, credit has to go to the Post Office for providing such a useful site. Armed with an address, users can get the proper zip code for the address. It doesn't sound like much, but you'll be amazed how often you use it.

BRANCHLESS AGENCIES

Legal Services Corporation

- *cyberspace:* lsc.gov
- *earth place:* Washington, DC
- *born on:* 05 May 1995 (middler)

*CHAPTER*FIVE

Law Firms

Overview

With more than 3,000 law firms listed in Yahoo's list of law firms, we had to draw the line somewhere. And we should probably reiterate that the purpose of this book is not to evaluate the quality of law firm Web sites. So that means we had to use an objective measure for including law firm Web sites in this chapter. We chose to use the *National Law Journal*'s NLJ 250, because it's a fairly consistent snapshot of private law firms over the years.

This chapter also includes some smaller law firms that are making a difference in the Internet marketspace. These sites provide good examples of how small law firms can level the playing field and show the big guys how it really should be done.

What purpose does this chapter serve? Primarily, it gives those in the profession an idea of the rate of adoption in the largest law firms. So what? These law firms are the ones who have the resources to do it right. They typically have a separate technology budget, they have a marketing budget, and their clients (*Fortune* 500 companies, government agencies, and high-profile individuals) are generally the leaders when it comes to adopting new technology to do more, and do it for less.

By looking at what the NLJ 250 are doing on the Internet, we get an idea of how far the profession has come in just a few short years. Many of the firms are using the Internet to actively solicit new business, and others are trying hard to make their existing clients feel more connected. For those who don't yet have a Web site, you can draw your own conclusions.

What makes a good law firm Web site? Generally, there are three purposes a law firm site can serve: marketing, client services, and recruiting.

From the marketing angle, firms recognize that they have a captive audience: for whatever reason, someone has shown up at their site and is willing to look around. In the few minutes that this visitor spends at the site, firms have an opportunity to show off. This is the chance to show how much the lawyers know about a particular practice area. Publish the full text of all those memos archived on somebody's hard drive. Give people the chance to be impressed by what the firm knows, and they probably will be.

Client services is less cut and dried. How do you make your existing clients feel more involved? Different firms take different approaches. Some go so far as to provide a "clients-only" section at the site that gives clients access to case-specific information (briefs, memos, etc.), and that facilitates lawyer-client communication. This is often referred to as an "extranet"—limited access to private information for a select group of people. Extranets will change the face of law practice. (For more on this, see the next section, "Extranets.") Other firms take a less involved approach that still yields positive results—by setting up e-mail distribution lists, for example, that send timely information to clients and keep them updated on events relevant to them.

Recruiting is straightforward. Law students are the most wired demographic in the legal community. Law firms who provide detailed information about their summer associate programs, hiring practices, and firm culture will be rewarded with more qualified applicants.

Tying this all together is not a simple task. Deciding on what content to publish is the first step, but there's much more. Agreeing on a presentation—how the site looks—is even more difficult. (Put ten lawyers in a room, and ask them what they think of something that is inherently subjective, and then try to achieve consensus. Best of luck.) If you get past those steps, you will likely have a first-rate site.

As you'll see from many of our synopses of sites that follow, several firms never really made it past the first step. We anticipate that the next year will bring most (if not all) of the NLJ 250 online. In addition, we expect that many of those firms who already have a presence on the Internet will create a second-generation site, supplementing their current site with more information, better presentation, and a more refined approach to leveraging the Web site as an integral part of their growth strategy. As this happens, clients will benefit, law students will benefit, but most importantly, law firms will benefit. We can't wait.

The law firms that include a review are displayed in italics in the listings on pages 80–88.

Extranets

What is an extranet, and why has it generated so much commotion in the last year? An extranet, at its core, is the use of a Web-based front end to provide limited access to otherwise private information. Some bench-marks follow:

Web-based front end

As with an intranet, an extranet takes advantage of the Web and its famil-iar interface to access underlying information.

Limited access

Only selected individuals (or, in some cases, organizations) may access the information. The information provider (the law firm) identifies these users. In the most typical situation, the users would be clients. Without a username and password (or some other form of user authentication), users may not access the information at all.

Otherwise private information

Though self-explanatory, this part of the definition is the most flexible. The most widely used example of an extranet is the FedEx Web site. Strictly speaking, their package-tracking site fits the definition of an extra-net. It uses a Web-based front end (users enter their package ID in the simple fill-out form on the FedEx site), it is limited, in that only custom-ers who have sent packages can use the site, and the information about a package is otherwise private. However, it is an extranet by only the strict-est use of the definition. It is limited in scope, since the only thing users can do is check the status of their packages.

So what is a better example of an extranet? Let's look at a law firm. Once a firm's network applications are integrated in an intranet (like bill-ing information), clients can be given access to the firm's extranet to check their monthly bill. Clients can also be given access to browse docu-ments related to their case that have been integrated with case or file management software. Clients can upload documents—ironically, saving thousands of dollars per month on FedEx charges. The extranet can even be a vehicle for collaboration with opposing counsel for file shar-ing, saving both time and money, which leads to savings for the client.

What does this mean down the road? As we predicted earlier, extra-nets have the potential to change how clients interact with their law firms. TrialNet, of Richmond, Vir-ginia, is a forward-looking company

Dr. HTML
(http://www2.imagiware.com/RxHTML/)
Not sure if your hand-coded HTML is correct? Or are you worried that the HTML authoring tool you used created mark-up tags that differ-ent browsers won't handle properly? Then stop by Dr. HTML. This is an online tool that will load your Web page and tell you where your code doesn't meet specs.

that provides outsourced extranet development for law firms and their clients. As more people learn about TrialNet's success, it is only a matter of time until law firms realize the cost-saving benefits of developing extranets for their clients. (Note: After completing this book, Rick joined TrialNet as its VP of Marketing & Development.)

Best Meta Sites

National Law Journal: NLJ 250 (http://www.ljx.com/lf250/nlj250index.html). The perennial horse race to identify the largest 250 law firms in the country. We used this list as the basis for our law firm Web site reviews, as it provided an objective benchmark.

FindLaw: Law Firms (http://www.findlaw.com/14firms/). FindLaw's list, with links to individual lawyers and law firms, provides a good cross-section of the variety of law firm Web sites.

Martindale-Hubbell (http://www.martindale.com/). The 800-pound gorilla of lawyer directories, Martindale-Hubbell's online companion allows users to search for law firms and lawyers, and can restrict searches by practice area, location, and other keywords. Updated more often than the Martindale-Hubbell books (which are updated once a year) and their CD-ROM product (updated four times per year), the Web site is a must for anyone who wants background on a lawyer, contact information for a firm, or other relevant information.

West Legal Directory (http://www.wld.com/). Not as comprehensive as Martindale-Hubbell, but still a good resource for finding law firms and individual lawyers. One advantage to WLD is that lawyers may update their listings for free, making the list in some cases more up-to-date than Martindale-Hubbell. Like Martindale-Hubbell, searches can be restricted to practice areas, and keywords and location can be used to narrow the search for someone.

Yahoo! Law Firms (http://www.yahoo.com/Business_and_Economy/ Companies/Law/). If you know the name of the law firm you're looking for, use Yahoo. If you don't, but still want to scroll through the names of 3,000-plus law firms, go nuts.

Visionaries

Davis Polk & Wardwell (dpw.com)
Heller, Ehrman, White & McAuliffe (hewm.com)
Morrison & Foerster, L.L.P. (mofo.com)
Nixon, Hargrave, Devans and Doyle (nhdd.com)
Wilson, Sonsini, Goodrich & Rosati (wsgr.com)

Early Adopters

Adams & Reese (arlaw.com)

Arent Fox Kinter Plotkin & Kahn (arentfox.com)

Arnold & Porter (aporter.com)

Brobeck Phleger Harrison (brobeck.com)

Cadwalader Wickersham and Taft (cadwalader.com)

Chapman and Cutler (chapman.com)

Choate, Hall & Stewart (choate.com)

Cooley Godward, L.L.P. (cooley.com)

Covington & Burling (cov.com)

Crosby, Heafey, Roach & May (chrm.com)

Day, Berry & Howard (dbh.com)

Dechert Price & Rhoads (dpr.com)

Faegre & Benson (faegre.com)

Finnegan, Henderson, Farabow, Garrett & Dunner (finnegan.com)

Foley, Hoag & Eliot (fhe.com)

Fried, Frank, Harris, Shriver & Jacobson (ffhsj.com)

Goodwin, Procter & Hoar (gph.com)

Gray Cary Ware & Freidenrich (gcwf.com)

Hale and Dorr (haledorr.com)

Hogan & Hartson (hhlaw.com)

Holme, Roberts & Owen (hro.com)

Hopkins and Sutter (hopsut.com)

Howrey & Simon (howrey.com)

Hunton & Williams (hunton.com)

Ice Miller Donadio & Ryan (imdr.com)

Latham and Watkins (lw.com)

Littler (littler.com)

Locke Purnell Rain Harrell (lprh.com)

Luce, Forward, Hamilton & Scripps (luce.com)

McGlinchey Stafford Lang (mcglinchey.com)

McGuire, Woods, Battle & Boothe (mwbb.com)

Milbank, Tweed, Hadley & Mcloy (milbank.com)

Morgan, Lewis & Bockius, L.L.P. (mlb.com)

Oppedahl & Larson (patents.com)

Paul, Hatings, Janofsky & Walker (phjw.com)

driving directions
See **Yahoo! Maps.**

e-mail
Electronic mail. An e-mail is (usually) a plain text message that is sent from a user on one computer over a network to a user on another computer. Internet e-mail is sent from one user on one computer network over the Internet to another user on another computer network.

Perkins Coie (**perkinscoie.com**)
Piper & Marbury (**pipermar.com**)
Reinhart, Boerner, et al. (**rbvdnr.com**)
Robert L. Sommers c/o Attorneys at Law (**taxprophet.com**)
Robins, Kaplan, Miller & Ciresi (**robins.com**)
Robinson & Cole (**rc.com**)
Rosenman & Colin (**rosenman.com**)
Schnader Harrison Segal & Lewis (**shsl.com**)
Sedgwick, Detert, Moran & Arnold (**sdma.com**)
Sonnenschein Nath & Rosenthal (**sonnenschein.com**)
Squire, Sanders & Dempsey (**ssd.com**)
Venable, Baetjer, Howard (**venable.com**)
Wiley, Rein & Fielding (**wrf.com**)
Wilmer, Cutler & Pickering (**wilmer.com**)
Winstead, Sechrest & Minick (**winstead.com**)
Winston & Strawn (**winston.com**)

Middlers
Akin, Gump, Strauss, Hauer & Feld, L.L.P. (**akingump.com**)
Alston & Bird (**alston.com**)
Altheimer & Gray (**altheimer.com**)
Arnold, White and Durkee (**awd.com**)
Arter & Hadden (**arterhadden.com**)
Baker & Botts (**bakerbotts.com**)
Baker, Donnelson, Bearman (**bdbc.com**)
Ballard Spahr Andrews & Ingersoll (**ballardspahr.com**)
Barnes & Thornburg (**btlaw.com**)
Benesch, Friedlander, Coplan & Aronoff (**bfca.com**)
Bingham Dana Gould (**bingham.com**)
Blackwell, Sanders, Matheny, Weary & Lombardi (**bsmwl.com**)
Blank, Rome, Comisky & McCauley (**brcm.com**)
Bogle & Gates (**bogle.com**)
Brown, Todd, and Heyburn (**bth-pllc.com**)
Buchanan Ingersoll (**bipc.com**)
Cahill Gordon & Reindel (**cahill.com**)
Calfee, Halter & Griswold (**calfee.com**)
Carlton Fields (**carltonfields.com**)
Chadbourne & Parke (**chadbourne.com**)
Coudert Brothers (**coudert.com**)
Cravath, Swaine & Moore (**cravath.com**)
Davis Wright Tremaine (**dwt.com**)

Dickinson Wright (dickinson-wright.com)
Dorsey & Whitney (dorseylaw.com)
Dow, Lohnes & Albertson (dlalaw.com)
Drinker Biddle & Reath (dbr.com)
Edwards and Angell (ealaw.com)
Fish & Richardson (fr.com)
Frost & Jacobs (frojac.com)
Fulbright & Jaworski, L.L.P. (fulbright.com)
Gardere and Wynne, L.L.P. (gardere-law.com)
Gardner, Carton and Douglas (gcd.com)
Gibson, Dunn & Crutcher (gdclaw.com)
Graham & James (gj.com)
Greenberg Traurig (gtlaw.com)
Haynes & Boone (hayboo.com)
Holland & Hart (hollandhart.com)
Holland and Knight Law Offices (hklaw.com)
Honigman, Miller, Schwartz, and Cohn (honigman.com)
Irell & Manella (irell.com)
Jackson & Walker (jw.com)
Jeff Kuester (kuesterlaw.com)
Jenkens and Gilchrist (jenkens.com)
Jones, Day, Reavis & Pogue (jonesday.com)
Katten Muchin & Zavis (kmz.com)
Kaye, Scholer, Fierman, Hayes, and
    Handler (ksfhh.com)
Kelley Drye & Warren (kelleydrye.com)
Kenyon & Kenyon (kenyonlaw.com)
Kilpatrick & Cody (kilcody.com)
King & Spalding (kslaw.com)
Kirkland & Ellis (kirkland.com)
Kirkpatrick & Lockhart (kl.com)
Kramer Levin Naftalis Nessen Kamin &
    Frankel (kramer-levin.com)
Lane, Powell, Spears & Lubersky
    (lanepowell.com)
Law Offices of Loeb and Loeb
    (loeb.com)
LeBoeuf, Lamb, Greene & MacRae
    (llgm.com)
Lewis, D'Amato, Brisbois & Bisgaard
    (ldbb.com)

EFF (http://www.eff.org/)
Electronic Frontier Foundation. Founded by
Lotus 1-2-3 creator Mitch Kapor and cattle
rancher/digerati John Perry Barlow, the EFF has
been called both the "ACLU of Cyberspace"
and the "NRA of Cyberspace." Originally created as a quasi-defense fund for individuals accused of computer crimes, the EFF grew into
an influential policy organization. This role was
solidified when the group moved its headquarters to Washington, DC (ironically across the
street from the FBI Building). In 1995, however, the policy arm of EFF (led by former ACLU
exec Jerry Berman) left and created its own organization. A divided EFF board then voted to
move the headquarters to San Francisco. EFF's
role in policy-making has been considerably
quieter since then.

Lord, Bissell & Brook (lordbissell.com)

Manatt, Phelps & Phillips (manatt.com)

Martin Howard Patrick, P.A. (dirtlaw.com)

Mayer, Brown & Platt (mayerbrown.com)

McCarter & English (mccarter.com)

McCutchen, Doyle, Brown & Enersen (mccutchen.com)

McDermott, Will & Emery (mwe.com)

Mendes and Mount (mendes.com)

Michael Best & Friedrich (mbf-law.com)

Mintz Levin Cohn Ferris Glovsky and Popeo, P.C. (mintz.com)

Montgomery, McCracken, Walker & Rhoads (mmwr.com)

Morrison, Mahoney and Miller (mm-m.com)

Moye Giles (mgovg.com)

Muchmore & Wallwork, P.C. (mmww.com)

Nelson Mullins Riley & Scarborough (nmrs.com)

O'Melveny & Myers/Information Technology (omm.com)

Oppenheimer Wolff & Donnelly (owdlaw.com)

Orrick Herrington and Sutcliff (orrick.com)

Palmer & Dodge (palmerdodge.com)

Paul, Weiss, Rifkind, Wharton & Garrison (paulweiss.com)

Pennie & Edmonds (pennie.com)

Pepper, Hamilton & Scheetz (constructlaw.com)

Phelps, Dunbar (phelps.com)

Pillsbury Madison & Sutro (pmstax.com)

Pitney, Hardin, Kipp & Szuch (phks.com)

Porter, Wright, Morris & Arthur (porterwright.com)

Powell, Goldstein, Frazer & Murphy (pgfm.com)

Preston Gates & Ellis (prestongates.com)

Proskauer Rose Goetz & Mendelsohn (proskauer.com)

Quarles and Brady (quarles.com)

Reed, Smith, Shaw & McClay (rssm.com)

Riker, Danzig, Scherer, Hyland, and Perretti (riker.com)

Rivkin, Radler & Kremer (rivkinradler.com)

Rogers & Wells (rw.com)

Ropes & Gray (ropesgray.com)

Ross & Hardies (rosshardies.com)

Rudnick & Wolfe (rudnickwolfe.com)

Saul, Ewing, Remick & Saul (saul.com)

Seyfarth, Shaw (seyfarth.com)

Shaw, Pittman, Potts & Trowbridge (shawpittman.com)

Shearman & Sterling (shearman.com)

Sheppard, Mullin, Richter & Hampton (smrh.com)

Shook Hardy & Bacon (shb.com)

Sidley & Austin (sidley.com)

Siskind and Susser, Attorneys at Law (visalaw.com)

Skadden Arps Slate Meagher & Flom (skadden.com)

Smith Helms Milluss & Moore, L.L.P. (shmm.com)

Snell & Wilmer, L.L.P. (swlaw.com)

Southerland, Asbill & Brennan (sablaw.com)

Steptoe & Johnson (steptoe.com)

Stoel Rives, L.L.P. (stoel.com)

Strasburger & Price, L.L.P. (strasburger.com)

Sullivan & Cromwell (sullcrom.com)

Swidler & Berlin (swidlaw.com)

Taft, Stettinius & Hollister (taftlaw.com)

Testa, Hurwitz & Thibeault (tht.com)

Thacher, Proffitt & Wood (thacherproffitt.com)

The Law Office of David Loundy (loundy.com)

Thelen, Marrin, Johnson & Bridges (tmjb.com)

Thompson Hine & Flory (thf.com)

Vedder, Price, Kaufman & Kammholz (vedderprice.com)

Verner, Liipfert, Bernhard, McPherson, Hand (verner.com)

Vorys, Sater, Seymour and Pease (vssp.com)

Wachtell, Lipton, Rosen & Katz (wlrk.com)

Warner Norcross & Judd (wnj.com)

Weil, Gotshal, & Manges (weil.com)

White & Case (whitecase.com)

Wildman, Harrold, Allen & Dixon (whad.com)

William A. Fenwick (fenwick.com)

Willkie Farr & Gallagher (willkie.com)

Wilson, Elser, Moskowitz, Edelman & Dicker c/o MDY Advanced Technologies (wemed.com)

Winthrop, Stimson (winstim.com)

Wolf, Block, Schorr & Solis-Cohen (wolfblock.com)

Womble Carlyle Sandridge and Rice (wcsr.com)

Wyatt, Tarrant & Combs (wyattfirm.com)

Late Adopters

Akerman, Senterfill & Eidson, P.A. (akerman.com)

Anderson, Kill, Olick & Oshinsky, P.C. (andersonkill.com)

Andrews & Kurth, L.L.P. (andrews-kurth.com)

Armstrong Teasdale (atsd.com)

Baker & Daniels (bakerdaniels.com)

Baker & Hostetler (bakerlaw.com)

Baker & McKenzie (bakerinfo.com)

Bell, Boyd, and Lloyd (bellboyd.com)

Bracewell & Patterson (bracepatt.com)

Brian T. Cullen (nowlan.com)

Broad and Cassel, P.A. (broadandcassel.com)

Brown and Wood, L.L.P. (bwllp.com)

Bryan Cave, L.L.P. (bryancave.com)

Clausen Miller, P.C. (clausen.com)

Cleary, Gottlieb, Steen & Hamilton (cleargolaw.com)

Cozen and O'Connor (cozen-oconnor.com)

Crowell & Moring (cromor.com)

Cummings & Lockwood (cl-law.com)

Curtis Mallet-Prevost, Colt & Mosle (cm-p.com)

Debevoise & Plimpton (debevoise.com)

Dewey Ballantine (dbtrade.com)

Dickstein Shapiro Morin & Oshinsky, L.L.P. (dsmo.com)

Dinsmore & Shohl (dinsmore-shohl.com)

Duane, Morris & Hecksher (duanemorris.com)

Dykema Gossett, P.L.L.C. (dykema.com)

Eckert Seamans Cherin and Mellott (escm.com)

Epstein Becker & Green, P.C. (ebglaw.com)

Fish & Neave (fishneave.com)

Foley & Lardner (foleylardner.com)

Fowler, White, Burnett, Hurley, Banick & Strickroot, P.A.
    (fowler-white.com)

Fox Rothschild, O'Brien & Frankel (frof.com)

Glass McCullough Sherrill & H. (gmshlaw.com)

Haight, Brown and Bonesteel (hbblaw.com)

Harris, Beach and Wilcox (harrisbeach.com)

Hodgson, Russ, Andrews, Woods & Goodyear, L.L.P. (hodgsonruss.com)

Hughes Hubbard & Reed, L.L.P. (hugheshubbard.com)

Hughes & Luce, L.L.P. (hughesluce.com)

Husch & Eppenberger (husch.com)

Jackson and Kelly (jacksonkelly.com)

Jackson, Lewis, Schnitzler & Krupman (jacksonlewis.com)

Jenner & Block (jenner.com)

Jones, Walker, Waechter, Poitevent, Carrere, and Denegre (jwlaw.com)

Kutak Rock (kutakrock.com)

Lathrop & Gage, L.C. (lathropgage.com)

Lewis, Rice & Fingersh (lewisrice.com)

Liddell, Sapp, Zivley, Hill, LaBoon (liddellsapp.com)

Marshall, Dennehey, Warner, Coleman & Goggin (mdwcg.com)

McKenna & Cuneo, L.L.P. (mckennacuneo.com)

Miles & Stockbridge (milesstockbridge.com)

Miller, Canfield, Paddock and Stone, P.L.C. (millercanfield.com)

Miller, Griffin & Marks, P.S.C. (horselaw.com)

Miller, Griffin & Marks, P.S.C. (kentuckylaw.com)

Moore & Van Allen, P.L.L.C. (mvalaw.com)

Patton Boggs, L.L.P. (pattonboggs.com)

Petree Stockton, L.L.P. (petree.com)

Phillips, Lytle, Hitchcock, Blaine & Huber (phillipslytle.com)

Plunkett & Cooney, P.C. (plunkettlaw.com)

Post Schell, P.C. (postschell.com)

Reid and Priest (reidpriest.com)

Schiff Hardin & Waite (schiffhardin.com)

Schulte, Roth and Zabel (srz.com)

Sharon Sooho, Esq., c/o Steven L. Fuchs (sooho.com)

Sills Cummis Zuckerman Radin Tischman & Gross (sillscummis.com)

Simpson Thacher & Bartlett
    (stblaw.com)

Steel Hector & Davis (steelhector.com)

Stroock & Stroock & Lavan
    (stroock.com)

Thompson Coburn
    (thompsoncoburn.com)

Thompson & Knight (tklaw.com)

Troutman Sanders, L.L.P.
    (troutmansanders.com)

Vinson & Elkins, L.L.P.
    (vinson-elkins.com)

White Williams (whitewms.com)

Whitman, Breed, Abbott & Morgan
    (financelaw.com)

Luddites
Morrison & Hecker, L.L.P. (none)

Longest Domain Names
Dickinson Wright
    (dickinson-wright.com)

encryption
Also known as "crypto," encryption is the process by which two correspondents encode their communication to render the message unreadable but to each other. Programs like Pretty Good Privacy (PGP) are robust enough that the government can't crack the code. (Of course, there are some who refute this claim, stating, "Well, that's just what they want you to believe." These are the same people who argue, "Just because you're paranoid doesn't mean they're not out to get you.") If everyone used encryption, much of the debate over attorney-client privilege and e-mail would be moot. Of course, most lawyers claim that encryption is too hard to use. These are the same people who would spend days learning how to program the presets in their BMW. See also **Clipper Chip.**

Miles & Stockbridge (milesstockbridge.com)
Thacher, Proffitt & Wood (thacherproffitt.com)
Troutman Sanders, L.L.P. (troutmansanders.com)

Shortest Domain Names
Graham & James (gj.com)
Jackson & Walker (jw.com)
Kirkpatrick & Lockhart (kl.com)
Latham and Watkins (lw.com)
Robinson & Cole (rc.com)
Rogers & Wells (rw.com)
Fish & Richardson (fr.com)

Most Memorable Domain Names
Frost & Jacobs (frojac.com)
Haynes & Boone (hayboo.com)
Hopkins and Sutter (hopsut.com)
Kilpatrick & Cody (kilcody.com)
Morrison & Foerster, L.L.P. (mofo.com)

BIG FIRMS—THE NLJ 250

Adams & Reese

- *cyberspace:* arlaw.com
- *earth place:* New Orleans, LA
- *born on:* 14 Dec 1994 (early adopter)
- *review:* The first main link off the home page—"About the Firm"—has been under construction for more than six months (and possibly much longer). To get to the real substance of the site, you have to click on "Main Menu," which brings up a list of subsections such as People, Newsletters, Practice Areas, and so on. Unfortunately, the only newsletters available are from—get this—1995.
- *practice areas:* professional liability, general business and financial, health care, maritime litigation, commercial litigation, corporate, tax and securities, toxic tort, general litigation, environmental, international, gaming, governmental relations, intellectual property

Akerman, Senterfill & Eidson, P.A.

- *cyberspace:* akerman.com
- *earth place:* Orlando, FL
- *born on:* 19 Oct 1996 (late adopter)

Akin, Gump, Strauss, Hauer & Feld, L.L.P.

- *cyberspace:* akingump.com
- *earth place:* Dallas, TX
- *born on:* 29 Oct 1995 (middler)

Alston & Bird

- *cyberspace:* alston.com
- *earth place:* Atlanta, GA
- *born on:* 14 Jan 1995 (middler)
- *review:* Alston & Bird maintains a second-generation site, which concentrates on making general information about the firm available to the visitor. There is no effort to publish original content. Descriptions of practice areas, lawyer biographies, and office information is all here, but not much else.
- *practice areas:* antitrust and investigations, capital markets, intellectual property, litigation, ERISA and employee benefits, bankruptcy, finance, trademarks, ERISA litigation, construction, communications and technology, transactional, estate planning and fiduciary, environmental, financial services, patent solicitation, exempt organizations, financial services litigation, health care, corporate, federal income tax, labor and employment, international, tax, medical products and services litigation, state and local tax, securities litigation, North Carolina transactional

Altheimer & Gray

- *cyberspace:* altheimer.com
- *earth place:* Chicago, IL
- *born on:* 28 Oct 1995 (middler)

▼▼▼▼▼

faxing

Yes, Virginia, you can receive faxes via the Web when you're away from (or at, for that matter) the office. FaxWeb (http://www.faxweb.net/) enables you to retrieve your faxes (and voice-mail) from anywhere in the world. You can even configure FaxWeb to notify you via e-mail or alphanumeric pager when faxes and voice-mail are received. For example, if you only want to use FaxWeb when you travel, you can simply use call-forwarding to forward your office's fax to your FaxWeb phone number. FaxWeb's interface is simple and intuitive. The service is priced reasonably at about $25/month.

Anderson, Kill, Olick & Oshinsky, P.C.

- *cyberspace:* andersonkill.com
- *earth place:* New York, NY
- *born on:* 31 Jul 1996 (late adopter)
- *review:* All of their 1996 and 1997 newsletters (covering lender, insurance, and employment law issues) are online, and they have announced plans to upload newsletters from 1994 and 1995. The insurance resources section contains links to a wealth of insurance-related Web sites. The Vacatur Center provides compelling arguments for why the policy of vacating legal precedents should be stopped. If you can get past the front page (proclaiming "We Are Not the Enemy") and the home page (containing rotating lawyer jokes), there is a lot of good content here.[1]
- *practice areas:* antitrust litigation and counseling, bankruptcy litigation, corporate and finance, employment and labor law, ERISA litigation, insurance coverage litigation, intellectual property, matrimonial and family law, products liability litigation, real estate, securities litigation, tax law, trusts and estates

Andrews & Kurth, L.L.P.

- *cyberspace:* andrews-kurth.com
- *earth place:* Houston, TX
- *born on:* 04 Jan 1996 (late adopter)

Arent Fox Kinter Plotkin & Kahn

- *cyberspace:* arentfox.com
- *earth place:* Washington, DC
- *born on:* 05 Oct 1994 (early adopter)

---

1. For a good example of how to use humor in a law-related Web site, see Russell & Tate (http://www.russelltate.com). Released on April 1, 1996, and based on the characters from NBC's Saturday Night Live (SNL), this may be the first law firm Web site parody. You've got to love their e-mail address: WeGetYoMoney@russelltate.com! All we can conclude about this site is that its creators must be SNL fans with way too much spare time on their hands. (If you guessed that we were involved with the development of this site, you're right!)

- *review:* This site has terrific content. The "Features of the Month" section can fairly be called an online community. Complete with articles, links to related information, and threaded discussion groups, the features focus on certain areas of law, legislation, or legal issues. When we reviewed the site, the feature was contests and sweepstakes law. They've got newsletters that you can read online or receive via e-mail. They also offer a tour, powered by JavaScript, of some of the firm's clients' sites. Very cool. Make no doubt about it, this site is great.

- *practice areas:* bankruptcy litigation, construction litigation, general litigation, white-collar criminal defense, advertising and trade regulation, agricultural law, antitrust and trade regulation, communications, cyberspace law, environmental, food and drug, government contracts, intellectual property, bank and financial institutions, corporate/securities, estate planning and probate, land use and zoning, real estate, sports and entertainment, taxation, energy and natural resources, government relations, international group, employment, ERISA, health, telemedicine, immigration

Armstrong Teasdale

- *cyberspace:* atsd.com
- *earth place:* St. Louis, MO
- *born on:* 21 May 1996 (late adopter)

Arnold & Porter

- *cyberspace:* aporter.com
- *earth place:* Washington, DC
- *born on:* 03 Aug 1993 (early adopter)
- *review:* Who would be able to claim that the other's domain name was confusingly similar: Arnold & Porter (**aporter.com**) or Pret-a-Porter Fashion (**pret-a-porter.com**)? Since neither of them have a Web site yet (shocking, isn't it?), we guess the question is moot.

free Internet
The Internet is not now—and never has been—free. Those that claimed that they had free Internet access in the past had their access provided by their employers or educational institutions. So if you want to spend $20,000/year on law school, you can still get "free" Internet access.

Arnold, White and Durkee

- *cyberspace:* awd.com
- *earth place:* Houston, TX
- *born on:* 08 Feb 1995 (middler)
- *review:* We're guessing that at least a few people end up at this site who were looking for information on all-wheel drive vehicles. Those who show up here looking for content—newsletters, publications, etc.—will be disappointed. Practice area profiles are solid, as are office locations, the client list, and lawyer biographies.
- *practice areas:* copyright, trademark and unfair competition, patent prosecution, trade-secret litigation, commercial contract and anti-trust litigation

Arter & Hadden

- *cyberspace:* arterhadden.com
- *earth place:* Cleveland, OH
- *born on:* 07 Jun 1995 (middler)
- *review:* A handful of newsletters can be found at Arter & Hadden's Web site, but the depth tends to be somewhat superficial. (Compare this with the quasi-law review articles published as newsletters at other firm's sites.) Biographies of lawyers are actually links directly to the lawyer's listing on Martindale-Hubbell's Web site (http://www.martindale.com).
- *practice areas:* appellate litigation, finance, bankruptcy, government affairs, business litigation, health care, commercial, insurance litigation, communications/utilities, intellectual property, construction, international, corporate and securities, medical products, director and officer liability, real estate, employment, tax services, environmental, workers' compensation

Baker & Botts

- *cyberspace:* bakerbotts.com
- *earth place:* Houston, TX
- *born on:* 28 Apr 1995 (middler)
- *review:* Though there's no original content to speak of, this site is a good example of how information about the firm can make up for

it. By talking about the technology used in the firm, giving a strong overview of the firm, and presenting detailed descriptions of practice areas and lawyers, Baker & Botts succeeds at using the site as a marketing tool. If it's intended as a client services tool, it has some work ahead of it.

- *practice areas:* bankruptcy and reorganization, corporate and securities, employee benefits, energy, environmental, financial transactions, government contracts, intellectual property and technology, labor and employment, legislation and policy, oil and gas, real estate, tax, trial

Baker & Daniels

- *cyberspace:* bakerdaniels.com
- *earth place:* Fort Wayne, IN
- *born on:* 03 Feb 1996 (late adopter)
- *review:* Baker & Daniels gives users the option of choosing what "headlines" they want in the "Newsstand"—a nice way of letting the user customize their page. Once selected, a dynamically generated page presents users with news articles relating to their choices. There are some good, relatively recent articles, though the number of choices for categories (19) outnumbers the number of total articles listed (12). Most practice areas have their own page, as do lawyer biographies and recruiting information.
- *practice areas:* antitrust, business planning, China practice, commercial, financial and bankruptcy, corporate finance, education, employee benefits, employment relations, environmental law, estate planning, family business, financial institutions, food and agriculture, food and drug, governmental affairs, health care, immigration, insurance, intellectual property, international law, litigation, medical device, mergers and acquisitions, nonprofit, occupational health, public finance, real estate, securities, sports, tax, transportation, utilities, energy, and telecommunications

Baker, Donnelson, Bearman

- *cyberspace:* bdbc.com
- *earth place:* Memphis, TN
- *born on:* 20 Feb 1995 (middler)

Baker & Hostetler

- *cyberspace:* bakerlaw.com
- *earth place:* Cleveland, OH
- *born on:* 24 Jul 1996 (late adopter)
- *review:* Another law firm has registered the confusingly similar baker-law.com.

Baker & McKenzie

- *cyberspace:* bakerinfo.com
- *earth place:* Hong Kong, China
- *born on:* 28 Aug 1996 (late adopter)

Ballard Spahr Andrews & Ingersoll

- *cyberspace:* ballardspahr.com
- *earth place:* Philadelphia, PA
- *born on:* 03 Apr 1995 (middler)
- *review:* Password protected.

Barnes & Thornburg

- *cyberspace:* btlaw.com
- *earth place:* Indianapolis, IN
- *born on:* 21 Jul 1995 (middler)
- *review:* The firm's 1997 Annual Report contains an interesting account of the firm's representation of the Federation of Bosnia and Herzegovina in an arbitration to determine control of Brcko, a city in northern Bosnia and Herzegovina. This nontraditional content puts a face on what is usually a faceless business. Other than the annual report, there really wasn't any substantive content to make visitors come back.
- *practice areas:* construction law, entrepreneurial services, financial institutions, health care, immigration services, international, media/publications, white-collar crime

Bell, Boyd, and Lloyd

- *cyberspace:* bellboyd.com
- *earth place:* Chicago, IL
- *born on:* 27 Nov 1996 (late adopter)

Benesch, Friedlander, Coplan & Aronoff

- *cyberspace:* bfca.com
- *earth place:* Cleveland, OH
- *born on:* 13 May 1995 (middler)
- *review:* You get one chance to make a first impression, and this site makes a great one. On the home page: "Laws of the Famous, 'Gomez's Law: If you don't throw it, they can't hit it.' —Lefty Gomez." The quotations appear to be rotating, so your mileage may vary. And so we chuckled and dug deeper into the site. Site navigation is aided by a nifty bit of JavaScript (and, unlike others we've seen, this navigation menu is not distracting). Advisories, articles, interviews, and books are listed in the "Publications" sections, but only the advisories are available online.
- *practice areas:* business reorganization, compensation and benefits, corporate and securities, environmental, estate planning and probate, financial institutions, gaming, health care, intellectual property, labor and employment, litigation, public law, real estate, tax

Bingham Dana Gould

- *cyberspace:* bingham.com
- *earth place:* Boston, MA
- *born on:* 23 Mar 1995 (middler)

Blackwell, Sanders, Matheny, Weary & Lombardi

- *cyberspace:* bsmwl.com
- *earth place:* Kansas City, MO
- *born on:* 19 Apr 1995 (middler)
- *review:* A fair amount of content in the form of quarterly advisors is available on such topics as securities, franchise, and employment law. No search engine, which is par for law firm Web sites, but no lawyer profiles either, which is subpar.

front page
A page on a Web site that sometimes appears before the home page. Often Web sites use a client pull to make the home page load automatically after the front page has been displayed for a few seconds. Also called "splash page."

FrontPage
A Microsoft program for designing and maintaining Web sites. Based on technology purchased from Vermeer, FrontPage '98 is an outstanding site creation and management tool, and provides unprecedented flexibility for non-programmers.

- *practice areas:* antitrust, franchise and distributorship disputes, unfair competition, architectural, engineering and construction law, corporate law, business and commercial litigation, employee benefits, creditors' rights and bankruptcy, energy law, education law, estate planning, trusts and probate, environmental compliance and litigation, international law, health law, real estate, insurance defense, securities law practice, labor and employment law, taxation, legal malpractice, technology and intellectual property, medical malpractice, white-collar criminal investigations and defense, product liability, workers' compensation

Blank, Rome, Comisky & McCauley

- *cyberspace:* brcm.com
- *earth place:* Philadelphia, PA
- *born on:* 18 Jul 1995 (middler)

Bogle & Gates

- *cyberspace:* bogle.com
- *earth place:* Seattle, WA
- *born on:* 08 Sep 1995 (middler)

Bracewell & Patterson

- *cyberspace:* bracepatt.com
- *earth place:* Houston, TX
- *born on:* 05 Jan 1996 (late adopter)
- *review:* A few newsletters covering education, environmental, and insurance law were available, but no lawyer profiles.
- *practice areas:* alternative dispute resolution, appellate practice, bankruptcy and creditors' rights, corporate and securities, early stage companies, educational institutions, employee benefits, energy, environmental, financial institutions, government contracts, health care, hospitality industry, intellectual property, international, labor and employment, legislative and governmental relations, not-for-profit organizations, power, pro bono activities, real estate, taxation, telecommunications, trial, trusts and estates

Broad and Cassel, P.A.

- *cyberspace:* broadandcassel.com
- *earth place:* Orlando, FL
- *born on:* 03 Mar 1996 (late adopter)

Brobeck Phleger Harrison

- *cyberspace:* brobeck.com
- *earth place:* San Francisco, CA
- *born on:* 05 Jan 1994 (early adopter)
- *review:* The home page employs a periodical style, with a monthly feature on a particular legal issue. For example, the November feature was about the need for focusing on trade-secret protection. Lots of articles are online on a wide variety of legal topics, including employment, securities, and environmental law. Special attention is paid to client services, with a clients-only form for submitting legal research questions to the firm's staff. Also contains in-depth information about the Securities and Exchange Commission's EDGAR filing process.
- *practice areas:* business and technology, financial services and insolvency, real estate group, tax and estate planning, antitrust and trade regulation, business litigation, environmental law group, insurance coverage litigation, intellectual property, labor and employment, product liability, real-estate litigation, securities litigation

Brown and Wood, L.L.P.

- *cyberspace:* bwllp.com
- *earth place:* New York, NY
- *born on:* 20 Dec 1996 (late adopter)
- *review:* Under construction.

Brown, Todd, and Heyburn

- *cyberspace:* bth-pllc.com
- *earth place:* Louisville, KY

FTP

File Transfer Program. FTP is a software program that allows users on one computer (the FTP client) to connect to another computer (the FTP server) for the limited purpose of copying files from (and sometimes to) the FTP server. FTP also stands for File Transfer Protocol, the standard protocol on which the FTP program runs.

- *born on:* 10 Aug 1995 (middler)

- *review:* Though not necessarily obvious, the "Legal Pad" provides visitors with some well-written articles about a variety of subject areas. The articles should be dated, so people know how recent they are, but they give you a good idea of what the firm can do. The lawyer directory consists of links to each lawyer profile at Martindale-Hubbell.

- *practice areas:* litigation, environmental practice, equine group, insurance litigation practice, labor and employment practice, national counsel practice, patent litigation, product liability litigation, corporate/business law, business acquisitions practice, commercial transactions, construction group, employee benefits practice, health-care group, international services group, public finance practice, securities capabilities, tax practice, real-estate practice, estate planning and administration

Bryan Cave, L.L.P.

- *cyberspace:* bryancave.com

- *earth place:* St. Louis, MO

- *born on:* 21 Mar 1997 (late adopter)

Buchanan Ingersoll

- *cyberspace:* bipc.com

- *earth place:* Pittsburgh, PA

- *born on:* 06 Dec 1995 (middler)

- *review:* The lawyer profile pages are huge (85 K, or approximately 43 printed pages), but the profiles themselves lack the navigational elements that are present on other pages in the site. Conspicuously absent is any content—newsletters or otherwise—that would compel a user to return.

- *practice areas:* beverage alcohol law group, beverage industry group, biotechnology, business and international group, business tax group, coal group, communications law group, computer technology ventures group, construction industry group, corporate finance group, corporate insurance and professional liability defense group, electronic security group, employee benefits group, energy sector services, environmental law group, family law group, financial institutions litigation group, financial institutions group, franchising group, government relations group, health care law group, health care mergers and acquisitions group, insurance regulatory law, intellectual property group, international banking and trade finance group, labor and employment law group, litigation group, medical device technology group, public offerings, real-estate group, real-estate litigation and development group, security guard practice team, technology ventures group, workers' compensation

Cadwalader Wickersham and Taft

- *cyberspace:* cadwalader.com
- *earth place:* New York, NY
- *born on:* 20 Jan 1994 (early adopter)
- *review:* It takes too many clicks to get to the substance in "Recruiting," but once there, there is as much (if not more) information here for eager law students than at most other sites. Profiles are not available for all lawyers, but those that are online provide a good narrative of the lawyer's background, as well as a mailing address and a direct-dial phone number. Publications are just listed here. To receive copies, you must fill out a form and get them by mail.
- *practice areas:* environmental, general corporate, securities and finance, banking, financial services, insurance, mergers and acquisitions, project finance, health care/not-for-profit, insolvency, insurance insolvency, Latin America, litigation, private client, real estate, finance, capital markets, tax

Cahill Gordon & Reindel

- *cyberspace:* cahill.com
- *earth place:* New York, NY
- *born on:* 03 Feb 1995 (middler)

Calfee, Halter & Griswold

- *cyberspace:* calfee.com
- *earth place:* Cleveland, OH
- *born on:* 29 Nov 1995 (middler)

▼▼▼▼▼

GIST TV Listings (http://www.gist.com/) Type in your zip code, and GIST tells you who your cable provider is. With one more click, you'll see what's playing on TV tonight. You can customize the display, so that you only see the channels you're interested in. A very useful site.

GNN
Global Network Navigator. One of the first major directories of the Internet that vied with Yahoo for dominance in the directory field. Then AOL bought GNN (from publisher O'Reilly & Associates) and tried to make it into something it was not. Yahoo is now the Internet's most popular Web site.

Carlton Fields

- *cyberspace:* carltonfields.com
- *earth place:* Tampa, FL
- *born on:* 21 Oct 1995 (middler)
- *review:* Password protected.

Chadbourne & Parke

- *cyberspace:* chadbourne.com
- *earth place:* New York, NY
- *born on:* 10 May 1995 (middler)

Chapman and Cutler

- *cyberspace:* chapman.com
- *earth place:* Chicago, IL
- *born on:* 18 Nov 1993 (early adopter)
- *review:* Chapman and Cutler may have some of the oldest content on the Web (for law firms, at least)—and that's a good thing. When combined with timely information (which these newsletters are), historical documents are a great way both to see how the firm has handled major developments in the law, and to gauge how important client communication is to the firm (How long have they been doing newsletters? Are they comprehensive, or just fluff?). When we saw that some newsletters from as far back as 1992 were available, we admit to being impressed. (The most recent were less than a month old.) Decent recruiting information is also available on-line, and there's a mysterious link to "Client Document Access"—making us wonder if the firm has some kind of extranet set up for their clients. If so, it was down when we tried to connect. There was nothing on the site that we could find explaining what it did.
- *practice areas:* banking, bankruptcy, workout and special litigation, corporate and general litigation, corporate and securities, corporate finance, employee benefits, environmental, health, educational and cultural institutions finance, public finance, public utilities, real estate, tax, trust and estate

Choate, Hall & Stewart

- *cyberspace:* choate.com
- *earth place:* Boston, MA

- *born on:* 15 Nov 1994 (early adopter)
- *review:* The news section contains articles and newsletters on a variety of topics, including health care and labor law. But the news section is not very well organized. (In some cases, the "Archives" section had newer articles than did the "Newsletters" section.) There are no navigational elements to speak of, and the lawyer directory contains only e-mail addresses.
- *practice areas:* business, patent and intellectual property, creditors' rights and bankruptcy, litigation, labor, employment and employee benefits, health care, real estate, land use and environmental, tax, state tax, fiduciary, the Choate group, investigative services

Clausen Miller, P.C.

- *cyberspace:* clausen.com
- *earth place:* Chicago, IL
- *born on:* 05 Apr 1996 (late adopter)

Cleary, Gottlieb, Steen & Hamilton

- *cyberspace:* cleargolaw.com
- *earth place:* New York, NY
- *born on:* 13 Dec 1996 (late adopter)

Cooley Godward, L.L.P.

- *cyberspace:* cooley.com
- *earth place:* San Francisco, CA
- *born on:* 17 Nov 1994 (early adopter)
- *review:* Plenty of articles—many about intellectual property law—appear under the "What's New" section, but the organization is chronological, not subject-oriented. A chronological listing isn't the easiest to browse. But this may be a limitation of the software powering this site, because the entire site appears to be driven by a database, not by static files. The site has a very nice layout on the lawyer profile pages. The inclusion of "Upcoming Seminars and Events" is a nice touch—it demonstrates the firm's commitment to educating its clients and keeping up on developments in the law. At the time visited, however, there was just one seminar listed. Not to be confused with The Thomas Cooley Law School (cooley.edu).

- *practice areas:* business, litigation, alternative energy project, financing, creditors' rights and bankruptcy, defense of regulatory, civil, and criminal enforcement, emerging growth companies, employee benefits and equity compensation, employment and labor, energy and environmental company, environmental, estate planning, family business, financial institutions, food industry, health care, immigration, information technologies, international law, life sciences, mergers and acquisitions, nonprofit organizations, pro bono, real estate, real-estate and construction litigation, retail industry, Rocky Mountain, securities litigation, southern California, sports law, tax, technology litigation, trade regulation, trademark, advertising and copyright, workout, troubled loan and asset representation

Coudert Brothers

- *cyberspace:* coudert.com
- *earth place:* San Francisco, CA
- *born on:* 21 Mar 1995 (middler)
- *review:* A total of two newsletters are online: one issue of a Construction newsletter, one of an Emerging Markets newsletter, and both are PDF files. The best information on this site is the office location information. They list not only practice areas in which they specialize but also recent matters at that location. This gives prospective clients a great feel for what the firm can do (and where). Laywer biographies are just links back to the *West Legal Directory*.
- *practice areas:* aerospace, banking, construction, energy and natural resources, entertainment, government contracts, high technology, hotel, insurance, investment funds, project finance, real estate, telecommunications

Covington & Burling

- *cyberspace:* cov.com
- *earth place:* Washington, DC
- *born on:* 08 Jul 1994 (early adopter)

Cozen and O'Connor

- *cyberspace:* cozen-oconnor.com
- *earth place:* Philadelphia, PA
- *born on:* 29 Oct 1996 (late adopter)

Cravath, Swaine & Moore

- *cyberspace:* cravath.com
- *earth place:* New York, NY
- *born on:* 14 Mar 1995 (middler)

Crosby, Heafey, Roach & May

- *cyberspace:* chrm.com
- *earth place:* Oakland, CA
- *born on:* 18 Jul 1994 (early adopter)
- *review:* The home page contains simple professional graphics and the firm's contact information (mailing address, phone, fax, e-mail), which is all too often buried with a law firm's site. Lawyer profiles contained only a phone number and e-mail address for each lawyer. There are some articles online, but it is difficult to find what you are looking for, because they are arranged chronologically (proof that there's more than one way to organize a Web site).
- *practice areas:* appellate, business and corporate, business litigation, environmental, finance and commercial, insurance, intellectual property, labor and employment, product liability, real estate, trusts and estates

Crowell & Moring

- *cyberspace:* cromor.com
- *earth place:* Washington, DC
- *born on:* 12 Mar 1996 (late adopter)

Good Times

Consider this our public service: GOOD TIMES IS NOT A VIRUS. For those of you who aren't familiar with netiquette, our use of all caps indicates that WE'RE SCREAMING. Several years ago, a college student (we'll call him Evil) circulated an e-mail indicating that a virus was circulating on the Internet by e-mail. This particularly nefarious virus would delete your hard drive the instant that you opened the message with the subject line "Good Times." Here's one thing that's always puzzled us: Didn't the original warning have the subject line "Good Times Virus: Don't Read!"? Anyway, the quick answer is that e-mail is incapable of deleting your hard drive. E-mail is text. Text can't do anything to your hard drive. (Now, if you receive an attachment to an e-mail message, and you run that attachment, it could be a virus.) Here's a polite request from those of us who receive way too many false alarms: Check out the Computer Incident Advisory Capability Web site at the U.S. Department of Energy, and see if the dire warnings you just read on e-mail are listed on this page. If they are, then save your friends a lot of trouble and resist the urge to forward the warning to everyone you've ever corresponded with. See http://ciac.llnl.gov/ciac/CIACHoaxes.html.

Cummings & Lockwood

- *cyberspace:* cl-law.com
- *earth place:* Hartford, CT
- *born on:* 24 Jun 1996 (late adopter)
- *review:* Seminar announcements are a nice touch, and two upcoming seminars were listed at the time we visited. In addition, a handful of "Legal Advisories" were available, but tended not to offer the kind of depth that allows readers to go beyond scratching the surface. Lawyer biographies were passable, but didn't go into the same level of detail that most other firms do.
- *practice areas:* commercial real estate, corporate, environmental, ERISA/benefits, finance and lending, intellectual property, labor and employment, litigation and dispute resolution, tax, workouts and bankruptcy, construction, financial institutions, health care, planned charitable giving, matrimonial and family law, residential real estate, trusts and estates group, environmental litigation, insurance litigation, intellectual property litigation, issues and appeals, labor and employment litigation, probate litigation, product liability and toxic tort litigation

Curtis Mallet-Prevost, Colt & Mosle

- *cyberspace:* cm-p.com
- *earth place:* New York, NY
- *born on:* 04 Sep 1996 (late adopter)
- *review:* The home page features elegant graphics and a three-sentence summary of what this firm is all about. The navigation bar, unfortunately, uses an old server-side image map. Oddly, the home page's navigation bar links to the offices section, but the subpages' navigation bar does not. There are some newsletters online, but they are arranged in the less-than-ideal chronological style.
- *practice areas:* international transactions, acquisitions, transnational offerings, domestic securities and finance, investment management, litigation, tax, admiralty, bankruptcy, real estate, environmental, intellectual property, employee benefits, trusts and estates

Davis Polk & Wardwell

- *cyberspace:* dpw.com
- *earth place:* New York, NY
- *born on:* 28 Jul 1989 (visionary)

Davis Wright Tremaine

- *cyberspace:* dwt.com
- *earth place:* Seattle, WA
- *born on:* 12 Sep 1995 (middler)
- *review:* Narrative-style lawyer profiles were nicely supplemented by links to each lawyer's fact-rich *Martindale-Hubbell Law Directory* listings. Much useful content is located in the "News to Use" section, including newsletters and articles arranged by legal topic.
- *practice areas:* admiralty and maritime, aircraft industry, antitrust, business practice, Canada practice, commercial transactions, communications and media law, construction and government contracts, credit recovery and bankruptcy department, education law, emerging business programs, employee benefits, employment law, energy, environmental and natural resources, government contracts, government investigations and criminal defense, health care law, hospitality, intellectual property, international law, legislative practice, litigation, municipal finance, newspaper group, real estate and land use, retail, securities, Shanghai, software, sports law, state and local tax, tax, technology, telecommunications and regulatory, trusts and estates

Day, Berry & Howard

- *cyberspace:* dbh.com
- *earth place:* Hartford, CT
- *born on:* 21 Dec 1993 (early adopter)

Debevoise & Plimpton

- *cyberspace:* debevoise.com
- *earth place:* New York, NY
- *born on:* 13 Jun 1996 (late adopter)
- *review:* A search engine on the home page is a nice touch. One of the graphics on the recruiting pages was broken. A small selection of memos appears online, but the organization (chronological) is poor.

Gopher

Developed at the University of Minnesota (the Gopher is their mascot), Gopher is a text-based system that was popular before the Web grew in popularity. Gopher servers employ a menu-driven user interface, much like an ATM at a bank. While some information still exists on Gopher servers, most Internet publishers (i.e., anyone making information available on the Internet) have long ago abandoned all Gopher development in favor of Web development. Gopher sites can be accessed with Web browsers. To browse GopherSpace, point your browser at the home of Gopher (gopher://gopher.micro.umn.edu/).

- *practice areas:* corporate, litigation, tax and employee benefits, trusts and estates, real estate

Dechert Price & Rhoads

- *cyberspace:* dpr.com
- *earth place:* Philadelphia, PA
- *born on:* 02 Sep 1994 (early adopter)
- *review:* For a site with a similar domain name, see Dan Paramore Racing Heads (**dpr-racing.com**). Cylinder heads (including redirected ports and multi-angle valve seats) and more for high-performance automotive enthusiasts.

Dewey Ballantine

- *cyberspace:* dbtrade.com
- *earth place:* Washington, DC
- *born on:* 20 Mar 1996 (late adopter)
- *review:* This firm's practice is international trade law, and their home page highlights current events. In this case, a U.S. dispute before the World Trade Organization about the Japanese film market. There were some articles and related materials on international trade law available.
- *practice areas:* international trade

Dickinson Wright

- *cyberspace:* dickinson-wright.com
- *earth place:* Detroit, MI
- *born on:* 16 Aug 1995 (middler)
- *review:* This large Michigan firm runs its site off of a Lotus Notes Domino server, which is puzzling, if only because there isn't much content to be found. (Clicking on "All, by Title" in the Document Library yields one title—an article about the year 2000 problem.)
- *practice areas:* general practice, energy regulation, tax, corporate matters, trademarks, federal government regulations, patent, patent litigation

Dickstein Shapiro Morin & Oshinsky, L.L.P.

- *cyberspace:* dsmo.com
- *earth place:* Washington, DC
- *born on:* 27 Jun 1996 (late adopter)
- *review:* The lawyer profiles were quite in-depth. The most interesting content here are the reprints of the firm's print advertisements (featuring various puzzles). Online publications cover legal topics such as high technology and intellectual property law.
- *practice areas:* litigation, bankruptcy and creditors' rights, business crimes and regulatory enforcement, communications, corporate and securities transactions, energy, environment and natural resources, financial institutions, government affairs, government contracts, health law, insurance litigation, intellectual property, international trade and transactions, labor/employment law, public policy/public sector litigation, real estate, securities litigation, tax

Dinsmore & Shohl

- *cyberspace:* dinsmore-shohl.com
- *earth place:* Cincinnati, OH
- *born on:* 12 Jun 1996 (late adopter)

Dorsey & Whitney

- *cyberspace:* dorseylaw.com
- *earth place:* Minneapolis, MN
- *born on:* 05 Mar 1995 (middler)
- *review:* Under "Legal Updates" you'll find articles, memos, and newsletters on a variety of topics including employment, environmental, and intellectual property law.
- *practice areas:* employee benefits, estate planning, health, private business succession planning, private companies, real estate, real estate workout, tax,

hardware
See **Computer ESP**.

Hieros Gamos
Dubbing itself the Comprehensive Law and Government Site, Hieros Gamos is the online presence for Lex Mundi, an international consortium of law firms. What Hieros Gamos has in comprehensiveness, it loses in comprehensibility. This site is too large for its own good, and as a result the organization suffers. We've always found FindLaw to be a more refined approach to cataloging legal information on the Internet.

banking and commercial, corporate trust, corporate, emerging companies, international, mergers and acquisitions, mutual funds/investment companies, public companies, public offerings, securities markets regulatory compliance, structured finance, Indian law and gaming, project finance, public finance, commercial lease and real estate tax appeals, complex commercial, construction, employment, environmental/natural resources, financial institution litigation, franchise, insurance, intellectual property, labor and employment, products liability, securities litigation, technology and intellectual property litigation

Dow, Lohnes & Albertson

- *cyberspace:* dlalaw.com
- *earth place:* Washington, DC
- *born on:* 18 Aug 1995 (middler)
- *review:* Useful information about their recruiting program, practice areas, and newsletters are all available from the front page. Lawyer biographies are relatively brief, but the overall concentration on content makes this site a useful tool for learning about the firm.
- *practice areas:* antitrust, aviation, bankruptcy and workouts, communications, compensation and benefits, computer and information technology, corporate, educational institutions, estate planning and administration, first amendment and libel, government grants and contracts, government relations, health care, intellectual property, interactive media and technology, labor and employee relations, litigation, public broadcasting and telecommunications, securities law and regulation, taxation

Drinker Biddle & Reath

- *cyberspace:* dbr.com
- *earth place:* Philadelphia, PA
- *born on:* 13 Aug 1995 (middler)

Duane, Morris & Hecksher

- *cyberspace:* duanemorris.com
- *earth place:* Philadelphia, PA
- *born on:* 20 Mar 1996 (late adopter)
- *review:* All the elements of a good site are here: recruiting information, practice area descriptions, and lawyer biographies. Most of the

newsletters are available as PDF files, and the entire site is driven by Active Server Pages, making the site search-engine hostile. Other than that, the site gives its visitors plenty to read.

- *practice areas:* administrative and regulatory law, affordable housing and community development, alternative dispute resolution, antitrust litigation, aviation litigation, class action litigation, commercial litigation, construction law and litigation, corporate compliance, corporate law, criminal law and litigation, employment law and management labor relations, energy law, environmental law, estates and asset planning, family law, fidelity and surety law, financial institution litigation, franchise litigation, health-care law, immigration law, insurance defense litigation, insurance law, intellectual property practice, international law practice, lawyer liability litigation, loan documentation, maritime litigation, medical malpractice litigation, mortgage lending and financial services, product liability litigation, professional and business ethics, professional liability, public finance, real-estate law, real-estate tax assessment litigation, reorganization and finance securities law, services for educational institutions, services for emerging businesses, services for trade associations, sports and entertainment law, taxation, workers' compensation

Dykema Gossett, P.L.L.C.

- *cyberspace:* dykema.com
- *earth place:* Detroit, MI
- *born on:* 12 May 1997 (late adopter)

Eckert Seamans Cherin and Mellott

- *cyberspace:* escm.com
- *earth place:* Pittsburgh, PA
- *born on:* 27 Mar 1996 (late adopter)

Edwards and Angell

- *cyberspace:* ealaw.com
- *earth place:* Providence, RI
- *born on:* 21 Mar 1995 (middler)

Epstein Becker & Green, P.C.

- *cyberspace:* ebglaw.com
- *earth place:* New York, NY

- *born on:* 19 Jan 1996 (late adopter)

- *review:* The site provides a general overview of the firm's practice areas, and serves as an archive for recent publications.

- *practice areas:* health care, labor and employment, corporate and securities law, litigation, government contracts, employee benefits, elder law

Faegre & Benson

- *cyberspace:* faegre.com

- *earth place:* Minneapolis, MN

- *born on:* 22 Nov 1994 (early adopter)

Finnegan, Henderson, Farabow, Garrett & Dunner

- *cyberspace:* finnegan.com

- *earth place:* Tokyo, Japan

- *born on:* 10 Nov 1994 (early adopter)

- *review:* A simple site that emphasizes content over presentation. Good information about patents and trademarks is available here. General background about the lawyers is presented as well. The mysterious "Charlie's Corner" is just a brief summary of what's going on at the Patent and Trademark Office.

- *practice areas:* litigation, appellate, trademark, licensing, copyright, regulatory, bio/pharmaceutical, chemical/metallurgical, mechanical, electrical, computer

Fish & Neave

- *cyberspace:* fishneave.com

- *earth place:* New York, NY

- *born on:* 03 Apr 1996 (late adopter)

- *review:* Password protected.

Fish & Richardson

- *cyberspace:* fr.com

- *earth place:* Boston, MA

- *born on:* 24 Jul 1995 (middler)

- *review:* One thing is for sure, we're glad this firm made it into the NLJ 250. Maybe now some other firms will see what Fish & Richardson is doing on their site and take a lesson or two. The most impressive feature at Fish & Richardson's site is the digest of patent opinions for the U.S. Court of Appeals for the Federal Circuit. This digest, which includes every case, dates back more than five years. Talk about content! This is no doubt one of the most impressive content-oriented sites of any law firm we've seen. A number of articles are available online (though we'd like to see dates on them), and lawyer biographies are arranged in just about any way you'd want to find them. And who could resist the ads that Fish & Richardson have been running in major technology publications (which are reprinted on the site). Now that's legal humor that works. (But see Anderson Kill.)

- *practice areas:* patents, trademarks, copyrights trials, federal communications commission regulation, food and drug administration regulation, U.S. International Trade Commission proceedings, biotechnology, chemistry, electronics and computer hardware, entertainment and new media, medical and radiological devices, computer programs and programmed systems

Foley, Hoag & Eliot

- *cyberspace:* fhe.com

- *earth place:* Boston, MA

- *born on:* 26 May 1994 (early adopter)

- *review:* This Boston-based law firm offers a well-designed site with some good sections of content. The "Legal Updates" section includes articles on "the law affecting businesses," including intellectual property, tax, employment, and product liability law. Businesses outside the United States (not to mention companies outside of Massachusetts) will appreciate the comprehensive guide entitled "Doing Business in Massachusetts."

- *practice areas:* accountants' professional liability practice, alter-

hits
Requests for information from a Web client to a Web server. If a Web home page contains some text and pointers to three graphics files, then there would be four hits on the Web server every time the home page was accessed by a Web client. The number of unique users that browse a particular Web server is less than the total number of hits on that server.

native dispute resolution, bankruptcy reorganization and insolvency practice, biomedical technology practice, corporate finance, energy and utilities, environmental compliance counseling and due diligence, environmental litigation and dispute resolution, immigration, international practice, intellectual property, labor and employment law services, product liability defense and prevention, public/private strategies group, real-estate land use and development, real-estate related litigation, securities and investment fraud litigation, tax, trial practice, trusts and estates department, estate planning

Foley & Lardner

- *cyberspace:* foleylardner.com

- *earth place:* Milwaukee, WI

- *born on:* 21 Mar 1997 (late adopter)

- *review:* Though there is not a lot of original content at this site, visitors seeking to learn about Foley & Lardner will go away satisfied. Information about their summer associate and recruiting programs is available, as is a wealth of information about their numerous practice areas. Many of the firm's 600 lawyers have biographies online, and the attempt to provide industry news is a good one except that much of the news is out of date.

- *practice areas:* antitrust, construction, creditors' rights, distribution, environmental/litigation, family law, intellectual property litigation, labor and employment, life, health and disability, product liability, public law, securities/litigation, regulatory department, energy, environmental/regulatory, insurance, legislative/administrative, tax and individual, planning department, employee benefits, estates and trusts, executive compensation, taxation, airport support, broker/dealer, financial institutions/finance, general corporate/commercial, government finance, heath-care finance, international, mergers/acquisitions, project finance, real estate, securities/public companies, health law department, health-care business, health-care payments, health-care payor, health-care provider operations, public hospitals and health systems, biotechnology and pharmaceutical, chemical, consumer and industrial products, electronics, trademark and copyright

Fowler, White, Burnett, Hurley, Banick & Strickroot, P.A.

- *cyberspace:* fowler-white.com
- *earth place:* Miami, FL
- *born on:* 24 Sep 1996 (late adopter)

Fox Rothschild, O'Brien & Frankel

- *cyberspace:* frof.com
- *earth place:* Philadelphia, PA
- *born on:* 09 Apr 1997 (late adopter)

Fried, Frank, Harris, Shriver & Jacobson

- *cyberspace:* ffhsj.com
- *earth place:* New York, NY
- *born on:* 31 Jan 1994 (early adopter)
- *review:* The search interface (unlike many) provides summary information for each of the found pages. The "Lawyer Listing" page provides lawyer profiles that are too short. A fantastic feature of this site is that newsletters covering such areas as banking, securities, and lending law are available online and by e-mail subscription. We wish more firms would provide services via e-mail.
- *practice areas:* bankruptcy and restructuring, benefits and compensation, pension benefit guaranty corporation, ERISA, corporate, securities offerings and financings, leveraged buyouts, directors' committees, business and financial restructurings, securities regulation, compliance and enforcement, mergers, acquisitions and dispositions, shareholder relations and proxy contests, financial institutions practice, international, Latin America, energy, estates and trusts, government contracts, insurance industry, regulatory compliance, complex corporate transactions, risk financing and specialized insur-

home page
The starting point for a particular individual's or organization's Web presence. The home page for the ABA is http://www.abanet.org/.

HomePage
A program by Claris for designing and maintaining Web sites.

ance structures, litigation and arbitration, reinsurance, federal and state legislative representation, insurer insolvency, international trade, litigation, environmental, antitrust, trade regulation and franchising, intellectual property, white-collar criminal and civil RICO defense, securities and shareholder litigation, arbitration, mediation and alternative dispute resolution, real-estate litigation, tax litigation, professional liability, commercial litigation, compliance programs, product liability, public interest litigation, real estate, capital markets, restructurings, leasing, development, portfolio transactions, tax practice, acquisitions, multinational corporations, international tax planning, real-estate transactions, counsel to individuals and other advisors, bankruptcy and restructuring, litigation, trust and estates

Frost & Jacobs

- *cyberspace:* frojac.com
- *earth place:* Cincinnati, OH
- *born on:* 20 Jul 1995 (middler)
- *review:* Another cool domain name. Lawyer profiles employ the narrative style effectively. Site navigation would be improved if the navigation bar included links to all major sections of the site. Helpful articles are available covering such areas as litigation, intellectual property, and environmental law.
- *practice areas:* business/corporate, commercial real estate, environmental law, health care, immigration, intellectual property, international practice group, labor and employment law, litigation, personal planning, and family business

Fulbright & Jaworski, L.L.P.

- *cyberspace:* fulbright.com
- *earth place:* Houston, TX
- *born on:* 04 Jun 1995 (middler)
- *review:* Fulbright & Jaworski, L.L.P., founded in 1919, is an international, full-service law firm. There is no original content at this site, but they do a good job of promoting their practice areas and their national rankings in various surveys.
- *practice areas:* alternative dispute resolution, admiralty, bankruptcy, corporate, employee benefits, energy and environment,

family, health care, international, intellectual property, labor and employment, litigation, oil and gas, project finance, public finance, real estate, tax, transportation, trusts and estates, venture capital

Gardere and Wynne, L.L.P.

- *cyberspace:* gardere-law.com

- *earth place:* Dallas, TX

- *born on:* 11 Sep 1995 (middler)

- *review:* The presentation of the lawyer profiles is quite pleasing, and the narrative style is informative and effective. Considerable attention is paid to recruiting, with frequently asked questions and answers provided to law students seeking summer or permanent employment. Under "Hot Topics" we found an intriguing article entitled "What do you mean I don't own my own web page?"

- *practice areas:* administrative law, admiralty, antitrust, appellate, aviation, business law, computer technology, construction, corporate and securities, employee benefits, energy, environmental, financial services, food and beverage, franchise and direct selling, government contracts, health care, high technology, immigration, insurance, intellectual property, international, labor and employment, real estate, securities litigation, tax, telecommunications, trial, trusts and estates

Gardner, Carton and Douglas

- *cyberspace:* gcd.com

- *earth place:* Chicago, IL

- *born on:* 08 Feb 1995 (middler)

- *review:* A relatively new addition to the world of NLJ 250 Web sites, the Gardner, Carton and Douglas site offers visitors information relating to their recruiting program, to a consortium they belong to called the World Law Group, and to lawyer biographies. The articles section provides some of the old-

HTML
HyperText Markup Language. The file format used on the World Wide Web. Many word processing programs now let the user save a particular file as type .HTML (or type .HTM), just as a file can be saved as type text or as RTF (Rich Text Format). See also **Dr. HTML.**

est online content we've seen at a law firm. At least one of the articles dates from 1963!

- *practice areas:* communications, corporate securities and financing transactions, creditors' rights and bankruptcy, employee benefits, environmental, estate planning and administration, health, intellectual property, international, labor and employment, litigation, public law, real estate

Gibson, Dunn & Crutcher

- *cyberspace:* gdclaw.com
- *earth place:* Los Angeles, CA
- *born on:* 25 Nov 1995 (middler)
- *review:* As a firm brochure, this site really sings. But unless we missed it (which is doubtful, because the site is so well organized), there were no memos, articles, or newsletters online.
- *practice areas:* antitrust and trade regulation, communications, environment and natural resources, intellectual property, legislative counsel and government relations, securities litigation, international trade and customs, aerospace industries, antitrust and trade regulation, appellate and constitutional law, bankruptcy and creditors' rights, business crimes and investigations, corporate tax, corporate transactions, employee benefits and executive compensation, entertainment, financial institutions, government and commercial contracts, insurance litigation, international project finance and privatizations, international transactions, labor and employment, legal malpractice defense, media, personal tax and estate planning, real estate, construction and technical litigation

Goodwin, Procter & Hoar

- *cyberspace:* gph.com
- *earth place:* Boston, MA
- *born on:* 07 Sep 1994 (early adopter)

Graham & James

- *cyberspace:* gj.com
- *earth place:* San Francisco, CA
- *born on:* 05 Jun 1995 (middler)

- *review:* Articles and newsletters covering a wide variety of legal topics—including intellectual property, international, and labor law—are available. The firm also maintains an e-mail distribution list for article dissemination—a tactic more firms should adopt.

- *practice areas:* antitrust, banking, bankruptcy and creditors' rights, corporate and commercial, employee benefits and stock ownership plans, energy, entertainment, environmental and land use, equipment leasing, estate planning, family law, financial services, food and drug, health care, immigration, insurance, intellectual property, international asset management, international trade and customs, labor and employment, legislative and regulatory, litigation and arbitration, maritime, mergers and acquisitions, product liability, public finance, public utilities, real estate, securities, tax, telecommunications, transportation

Gray Cary Ware & Freidenrich

- *cyberspace:* gcwf.com

- *earth place:* San Diego, CA

- *born on:* 07 Mar 1994 (early adopter)

- *review:* Gray Cary Ware & Freidenrich sponsor a number of seminars for their clients, and take advantage of the Web to make signing up for the seminars straightforward. The "Cyberspace Legal Issues" link promises to be interesting reading, except that the material is more than a year old, which is more than a generation on the Net! Most other content is similarly out of date.

- *practice areas:* commercial law and financial institutions, corporate and securities, employment law, environmental and real estate, international legal, litigation, products, technology, and multimedia, securities litigation, tax and trusts, technology and intellectual property services

Greenberg Traurig

- *cyberspace:* gtlaw.com

- *earth place:* Miami, FL

- *born on:* 10 Sep 1995 (middler)

Haight, Brown and Bonesteel

- *cyberspace:* hbblaw.com
- *earth place:* Santa Monica, CA
- *born on:* 07 Sep 1996 (late adopter)

Hale and Dorr

- *cyberspace:* haledorr.com
- *earth place:* Boston, MA
- *born on:* 25 Jun 1993 (early adopter)
- *review:* There is a WAIS search engine to search content on the site, and lawyer profiles employ an effective narrative style. There are few navigational elements beyond the home page. About a dozen newsletters and a handful of other articles are available online.
- *practice areas:* biotechnology, family business, corporate finance, emerging companies, international securities, partnership, tax and business law, publicly traded companies, telecommunications, software, antitrust, government enforcement, compliance, bankruptcy and commercial law, environmental, government relations, intellectual property, international, investment management group, labor and employment, real estate, tax, trusts and estates

Harris, Beach and Wilcox

- *cyberspace:* harrisbeach.com
- *earth place:* Rochester, NY
- *born on:* 10 Jul 1996 (late adopter)
- *review:* A few articles are scattered throughout the site, though not enough to encourage visitors to return. The "in-depth" discussion of issues relating to the law of the Internet consisted of two paragraphs. Parts of the site were still under construction when we stopped by.
- *practice areas:* collections law, commercial real-estate development and finance, construction and surety law, corporate law, environmental law, financial restructuring, bankruptcy, and creditors' rights law, foreclosures, health services, intellectual property law, international law, labor and employment law, legislation and government relations (Harris Beach Associates, L.L.C.), litigation, personal legal services, public finance law, residential real estate, tax

law, technology and emerging businesses, telecommunications and media law, trusts and estates

Haynes & Boone

- *cyberspace:* **hayboo.com**
- *earth place:* Dallas, TX
- *born on:* 05 May 1995 (middler)
- *review:* Another one of our favorite domain names. The results page for the lawyer search is the best we've ever seen, with summary information provided for each found lawyer. Some sections of the site ("Connections," "Leading Edge," and "Briefings") provide little clue about what might be inside. We looked, of course, but we wonder if nonreviewers would be as patient. The bulk of the I'll-be-back content is under "Briefings," including newsletters about litigation, health care, and intellectual property law.
- *practice areas:* appellate, business litigation, business planning and taxation, business reorganization and bankruptcy, energy, environmental, finance, health care, international, intellectual property, labor, employment and employee benefits, real estate, regulated industries and government practice, specialized litigation and government investigation, technology

Heller, Ehrman, White & McAuliffe

- *cyberspace:* **hewm.com**
- *earth place:* San Francisco, CA
- *born on:* 09 Jan 1990 (visionary)
- *review:* Lawyer profiles included links to representative cases. There are articles online in most of their practice areas, and a little more than a dozen articles appear in the "Library" section. Other content worth coming back for is harder to get to, tucked several clicks away under "Practice Areas."
- *practice areas:* alternative dispute resolution, antitrust, bank-

HTTP
HyperText Transport Protocol. The standard protocol on which Web clients and servers run. Unlike FTP and Gopher, where the protocols and the programs that run them use the same name, the World Wide Web uses different names for each. This is why an FTP URL uses the word FTP twice—once for the protocol, once for the program.

ruptcy/reorganizations/workouts, corporate governance and securities litigation, corporate/securities/mergers and acquisitions, energy, environmental, estates and trusts, finance, financial institutions, information technology, insurance coverage, intellectual property/patent and trademark, international, labor and employment, life sciences, litigation, product liability, professional liability, real estate/land use/real-estate investment trusts, tax/federal and state, white-collar crime

Hodgson, Russ, Andrews, Woods & Goodyear, L.L.P.

- *cyberspace:* hodgsonruss.com
- *earth place:* Buffalo, NY
- *born on:* 18 Dec 1996 (late adopter)
- *review:* This site has the right subsections, but makes little attempt to provide any detail. The lawyer biographies are similar to their Martindale-Hubbell entries, but the practice area page lists practice areas without any in-depth information about the firm's experience in that section. The same is true of the locations. There is no information about the cities in which the firm has offices.
- *practice areas:* administrative law, antitrust, banking, bankruptcy, benefits, including ERISA, business law, Canada/U.S. cross-border counseling, computer law, construction, corporate law, education law, electronic commerce, employee benefits, environmental law, estate planning and administration, executive compensation, federal tax, financial services, government relations, health-care law, homeowner association/condominium, immigration, insolvency and creditors' rights, insurance, insurance coverage, intellectual property law, international law, joint ventures, labor and employment, land use and zoning, licensing, litigation, New York state tax, nonprofit organizations, patent, trademark, copyright, pension, personal injury, product liability, professional corporations, public finance, public utility law, real estate, securities, special education, state and local tax, tax, technology, white-collar criminal defense

Hogan & Hartson

- *cyberspace:* hhlaw.com
- *earth place:* Washington, DC
- *born on:* 11 Aug 1993 (early adopter)

- *review:* Another law firm, Houston Harbaugh, has registered the confusingly similar hh-law.com. This just goes to show why hyphens in domains are generally a Bad Thing.

Holland & Hart

- *cyberspace:* hollandhart.com
- *earth place:* Denver, CO
- *born on:* 22 Sep 1995 (middler)
- *review:* There's not much of substance at this site. Indeed, though they write several employment law newsletters for commercial publisher M. Lee Smith, the content is available by subscription only. Some information about the practice areas is also available at their site, but the site itself is rather light.
- *practice areas:* business and corporate law, international law, labor law, natural resources and environmental law, intellectual property law

Holland and Knight Law Offices

- *cyberspace:* hklaw.com
- *earth place:* Lakeland, FL
- *born on:* 28 Jul 1995 (middler)
- *review:* The lawyer search feature (powered by Excite) produces output with detailed information for each lawyer—it's almost too complete! Many newsletters are online covering such topics as alcoholic beverage, construction, and international trade law.

  note: Another law firm, Haglund & Kirtley, picked up the hk-law.com domain, making it a lot like the larger firm, Holland & Knight. Here's hoping that no privileged communication intended for hklaw.com finds itself misaddressed!

information superhighway

As far as we can tell, this term was first used in 1988 by Mitch Kapor to describe a national network used for transporting information in multiple forms, including sound, pictures, words, and numbers. Mitch Kapor, who founded Lotus Development Corp. in 1982, left Lotus in 1986, and later went on to form the Electronic Frontier Foundation. Kapor properly referred to the information superhighway as the *medium* for exchanging information, not the information itself. The popular press has used and abused the term to mean both the *medium* and the *message.* Besides, the analogy of the Internet to a highway is not a good one. Unlike the premise in the book *Zen and the Art of Motorcycle Maintenance,* on the Internet we care about the destination, not the journey. The satisfaction lies in getting to the information quickly and not worrying about the underlying network that transmitted the information request.

- *practice areas:* administrative and rulemaking, agriculture, alternative dispute resolution, antitrust and trade regulation, appellate, aviation, beverage alcohol, bond financing [public finance], cash flow and asset-based lending, class action, commercial leasing, community services, computer and telecommunications, construction and engineering; public contract, corporate and securities, creditors' rights, bankruptcy and workouts, criminal defense, general, Cuba action team, development of regional impact, education, energy practice, entertainment law, environmental law, ERISA/employee benefits, family and marital law, federal legislative, financial institutions, franchise, government contracting, growth management, concurrency and land use, health care, hotel development, HUD-FHA, FNMA-FHLMC and governmental housing programs, immigration, insurance, intellectual property, international, international trade and customs regulatory practice, labor and employment law, Latin American focus group, legislative (federal), state legislative (Florida), litigation, marine, aviation and international litigation, media and communications, mining law, mortgage banking, personal injury and wrongful death, power plant/transmission line siting, product liability, public utility practice, real-estate development and finance (Washington, DC, and Florida), REITs, sports representation and management, state and local taxation, taxation, telecommunications, timeshare and resort development and finance, transportation, trusts and estates, white-collar crime, workers' compensation

Holme, Roberts & Owen

- *cyberspace:* hro.com
- *earth place:* Denver, CO
- *born on:* 03 Mar 1994 (early adopter)
- *review:* Lawyer profiles were supplemented nicely with links to the *Martindale-Hubbell Law Directory* listings for each lawyer. We wish more firms would take advantage of this feature. A handful of newsletters were available in the "What's New" section, but there was no section dedicated to the firm's publications (that is, what's old).

  note: Yet another firm that has had a smaller firm register a domain that differs by a hyphen from a larger firm's domain. In this case, hr-o.com has been registered by another law firm. Surely there's a better answer.

- *practice areas:* commercial law and securities, complex commercial litigation, community resources, environmental, ERISA, federal income, state and local tax, individuals, trusts and family businesses, intellectual property, international, labor and employment, natural resources, public law and land use, real estate, development land use and financing

Honigman, Miller, Schwartz, and Cohn

- *cyberspace:* honigman.com
- *earth place:* Detroit, MI
- *born on:* 03 Oct 1995 (middler)

Hopkins and Sutter

- *cyberspace:* hopsut.com
- *earth place:* Chicago, IL
- *born on:* 20 Dec 1994 (early adopter)
- *review:* Another memorable domain name. The "Executive Briefings" section includes summaries of legal developments in areas such as employee benefits, tax, and insurance law.
- *practice areas:* airport services, antitrust, banking, bankruptcy, corporate transactions, employee benefits, employment law, energy and telecommunications, environmental, gaming law, insurance, international law, legislative, litigation, public law and finance, real estate, securitization, taxation, transportation, trusts and estates

internet
An internet (lowercase "i") is a series of interconnected computer networks.

Internet
The Internet (uppercase "I") is the international network of interconnected computer networks. Estimates of the number of individuals on the Internet vary widely, but it is safe to say there are probably 75 million users worldwide. This makes the Internet the world's second-largest communication network, after the telephone network. Erik's first time was in 1984. It was not very crowded then. Not too many businesses—or obtrusive advertising. The early adopters were mostly government and educational professionals. But above all, etiquette was taken for granted. Everyone was polite and friendly. People knew each other on a first-name basis. Those of us who were there early felt a sense of community. In the next decade or so, things began to change. More commerce. More people. More traffic. And even some crime, although it never made the cover of *Time*. Those of us who were the "originals" began to resent the newcomers. The new arrivals didn't understand this great resource. They just wanted to exploit it. They had no sense of community, and etiquette was tossed out the window. The Bush administration was a turning point, for obvious reasons. Sometimes we wish he had never discovered it. See also **Maine.**

Howrey & Simon

- *cyberspace:* howrey.com
- *earth place:* Washington, DC
- *born on:* 02 Nov 1994 (early adopter)

Hughes Hubbard & Reed, L.L.P.

- *cyberspace:* hugheshubbard.com
- *earth place:* New York, NY
- *born on:* 13 Aug 1996 (late adopter)
- *review:* The challenge in developing a Web site for firms this large is managing the volume of information. Howrey & Simon's recent addition to the NLJ 250 Web sites does just that. Clean organization makes finding the content fairly simple. Articles are online, but aren't as recent as they could be. Good information about their recruiting efforts is also available.
- *practice areas:* antitrust, arbitration and alternative dispute resolution, art law, aviation, corporate reorganization, derivatives, employee benefits and executive compensation, environmental, equipment finance, financial services, gaming industry, government relations, intellectual property, international trade, joint ventures, labor and employment, Latin America, litigation, mergers and acquisitions, not-for-profit, Pacific Basin, personal legal affairs, product liability, professional liability, project finance, public finance, real estate, securities, tax, technology law

Hughes & Luce, L.L.P.

- *cyberspace:* hughesluce.com
- *earth place:* Dallas, TX
- *born on:* 05 Jul 1996 (late adopter)

Hunton & Williams

- *cyberspace:* hunton.com
- *earth place:* Richmond, VA
- *born on:* 15 Jun 1994 (early adopter)
- *review:* The layout of the lawyer profile pages is good, but the titles of these and other pages did not include the name of the firm, and no navigational elements were included. The firm's publications are

included in the "Currents" section, which we would rename "Publications." Articles are listed, but not reprinted, on the site. A few newsletters are online.

- *practice areas:* admiralty and maritime, airline, alternative dispute resolution, antitrust, appellate, asset securitization, banking and finance, bankruptcy and creditors' rights, biotechnology, coal, constitutional and civil rights law, construction and procurement, consumer law, corporate and securities, corporate trust, criminal defense, domestic relations, due diligence, employee benefits, employee benefits litigation, energy, environmental, European competition, exempt organizations, franchising, government contracts, hazardous waste and toxic tort, health care, immigration, intellectual property, international, international environmental, labor and employment, litigation, loan workouts, mergers and acquisitions, patent, product liability litigation, project finance and leveraged leasing, public finance, real estate, real-estate investment trusts, securities litigation, state and local government law, syndications and joint ventures, tax and ERISA, federal, state, and local taxation, telecommunications

Husch & Eppenberger

- *cyberspace:* husch.com
- *earth place:* St. Louis, MO
- *born on:* 28 Jan 1996 (late adopter)

Ice Miller Donadio & Ryan

- *cyberspace:* imdr.com
- *earth place:* Indianapolis, IN
- *born on:* 06 Oct 1994 (early adopter)
- *review:* Lawyer profile pages lack the look-and-feel and navigational elements present on other pages. Labor, health, and construction law are among the topics covered in the "Publications" section. A few broken links in text navigation elements hindered site navigation.
- *practice areas:* advanced technology services, antitrust and trade regulation, creditors' rights and commercial law, business transactions, college and university, computer law, construction and development, drug, device and chemical products, employee benefits,

entrepreneurial services, environmental, government services, health law, insurance law, intellectual property, international, labor and employment, litigation, municipal finance, personal services (wills, estate planning, domestic law), products liability, real estate, securities law, sports and entertainment, tax law, utility regulation, venture finance services, workers' compensation

Irell & Manella

- *cyberspace:* irell.com
- *earth place:* Los Angeles, CA
- *born on:* 13 Oct 1995 (middler)

Jackson and Kelly

- *cyberspace:* jacksonkelly.com
- *earth place:* Charleston, WV
- *born on:* 28 Feb 1996 (late adopter)
- *review:* This West Virginia firm does a good job of providing some content without overwhelming the visitor. The content is current, though not particularly in-depth. Lawyer biographies are well presented, and the practice areas are informative and easy to navigate.
- *practice areas:* business and commercial, international law, labor and employment, business dispute, legislative services, employee benefits, litigation, environmental, federal and workers' compensation, medical professional liability, government contracts, natural resources, health law, safety and health, intellectual property, taxes, estates and trusts

Jackson, Lewis, Schnitzler & Krupman

- *cyberspace:* jacksonlewis.com
- *earth place:* White Plains, NY
- *born on:* 11 Jul 1996 (late adopter)
- *review:* This firm represents management on workplace issues. (Translation: employment, labor, and benefits law.) Navigation is simple and intuitive, like many sites created with Microsoft FrontPage. Of the lawyers listed, only one appeared to have a profile online. A handful of substantive articles from the firm's newsletter were available.

- *practice areas:* employee benefits law services, wage and hour standards practice, services for union-free employers, employment law and litigation services, occupational safety and health standards practice, services for unionized employers

Jackson & Walker

- *cyberspace:* jw.com
- *earth place:* Dallas, TX
- *born on:* 28 Apr 1995 (middler)

Jenkens and Gilchrist

- *cyberspace:* jenkens.com
- *earth place:* Dallas, TX
- *born on:* 09 Sep 1995 (middler)
- *review:* Very little content, and what is available is mostly six to twelve months old. Lawyer profiles do not provide much detail.
- *practice areas:* administrative law, bankruptcy and reorganization, commercial transactions/real estate, construction law, corporate and securities, employee benefits, energy, environmental law, estate planning, probate and trusts, federal practice, financial institutions, financial services (lending and credit transactions), franchise and distribution law, health law, immigration, intellectual property, international law, labor and employment law, land use and municipal law, legislative affairs, litigation, media law, taxation, white-collar criminal law defense

Jenner & Block

- *cyberspace:* jenner.com
- *earth place:* Chicago, IL
- *born on:* 13 Mar 1996 (late adopter)
- *review:* Only the Environmental Group of the law firm is online. Within this practice area

▼▼▼▼▼

Internet Town Hall
The home of both the original EDGAR archive on the Internet, and Internet Talk Radio (Carl Malamud's "radio" program, distributed on the Web in 20-megabyte sound chunks—makes you appreciate RealAudio). The Internet Town Hall (http://town.hall.org/) is no longer available, though we like Carl's <title> to this page: "World Wide Cobweb." The text begins, "The information you are accessing is archival and is no longer available on-line."

there is a wealth of information about each subgroup, as well as newsletters and memos pertaining to related topics.

- *practice areas:* environmental

Jones, Day, Reavis & Pogue

- *cyberspace:* jonesday.com
- *earth place:* Cleveland, OH
- *born on:* 03 Oct 1995 (middler)
- *review:* This well-designed site offers great summaries of their publications, but no full-text articles. The office home pages are informative, as they provide contact information for each office, the history of the office's development, and highlights of the office's accomplishments.
- *practice areas:* bankruptcy/restructuring, business transactions, corporate finance, financial transactions, health care, institutional investors, private business and investment, real estate, antitrust and trade regulation, environmental, health and safety, health care, trade and regulatory law, corporate criminal investigation, intellectual property, labor and employment, product liability regulation, tax, employee benefits

Jones, Walker, Waechter, Poitevent, Carrere, and Denegre

- *cyberspace:* jwlaw.com
- *earth place:* New Orleans, LA
- *born on:* 24 Feb 1996 (late adopter)

Katten Muchin & Zavis

- *cyberspace:* kmz.com
- *earth place:* Chicago, IL
- *born on:* 22 May 1995 (middler)

Kaye, Scholer, Fierman, Hayes, and Handler

- *cyberspace:* ksfhh.com
- *earth place:* New York, NY
- *born on:* 02 Dec 1995 (middler)

Kelley Drye & Warren

- *cyberspace:* kelleydrye.com

- *earth place:* New York, NY

- *born on:* 03 Oct 1995 (middler)

- *review:* A remarkably comprehensive list of articles shows just how powerful a commitment to content can be. Not only do the articles showcase the firm's contribution to various fields of law, they demonstrate how content can bring people back to a site. We don't like the lawyer page as a list of links to the *West Legal Directory,* but there needs to be some room for improvement.

- *practice areas:* antitrust and trade regulation, Asia, aviation law, commercial litigation, emerging growth company, employee benefits, environmental law, financial institutions, government contracts, health care, immigration, India, insurance industry, intellectual property, labor/employee relations, maritime law, mergers and acquisitions, private clients, product liability, project finance and infrastructure, real estate, restructuring and creditor's rights, securities, securities litigation, tax, telecommunications, white-collar crime/corporate investigation practice group

Kenyon & Kenyon

- *cyberspace:* kenyonlaw.com

- *earth place:* New York, NY

- *born on:* 31 Jan 1995 (middler)

InterNIC

To have your own ".com" domain name you have to register it (or have somebody register it for you) with the InterNIC (http://www.internic .net/). The InterNIC used to stand for Internet Network Information Center, and it used to be a nonprofit organization run by a group of volunteer organizations. Now it is a thriving commercial monopoly. Basically, the InterNIC maintains a database of top-level DNS servers (computers). Each of these servers tells lower level servers about officially registered domain names. And they tell two servers, and they tell two servers, and so on, and so on. The DNS database is distributed to hundreds of thousands of computers around the Internet, but the historical home for the top-level servers has been the InterNIC. So after you register a domain name, it takes a few days for the change to propagate to all the other DNS servers on the Net. The InterNIC has a simple method for determining who gets to register certain domain names: First-come first-served. Recently, the InterNIC has modified this rule to the following: Registration of domain names is on a first-come first-served basis except when it isn't. But seriously, their current policy is very confusing and much worse than what preceded it. But that's what happens when you start charging for a service over which you have historically held a monopoly. The bottom line remains that the sooner you register your domain name the better. See also **monopoly.**

Kilpatrick & Cody

- *cyberspace:* kilcody.com
- *earth place:* Atlanta, GA
- *born on:* 24 Apr 1995 (middler)
- *review:* This domain name probably upsets the Giffords.

King & Spalding

- *cyberspace:* kslaw.com
- *earth place:* Atlanta, GA
- *born on:* 30 Jul 1995 (middler)
- *review:* Lawyer profiles employ an effective narrative style. Almost overlooked on a ho-hum page of links to other law-related sites includes links to the firm's Web site Request for Proposal and Web site development contract (and boy we'd love to see some standards in this area). Articles cover several legal topics including construction, intellectual property, and communications law.
- *practice areas:* antitrust, intellectual property and technology, banking and finance, international, bankruptcy and commercial litigation, international trade regulation and customs, biotechnology, investment funds, communications practice, Islamic finance and investment, contracting, labor ERISA and employment law, corporate, litigation, electric utility industry financing practice, product liability, energy, public finance, environmental, real estate, food and drug, securities and shareholder litigation, government contracts, special matters, governmental, tax, health care, toxic tort, insurance, trusts and estates

Kirkland & Ellis[2]

- *cyberspace:* kirkland.com
- *earth place:* Chicago, IL
- *born on:* 23 Jan 1995 (middler)
- *review:* Lawyer profiles are merely links to the firm's *Martindale-Hubbell Law Directory* listing. No supplemental narratives are pro-

---

2. We're not sure, but we're willing to bet that this Lingerie Catalog of Kirkland, WA-based "Ooh La La" (**http://www.oohlala-kirkland.com**) gets more hits per week than the more mundane Kirkland & Ellis at kirkland.com.

vided. Much to our chagrin, the "Publications" section was under construction, so there was little content to compel us to visit again.

- *practice areas:* alternative dispute resolution, appellate, banking and financial services, communications, competition and antitrust, mergers and acquisitions, private equity, securities, corporate, workout and bankruptcy, derivatives, employee benefits, employment and labor, environmental, estate planning, government contracts, health care, intellectual property, international, litigation, mass tort, real estate, tax, white-collar crime

Kirkpatrick & Lockhart

- *cyberspace:* kl.com
- *earth place:* Pittsburgh, PA
- *born on:* 24 May 1995 (middler)
- *review:* A comprehensive list of publications is provided on the Web site, but visitors must complete an order form to receive copies (we assume hard copy) of the articles. One of the cleanest search engines we've seen in searching for lawyers, the results act as a front end to all lawyer biographies.
- *practice areas:* antitrust, appellate litigation, bankruptcy, construction, corporate and general business, criminal defense/white-collar crime, energy, environmental, ERISA, ESOP, executive compensation, financial institutions, government affairs/legislation, government contracts, health care, insurance coverage, intellectual property/patents, international law, investment management, labor relations/employment, litigation, media and entertainment law, mergers and acquisitions, mortgage banking, nonprofit organizations, product liability, real es-

intranet

Generally, this term describes an internal information system based on Internet technology. But, as with the Internet, definitions of intranets tend to focus too heavily on the underlying technology rather than on what that technology can do for you. Don't get us wrong, we think Internet and intranet technology are really cool. But we prefer definitions that focus on the functions and benefits of the technology, not on the technology itself. The functions and benefits of technology are the logical layer. The underlying components are the physical layers. It is important to separate the logical layer (what do you want to do) from the physical layer (wires, computers, software).

tate, rotation program, securities enforcement, securities (general), taxation (general), technology, telecommunications, toxic tort, transportation, trusts and estates

Kramer Levin Naftalis Nessen Kamin & Frankel

- *cyberspace:* kramer-levin.com
- *earth place:* New York, NY
- *born on:* 04 Feb 1995 (middler)
- *review:* A site that favors content over presentation, Kramer Levin's site is starting to show its age. There is nevertheless good general information about the firm under "Firm Brochure," and all lawyers have biographies. (We can't understand why the lawyer photos are hyperlinked in each biography to a larger picture of the lawyer!)
- *practice areas:* antitrust, appellate, asset securitization, banking, bankruptcy and restructuring, corporate securities and finance, employee benefits, employment and labor, environmental, financial services, individual client group, insurance defense, insurance restructuring, intellectual property, litigation, product liability, real estate, tax, white-collar criminal defense, pro bono

Kutak Rock

- *cyberspace:* kutakrock.com
- *earth place:* Omaha, NE
- *born on:* 11 Jan 1996 (late adopter)
- *review:* The "Publications" section contains no substantive content, but is just a bibliography. Lawyer profiles are available for the firm's technology law and health-care law groups, but we'd like to see them more easily accessible from the home page and broken up into separate pages. Other lawyer profiles are available, buried under "Practice Areas." A handful of undated memos are available on various legal issues, including public finance and health-care law.
- *practice areas:* banking and commercial lending, bankruptcy, blue sky, corporate finance, corporate practice, employment law, environmental law, government relations, health-care practice, insurance group, international practice, litigation, public finance, real estate and commercial practice, structured finance, securities law, securities litigation, arbitration and regulatory practice, tax, technology law practice, workouts and surveillance.

Lane, Powell, Spears & Lubersky

- *cyberspace:* lanepowell.com
- *earth place:* Seattle, WA
- *born on:* 30 Nov 1995 (middler)

Latham and Watkins

- *cyberspace:* lw.com
- *earth place:* Los Angeles, CA
- *born on:* 25 Oct 1994 (early adopter)
- *review:* The firm's newsletters are listed under "Publications," but they are available only in Adobe Acrobat PDF format. Acrobat is a good supplemental format for some purposes, but it does not make a good primary format, and it is certainly not the ideal format for Web browsing. And many of the subpages could stand to be broken up into more easily browsed chunks. Lawyer profiles were nowhere to be found. This site is not to be confused with *Lawyers Weekly* (lweekly.com).
- *practice areas:* corporate law, finance and real-estate law, litigation, tax law, environmental law, international law

Lathrop & Gage, L.C.

- *cyberspace:* lathropgage.com
- *earth place:* Kansas City, MO
- *born on:* 17 Jul 1996 (late adopter)

Law Offices of Loeb and Loeb

- *cyberspace:* loeb.com
- *earth place:* Los Angeles, CA
- *born on:* 24 Aug 1995 (middler)

LeBoeuf, Lamb, Greene & MacRae

- *cyberspace:* llgm.com
- *earth place:* New York, NY
- *born on:* 22 Sep 1995 (middler)
- *review:* The home page employs a creative newspaper-like style that combines short narratives of the site's major sections with links to

areas in each major section. And more than once we had to return to the home page to get our bearings, because site navigation elements didn't show us where we were or where we'd been. If lawyer profiles were there, we couldn't find them, and there was no search engine to help us.

- *practice areas:* intellectual property, media practice, litigation, energy and utilities, corporate and finance, bankruptcy, Commonwealth of Independent States (CIS), international, municipal bond, real estate, tax, trust and estates

Lewis, D'Amato, Brisbois & Bisgaard

- *cyberspace:* ldbb.com
- *earth place:* Los Angeles, CA
- *born on:* 03 May 1995 (middler)

Lewis, Rice & Fingersh

- *cyberspace:* lewisrice.com
- *earth place:* St. Louis, MO
- *born on:* 10 Feb 1997 (late adopter)

Liddell, Sapp, Zivley, Hill, LaBoon

- *cyberspace:* liddellsapp.com
- *earth place:* Houston, TX
- *born on:* 23 Jan 1996 (late adopter)
- *review:* Bullet-style lawyer profiles are available, but we prefer the more readable narrative style. Oddly, a link to the firm's *Martindale-Hubbell Law Directory* listing is provided, but not for individual lawyers or even from the "Attorneys" page. You have to go to the table of contents to find it. A handful of the firm's publications are listed, though they are generally out of date and of little use.
- *practice areas:* antitrust, banking and financial services, bankruptcy and workouts, corporate, energy/oil and gas, environmental, ERISA/employee benefits, insurance and maritime, intellectual property and technical litigation, international transactions, labor and employment, legislative counseling, litigation and appellate practice, print and broadcast media, real estate, taxation, trusts, and estates

Littler

- *cyberspace:* littler.com

- *earth place:* San Francisco, CA

- *born on:* 16 Aug 1994 (early adopter)

- *review:* "The 1996 Employer[sm]," an incredibly in-depth treatise on employment law, is available via a Folio Infobase Web server. Hard copies can be purchased from the firm online, making the firm one of the few offering both products and services. PowerPoint presentations from some of their seminars are also available online. They even sell a board game, "The Littler Employment Law Challenge[tm]," which is a tool for learning about employment law.

- *practice areas:* Age Discrimination in Employment Act (ADEA), alternative dispute resolution, Americans with Disabilities Act (ADA), arbitration, background investigations, benefits, civil rights litigation, Cobra, collective bargaining, compensation, conduct investigations, contracts, disabilities, discrimination, drugs and alcohol, elections, equal employment opportunity, ERISA, handbooks, harassment, independent contractor status, immigration, international employment, labor-management relations, litigation, manuals, mediation, National Labor Relations Board (NLRB), negotiations, Occupational Safety and Health Agency (OSHA), organizing drives, policies, problem prevention, privacy, railway labor act, sexual harassment, taxation, unemployment and disability benefits, unfair labor practices, wage and hour, workers' compensation, workplace violence, wrongful termination

Locke Purnell Rain Harrell

- *cyberspace:* lprh.com

- *earth place:* Dallas, TX

- *born on:* 29 Aug 1994 (early adopter)

- *review:* A handful of articles are available, including some on real-estate law. Some information about the firm from news sources is available, though it hadn't been updated in more than six months.

ISDN
Integrated Services Digital Network. The functional equivalent of digital modems. ISDN technology turns an ordinary analog phone line into two 64 kilobit/second channels that can be used for voice or data. ISDN allows for faster transmission feeds than analog modems provide.

ISP
Internet Service Provider. Companies that sell various levels of Internet services. National ISPs include UUNet, PSI, and NetCom. See also **TheList.Com.**

- *practice areas:* administrative/regulatory law, affordable housing, banking, bankruptcy, corporate and securities, employee benefits, environmental, estate planning, franchise and distribution, health care, intellectual property, international law, Mexican legal practice, labor and employment, litigation, media and communications, oil and gas, real estate, tax, technology, telecommunications, transportation

Lord, Bissell & Brook

- *cyberspace:* lordbissell.com
- *earth place:* Chicago, IL
- *born on:* 02 Sep 1995 (middler)

Luce, Forward, Hamilton & Scripps

- *cyberspace:* luce.com
- *earth place:* San Diego, CA
- *born on:* 25 Jun 1994 (early adopter)
- *review:* The lawyers are listed in multiple places (under "Attorney Resumes" and then again under "Attorney Lists"), which doesn't seem to be very intuitive. The "Publications" page suffers from poor organization, but several useful items are available, including newsletters on franchise law.
- *practice areas:* bankruptcy, finance and commercial, business (includes the public finance group and the international services group), business litigation (includes white-collar criminal defense group), environmental, insurance and reinsurance (includes science advisory group), labor and employment law, personal litigation, product liability and warranty, real estate, real-estate litigation, trusts and estates

Manatt, Phelps & Phillips

- *cyberspace:* manatt.com
- *earth place:* Los Angeles, CA
- *born on:* 23 Feb 1995 (middler)
- *review:* Navigating this site isn't all that simple, and there isn't much content behind the many menu options. Other than the focus on the various practice areas, the site operates more as a brochure than as an archive of any original content.

- *practice areas:* bankruptcy and financial restructuring, environmental and natural resources, estates and trusts, family law, intellectual property, international trade, labor/employment law, land use, litigation, political, election and campaign, tax, white-collar criminal defense

Marshall, Dennehey, Warner, Coleman & Goggin

- *cyberspace:* mdwcg.com
- *earth place:* Philadelphia, PA
- *born on:* 20 Sep 1996 (late adopter)
- *review:* No substantive content is available except for one newsletter in Adobe Acrobat PDF format. A long list of articles authored by the firm is online—along with a form that the visitor must fill out to request that a copy be mailed to them. This approach makes little sense if the goal is to show off your expertise. Can a firm really expect people to go through that hassle to obtain an article?
- *practice areas:* appellate advocacy, civil rights/municipal liability, commercial litigation, construction litigation, employment law, environmental and toxic tort, general liability, health-care liability, insurance coverage/bad faith, liquor liability, product liability, professional liability, retail liability, special investigations litigation, sports and entertainment, transportation litigation, workers' compensation

Mayer, Brown & Platt

- *cyberspace:* mayerbrown.com
- *earth place:* Chicago, IL
- *born on:* 28 May 1995 (middler)
- *review:* Though the presentation is decidedly unimpressive, there is some good content to be found here. Given the difficult presentation, however, it is unlikely that many will wade through the text-heavy pages to find it. On the positive side, it's worth a trip to this site for the

Java
A programming language. Many Web browsers come complete with a Java interpreter. So unlike most computer programs (which must be compiled into executable binary code by a compiler), Java programs (or "applets") are interpreted in real time by the client's Web browser. For more information on how Java works, see the Web site of Sun Microsystems (http://www.sun.com), the folks who wrote Java. Java is to the World Wide Web as the graphical user interface was to the personal computer. It is changing the way people communicate, compute, and publish. See also **computer virus.**

Supreme Court Docket Report alone, which would be even more useful if it were available via e-mail subscription.

- *practice areas:* antitrust, banking and finance, bankruptcy, corporate, criminal defense, derivatives, environmental, ERISA, franchise, government, health care, information technology, insurance, intellectual property, international, labor and employment, litigation, natural resources, pro bono, real estate, regulated industries, religious and human services, taxation, telecommunications, wealth management

McCarter & English

- *cyberspace:* mccarter.com
- *earth place:* Newark, NJ
- *born on:* 16 Aug 1995 (middler)

McCutchen, Doyle, Brown & Enersen

- *cyberspace:* mccutchen.com
- *earth place:* San Francisco, CA
- *born on:* 29 Dec 1995 (middler)
- *review:* Output from the search engine is among the best we've seen. The found pages' titles, URLs, and summaries are displayed, and output is sorted by relevance. Lawyer profiles have a nice page layout and employ a narrative style. There is substantive content on the site, but it is buried deep under "Industry and Practice Groups" (not where we'd look for publications). There is good content here, such as how to conduct patent searches on the Internet.
- *practice areas:* agribusiness, antitrust, bankruptcy, bioscience, business and transactions, communications, computers and software, construction, energy and resources, environmental, estate planning, financial services, health care, insurance, intellectual property and technology, labor and employment, land use, litigation, real estate, securities, tax

McDermott, Will & Emery

- *cyberspace:* mwe.com
- *earth place:* Chicago, IL
- *born on:* 01 Sep 1995 (middler)

- *review:* The page listing all of the firm's lawyers took a long time to load, but the lawyer profiles were in-depth and employed a nice page layout. The articles are generally up to date, and provide comprehensive information about relevant topics within the practice areas.

- *practice areas:* corporate, employee benefits, estate planning, health law, intellectual property, international, legislative/government regulation, litigation/regulatory practices, tax

McGlinchey Stafford Lang

- *cyberspace:* mcglinchey.com

- *earth place:* New Orleans, LA

- *born on:* 25 Aug 1993 (early adopter)

McGuire, Woods, Battle & Boothe

- *cyberspace:* mwbb.com

- *earth place:* Richmond, VA

- *born on:* 11 Aug 1993 (early adopter)

- *review:* The publications section contains one of the most up-to-date lists of news items that we've seen at a law firm Web site. The publications section is similarly current, with newsletters from some of the primary practice areas at McGuire Woods.

- *practice areas:* admiralty and maritime, antitrust and trade regulation, automotive, banking and financial institutions, bankruptcy and workouts, business taxation, commercial litigation, corporate and business, corporate finance, distribution and franchising, education, energy and public utilities, entertainment group, environmental, executive compensation and employee benefits, government relations, elections and voting rights, health care, insurance, intellectual property, international, labor and employment, mergers and acquisitions, product liability, public finance, real

Law Lists

"Law Lists" (http://www.lib.uchicago.edu/ ~llou/lawlists/info.html) is the best compilation of law-related electronic mailing lists and Usenet newsgroups. It is maintained by Lyonette Louis-Jacques, Foreign and International Law Librarian and Lecturer in Law at the University of Chicago (llou@midway.uchicago .edu). It is also searchable (http://www.lib .uchicago.edu/cgi-bin/law-lists).

estate, retailing, securities regulation and enforcement, technology, taxation, transportation, trusts and estates, white-collar crime

McKenna & Cuneo, L.L.P.

- *cyberspace:* mckennacuneo.com
- *earth place:* Washington, DC
- *born on:* 13 Jun 1996 (late adopter)
- *review:* Layout of the lawyer profiles is among the best we've seen, and the narrative style is supplemented nicely by links to *Martindale-Hubbell Law Directory* listings for individual lawyers. More firms should follow this approach. The "New Articles" page contains substantive material that appears to be dynamically generated from a back-end database. An Excite search engine is available, though the look-and-feel of the output does not match the rest of the site, and only titles of found pages are listed.
- *practice areas:* government contracts, litigation, environmental, international trade and business, labor and employment, food and drug, energy, health care, general business, insurance recovery, IT/GSA contracting, qui tam defense

Mendes and Mount

- *cyberspace:* mendes.com
- *earth place:* Larkspur, CA
- *born on:* 10 May 1995 (middler)

Michael Best & Friedrich

- *cyberspace:* mbf-law.com
- *earth place:* Milwaukee, WI
- *born on:* 29 May 1995 (middler)

Milbank, Tweed, Hadley & Mcloy

- *cyberspace:* milbank.com
- *earth place:* New York, NY
- *born on:* 30 Mar 1994 (early adopter)
- *review:* The information is here, but it is not always laid out intuitively. The recruiting information is solid, but the site lacks any substantive information (articles, newsletters, and so on) that

would display the firm's expertise. Information about the practice areas is buried underneath "Firm Brochure," meaning that it isn't available from the home page.

- *practice areas:* banking and institutional investment, capital markets, environmental, financial restructuring, intellectual property/technology, leasing, litigation, mergers and acquisitions, project finance, public utilities, real estate, special services, structured finance, tax, telecommunications, trusts and estates

Miles & Stockbridge

- *cyberspace:* milesstockbridge.com
- *earth place:* Baltimore, MD
- *born on:* 13 Dec 1996 (late adopter)
- *review:* Contact information is located under "Inquiries." We'd like to see at least a phone number and address on the home page for quicker reference. The publications are well laid out and read easily online; however, they have not been updated since the site's initial release (most are dated between December 1996 and February 1997). Surprisingly, the firm did not include any lawyer biographies, though this is remedied somewhat by including a link to their *Martindale-Hubbell* listing where visitors can then browse the firm's 185 lawyers.
- *practice areas:* alternative dispute resolution, bankruptcy and creditors' rights, commercial and business litigation, commercial finance and leasing, construction contracts and construction litigation, environmental law, estate planning and probate and income tax planning, family law, general tort, risk management and insurance, government relations, health-care related industries, international representation and transactions, labor, employment and employee benefits, medical malpractice defense, product liability and toxic tort, public finance, real-estate lending, securities and franchise, special litigation, criminal defense and government agency investigations, title insurance defense, corporate

Miller, Canfield, Paddock and Stone, P.L.C.

- *cyberspace:* millercanfield.com
- *earth place:* Detroit, MI
- *born on:* 12 Apr 1996 (late adopter)

- *review:* Lawyer biographies are well presented, including a nifty Java applet that simplifies the retrieval of a particular lawyer's resume. Their "Hot Points" newsletter is published quarterly, and is available in its entirety online. The content is somewhat superficial, however, and includes unnecessary clipart images in the layout.

- *practice areas:* business services (east Michigan), business services (west Michigan), bankruptcy/workout, employee benefits, environmental, estate planning, federal tax, finance and development, health, intellectual property, international business services, labor and employment, litigation (product liability/tort), litigation (west Michigan), litigation and dispute resolution, public law, state and local tax

Mintz Levin Cohn Ferris Glovsky and Popeo, P.C.

- *cyberspace:* mintz.com

- *earth place:* Boston, MA

- *born on:* 04 Apr 1995 (middler)

- *review:* While Mintz Levin publishes a wealth of content, it is almost exclusively published in PDF format, which tends to be somewhat browser-unfriendly. The search interface is fantastic, allowing users to browse through their hits, one by one (instead of viewing one file, clicking "back," and viewing the next). Content is updated often, as evidenced by the "last updated" banners at the top of most pages, the "News" section, which is full of timely information (date headings are a big help), and the drop-down bar on the home page with links to the most recent information.

- *practice areas:* antitrust and trade regulation, biotechnology, business law, commercial law, communications law, employee benefits and executive compensation, employment and labor law, environmental law, government and public affairs, health-care fraud and abuse, health law, immigration, international practice, litigation, public finance, real-estate law, retirement and estate planning, securities law practice

Montgomery, McCracken, Walker & Rhoads

- *cyberspace:* mmwr.com

- *earth place:* Philadelphia, PA

- *born on:* 15 Apr 1995 (middler)

Moore & Van Allen, P.L.L.C.

- *cyberspace:* mvalaw.com

- *earth place:* Charlotte, NC

- *born on:* 10 Jan 1996 (late adopter)

- *review:* The firm's publications are out of date—many show a "last updated" date of 1995. The feedback form offers no option for writing a message, just a list of practice areas to choose from to request more information. On the positive side, office locations are prominently displayed (they are one of the four main subsections in the navigation frame), which makes getting contact information and directions to the offices straightforward.

- *practice areas:* banking, government contracts, bankruptcy, health care, business and corporate, intellectual property, commercial real estate, international, construction and surety, litigation, employment and employee benefits, regulatory and legislative, energy, taxation, environmental, trusts and estates

Morgan, Lewis & Bockius, L.L.P.

- *cyberspace:* mlb.com

- *earth place:* Philadelphia, PA

- *born on:* 01 Nov 1994 (early adopter)

- *review:* With a firm of this size (850 lawyers worldwide), there should be more content. When reviewed, the site had a dozen or so newsletters and other publications available for viewing. Their "What's New" section is refreshingly up to date, including press releases that were less than two weeks old. What articles they do have are very well written, timely (all have dates included, a surprisingly rare occurrence), and thoroughly footnoted. Strangely enough,

Legal Domain Network
One of the bright lights in the early days of legal information on the Internet, the LDN had a simple but brilliant idea. Recognizing the number of law-related discussion lists, Usenet groups, and other information sources available on the Internet (and this was in 1994—imagine what it would be like today!), the good folks at Chicago-Kent School of Law decided to "mirror" every list (a mirror is an archive of material that lives somewhere else) that gave permission. Soon after, you had a one-stop shopping place to go for information—to look up names, topics for discussion, etc. Some of their key people left, and the LDN has been up only sporadically since then.

the "Practice Area" section offers no in-depth information—it just lists the firm's practice area titles.

- *practice areas:* antitrust, banking, bankruptcy and reorganization, business and corporate, construction, corporate finance, customs, emerging business, employee benefits, energy, entertainment, environmental, food and drug regulation, government contracts, government relations, health care, immigration, insurance and reinsurance, intellectual property and technology, international trade, investment management, labor and employment, litigation, mergers and acquisitions, patents, personal law, project finance, public finance, real estate, securities regulation, tax, tax-exempt organizations, trade regulation, transportation

Morrison & Foerster, L.L.P.

- *cyberspace:* mofo.com

- *earth place:* San Francisco, CA

- *born on:* 30 Oct 1992 (visionary)

- *review:* Our favorite law firm domain name. In fact, if you search AltaVista for "mofo," you will find lots of interesting sites. Questionable domain names aside, Morrison & Foerster's site demonstrates some interesting uses of technology. The first option, the guided tour, is an excellent way to familiarize users with your site, not to mention a nice use of server-push technology (which refreshes the browser's screen without requiring the user to click anywhere). Publications are not published online (a mistake, in our opinion). Instead, an order form is provided so you can request particular newsletters.

- *practice areas:* bankruptcy, communications, corporate finance, energy, financial services, financial transactions and lending, intellectual property, international, investment management, labor and employment, land use and environmental, litigation and dispute resolution, project development and finance, real estate, tax

Morrison & Hecker, L.L.P.

- *cyberspace:* none

- *earth place:* Overland Park, KS

- *born on:* (Luddite)

- *review:* Missing in action.

Morrison, Mahoney and Miller

- *cyberspace:* mm-m.com
- *earth place:* Boston, MA
- *born on:* 24 Aug 1995 (middler)

Nelson Mullins Riley & Scarborough

- *cyberspace:* nmrs.com
- *earth place:* Columbia, SC
- *born on:* 27 May 1995 (middler)
- *review:* Information is easily accessible. The home page presents each of the major items in a law firm home page—Practice Areas, Attorney Directory, Firm Offices, Bulletins, and What's New. The "What's New" section is updated often. The items in the list were less than a week old when it was reviewed. There are numerous articles on the site, which demonstrates a commitment on the part of the firm to produce good content. The articles are not dated, however, which makes browsing the content difficult.
- *practice areas:* alternative dispute resolution, automotive products, aviation, banks and financial institutions, bankruptcy, business litigation, computers, construction, corporate and securities, creditors' rights, environmental, ERISA and employee benefits, governmental relations, health care, immigration, insurance, intellectual property and technology, international, labor and employment, mergers and acquisitions, officers' and directors' liability, pharmaceuticals and medical devices, premises liability, product liability, real estate, securities, taxation, technology, telecommunications, toxic torts, trade regulation, workers' compensation

Nixon, Hargrave, Devans and Doyle

- *cyberspace:* nhdd.com
- *earth place:* Rochester, NY
- *born on:* 03 Oct 1990 (visionary)

Legal List
See **The Legal List.**

LII
Along with Chicago-Kent, one of the clear early adopters in the legal profession when it came to the Internet. Cornell showed others how to do it—whether "it" was publishing primary law on-line (U.S. Code, U.S. Supreme Court opinions), or categorizing links to external sites, or hosting legal discussion lists.

mailing lists
See **Cyberia-L, "Law Lists," Legal Domain Network,** and **Net-Lawyers.**

- *review:* The site structure is solid. Just about everything is exactly where you would expect it. The contact information, while not on the home page, is conveniently available and displays all relevant information, and even links to the firm's *Martindale-Hubbell* entry for each office. Numerous articles are available, but none has a date, which reduces their usefulness because the reader doesn't know how current they might be.

- *practice areas:* antitrust, banking and lending, bankruptcy and workouts, business, construction, corporate finance, education, emerging business, energy and project finance, environmental, franchising, government relations, health services, immigration matters, international, labor and employee benefits, litigation, mergers and acquisitions, not-for-profit, personal services, public finance, real estate, regulated industries, tax, technology and intellectual property, telecommunications, white-collar criminal defense and internal investigations

O'Melveny & Myers/Information Technology

- *cyberspace:* omm.com
- *earth place:* Los Angeles, CA
- *born on:* 30 Aug 1995 (middler)
- *review:* We can't resist quoting the graphic on the home page when we reviewed this site (after all, they said it): "This site still under construction." Well, they ought to get points for being blunt.

Oppenheimer Wolff & Donnelly

- *cyberspace:* owdlaw.com
- *earth place:* Minneapolis, MN
- *born on:* 16 Sep 1995 (middler)
- *review:* There isn't much content to speak of on this well-designed site. It appears as though the focus was on designing a clean brochure that would describe the abilities of the various practice areas. Other than that, the site is thin on content of any value.

- *practice areas:* benefits, ESOPs and tax, business litigation, commercial finance and real estate, commercial law, banking and bankruptcy, corporate finance and transactions, emerging business, environmental, health care, insurance, intellectual property, international, labor and employment, medical devices, product liability, transportation

Orrick Herrington and Sutcliff

- *cyberspace:* orrick.com

- *earth place:* San Francisco, CA

- *born on:* 13 Dec 1995 (middler)

- *review:* Generally, "What's New" sections do little for sites that don't provide much new information. Making a visitor click on a link to see one or two items of little significance isn't really useful. Orrick Herrington and Sutcliff, on the other hand, have figured out how to provide news without hindering the visitor—they make the headlines part of the home page. This is an effective technique, and it gives people a reason to visit often. There is some good information about their recruiting program, and a lot of information relating to their practice areas. Lawyer biographies provide basic information, but could be presented better.

- *practice areas:* bankruptcy and restructuring, commercial and institutional finance, complex commercial litigation, general corporate, derivative products, electric industry restructuring, employment, emerging companies/venture capital, financial services, insurance and insurance insolvency, intellectual property, mergers and acquisitions practice, market regulation, project and infrastructure finance, public finance, public power, real-estate finance practice, securities practice, structured finance, taxation, white-collar criminal defense group

Palmer & Dodge

- *cyberspace:* palmerdodge.com

- *earth place:* Boston, MA

- *born on:* 15 Jan 1995 (middler)

Patton Boggs, L.L.P.

- *cyberspace:* pattonboggs.com

- *earth place:* Washington, DC

- *born on:* 07 May 1996 (late adopter)

Maine

Erik's first time was in 1972. It was not very crowded then—not too many businesses or obtrusive advertising. The early adopters were mostly government and educational professionals. But above all, etiquette was taken for granted. People knew each other on a first-name basis. Those of us who were there early felt a sense of community. In the next decade or so, things began to change. More commerce. More people. More traffic. And even some crime, although it never made the cover of *Time*. Those of us who were the "originals" began to resent the newcomers. The new arrivals didn't understand this great resource. They just wanted to exploit it. No sense of community, and etiquette was tossed out the window. The Bush administration was a turning point, for obvious reasons. Sometimes we wish he had never discovered it. See also **Internet.**

Paul, Hatings, Janofsky & Walker

- *cyberspace:* phjw.com

- *earth place:* Los Angeles, CA

- *born on:* 29 Nov 1994 (early adopter)

- *review:* Most importantly, there is consistent "fresh" content—a good sign that the firm has committed to the Web site as a way to attract repeat visitors, not to mention as a way to forge a stronger relationship with its clients. Seminar announcements, as well as immigration and intellectual property newsletters, are available on the Web site.

- *practice areas:* aircraft finance practice, Asia-Pacific, banking and financial services, computer law, corporate finance, creditor's rights and bankruptcy, customs, international trade and export control, emerging growth and technology, energy, federal legislative, health care, international energy/utility/infrastructure, international trade, Internet, cyberlaw and electronic commerce, investment management, Japan practice for U.S.-based clients, Latin America, lease and asset-based finance, mergers and acquisitions, project and infrastructure finance, structured finance and asset securitization, telecommunications and media, timber, paper and packaging, trade regulation and proprietary rights, employee benefits, immigration, railroad labor and employment law, accountant's liability, alternative dispute resolution, antidumping, countervailing duty and related trade proceedings, antitrust litigation and government enforcement, appellate, aviation, entertainment, environmental, government contracts, insurance coverage, intellectual property and technology licensing and litigation, intellectual property and technology, intellectual property trade secret, securities and corporate finance litigation, white-collar corporate criminal defense, affordable housing, land use, real estate acquisition and disposition, resort, restaurant and recreation, retail leasing, international tax, tax litigation

Paul, Weiss, Rifkind, Wharton & Garrison

- *cyberspace:* paulweiss.com

- *earth place:* New York, NY

- *born on:* 29 Jul 1995 (middler)

Pennie & Edmonds

- *cyberspace:* pennie.com
- *earth place:* New York, NY
- *born on:* 15 Aug 1995 (middler)
- *review:* Though the articles are undated, there are still enough articles here to demonstrate the firm's expertise—a good start. Under "What's New," however, we found a headline announcing a court decision in a case dated April 15, 1996.

Pepper, Hamilton & Scheetz

- *cyberspace:* constructlaw.com
- *earth place:* Philadelphia, PA
- *born on:* 22 Aug 1995 (middler)
- *review:* This is the Web site for the firm's construction law department. There is very limited information available here—a few paragraphs about their experience in construction law, contact information for the group, and issues of the *Construction Law Review,* which is a publication of Law Journal Extra! but edited by Pepper, Hamilton & Scheetz's construction law department. The page claims it has not been updated in almost a year, so it's not clear whether this page is being used much by the firm.
- *practice areas:* construction

Perkins Coie

- *cyberspace:* perkinscoie.com
- *earth place:* Seattle, WA
- *born on:* 22 Mar 1994 (early adopter)
- *review:* So you want information about electronic commerce? Digital signatures? Court cases involving the Internet? Look no further than Perkins Coie, the law firm with arguably the best con-

math phobia
The source of all fear of technology, including the belief that computers and the Internet are magic. The technology underlying the Internet *is not magic.* The Internet works because the computers connected to it communicate via computer programs that operate according to preset rules, not because of magic. When taken out of context or not properly defined, terms like "information superhighway" and "cyberspace" confuse or mislead the reader and perpetuate the myth that the Internet is somehow "magical." The unfortunate result of using the magical metaphor is that people may be discouraged from using or learning about the Internet.

tent strategy of the NLJ 250. Using a Folio Infobase Web server, Perkins Coie has an exhaustive library of Internet cases (and links to more information, if available). This is the best collection on the subject that a law firm has put together. The other topics are equally impressive, and current—they were all updated within two weeks of this review.

- *practice areas:* banking and financial, commercial law and bankruptcy, business transactions tax, China practice group, commercial/finance, corporate finance and securities, construction law, electronic commerce and Internet law, energy and utilities, environmental and natural resources law, family businesses, government contracts, health care, immigration, international, intellectual property, international trade, labor and employment, life sciences, litigation, personal planning, product liability, project finance, public finance, real estate and land use, securities litigation, software, telecommunications, white-collar defense

Petree Stockton, L.L.P.

- *cyberspace:* petree.com
- *earth place:* Morrisville, NC
- *born on:* 18 Jan 1996 (late adopter)

Phelps, Dunbar

- *cyberspace:* phelps.com
- *earth place:* New Orleans, LA
- *born on:* 19 Jan 1995 (middler)

Phillips, Lytle, Hitchcock, Blaine & Huber

- *cyberspace:* phillipslytle.com
- *earth place:* Buffalo, NY
- *born on:* 23 Jun 1996 (late adopter)
- *review:* Publications covering the last six months are online and dated. The majority of the articles provide substantial treatment to the issues covered. Current clients will find useful information here, and prospective clients will likely be impressed by the breadth of coverage. Lawyer biographies are detailed, and provide both phone and e-mail contact information.

- *practice areas:* banking and commercial, bankruptcy and creditors' rights, commercial, civil and criminal litigation, corporate and tax, employee benefits, environmental, health care, intellectual property, labor and employment, medical device and pharmaceuticals, real estate, trusts and estates

Pillsbury Madison & Sutro[3]

- *cyberspace:* pmstax.com
- *earth place:* San Francisco, CA
- *born on:* 06 Sep 1995 (middler)
- *review:* This is not the site for the entire firm, but just for the Tax Section. That said, there is some good tax-related information here. Design is fairly spartan, and the emphasis appears to be on simply presenting the information. There is a link to the firm's intellectual property group, Cushman, Darby & Cushman, but that's a separate site: **www.cushman.com**. The content here is fairly recent—available in either HTML or PDF formats—and is likely to be of great utility to clients and colleagues alike.
- *practice areas:* tax

Piper & Marbury

- *cyberspace:* pipermar.com
- *earth place:* Baltimore, MD
- *born on:* 15 Nov 1994 (early adopter)
- *review:* The basics are all here—recruiting information, descriptions of the practice areas, and lawyer biographies—but the site comes across as unimaginative. There's no hook to the site. The site contains no publications or other original content, and there seems to have been no effort to enhance the site's appearance with graphics. We like the inclusion of "Firm Technology" as a separate component of the site. Though just one page, it does a good job of outlining the firm's abilities. The lawyer biographies are concise, and the

3. Our search for this firm also turned up Positive Minded Sisters, which has registered pmszone.com.

addition of the lawyer's e-mail address is a welcome feature. Too few firms indicate how to reach their lawyers electronically.

- *practice areas:* antitrust and trade regulation, business tax, commercial lending, bankruptcy and creditors' rights, commercial litigation, communications, information and intellectual property, employee benefits and executive compensation, environmental, estates and trusts, finance, corporate and securities, financial services and products, food and drug, government contracts, health care, international commercial and maritime dispute resolution, labor and employment, mergers and acquisitions, product liability and toxic torts, public law, tax-exempt and project finance, real-estate development, finance and securities, securities and business litigation, state legislation and public policy, venture capital and emerging companies, white-collar and public law litigation

Pitney, Hardin, Kipp & Szuch

- *cyberspace:* phks.com
- *earth place:* Florham Park, NJ
- *born on:* 28 Aug 1995 (middler)
- *review:* Meet Judge Wally! Play a Trivia Game! Try and score higher than someone named "Hooters"! Such is the life when you visit the New Jersey law firm of Pitney, Hardin, Kipp & Szuch, home of the strangest content strategy we've seen. It's not all bad, however. The trivia game notwithstanding, there are some good, timely client bulletins.
- *practice areas:* litigation and alternate dispute resolution, corporate, financial services, environmental, labor and employment law, real estate, trusts and estates

Plunkett & Cooney, P.C.

- *cyberspace:* plunkettlaw.com
- *earth place:* Detroit, MI
- *born on:* 23 Aug 1996 (late adopter)

Porter, Wright, Morris & Arthur

- *cyberspace:* porterwright.com
- *earth place:* Columbus, OH
- *born on:* 17 Apr 1995 (middler)

Post Schell, P.C.

- *cyberspace:* postschell.com

- *earth place:* Philadelphia, PA

- *born on:* 20 Feb 1997 (late adopter)

- *review:* Nothing remarkable at Post & Schell's Web site, though they do cover most of the basics. Practice profiles are brief, and don't provide much detail about the firm's expertise. Lawyer biographies are clearly listed. Contact information is provided immediately, with the option of clicking on the lawyer name for a short biography. One nice touch is that the firm gives visitors maps, so that finding the various offices won't be difficult at all.

- *practice areas:* automobile, premises, toxic tort, product liability, property, workers' compensation, employment law, professional malpractice, directors and officers, coverage, appellate

Powell, Goldstein, Frazer & Murphy

- *cyberspace:* pgfm.com

- *earth place:* Atlanta, GA

- *born on:* 22 Dec 1995 (middler)

- *review:* The "What's New" section contained reasonably up-to-date information, though some of the "announcements" are buried and could be brought into the "What's New" section itself. The newsletters are very good, though there are gaps in the coverage. We like allowing visitors to subscribe to the newsletters. This builds a good database of contact names for the firm, and is still the best example of "push" technology in use today. The lawyer biographies are good, though we don't understand why the e-mail addresses are hidden. You must click on a picture of a mailbox to go to another file, where you can fill in a form. At no time is the lawyer's e-mail address disclosed.

misc.legal.moderated
The only useful Usenet newsgroup, misc .legal.moderated is moderated by a team of lawyers (including one of the first net.lawyers, Mark Eckenweiler), and is home to some very cogent legal discussion. Thanks to the moderators, much of the nonlegal discussion is filtered out so that the reader does not need to sift through it, and what remains are some genuinely interesting discussions that alternate between academic and practical.

monopoly
See **InterNIC.**

- *practice areas:* business law, litigation, health care, real estate, employment, government and regulatory, international, individual representation

Preston Gates & Ellis

- *cyberspace:* prestongates.com
- *earth place:* Seattle, WA
- *born on:* 19 Jun 1995 (middler)
- *review:* Visitors get the choice of choosing "high graphics" or "low graphics," which you'll definitely appreciate if you're surfing at 28.8. Once you get through the initial set of screens, many of the sections ("News of Note," for example) provide good current information about the firm, including recent speeches and publications the firm has produced, and awards the firm has received. Lawyer biographies are well done, providing background information as well as a photo of the lawyer and contact information.
- *practice areas:* business, environment/land use, federal/regulatory/legislative, information technology, litigation, municipal, real estate/finance

Proskauer Rose Goetz & Mendelsohn

- *cyberspace:* proskauer.com
- *earth place:* New York, NY
- *born on:* 31 Jan 1995 (middler)
- *review:* Compared to some of the cluttered sites we've reviewed, we actually like Proskauer's understated approach—it places the emphasis on the information and makes it easily accessible. Browsing through the content, the simplicity of organization is a big plus— you always know where you are. The firm publishes several topic-specific newsletters, and has made a couple of White Papers available as well.
- *practice areas:* accountants' liability, airline labor law, asset securitization and finance, banking practice, bankruptcy and reorganization, corporate department, defense industry practice, employee benefits, environmental, land use and environmental insurance coverage practice, fashion industry, franchise law, health-care law, health-care litigation, hospitality practice group, immigration and nationality law, information technology law, initial public offer-

ings, institutional investing and investment funds, intellectual property and computer law, international arbitration, international practice, international securities practice, Internet and technology law, Israel practice, labor and employment law, labor litigation, legal ethics counseling, lender liability litigation, libel, copyright and first amendment litigation, litigation and dispute resolution department, litigation technology at Proskauer, Los Angeles labor practice, matrimonial law, media and publishing acquisitions and financings, mergers and acquisitions, nonprofit/exempt organizations, occupational safety and health law practice, personal planning, privatization projects, pro bono activities, probate and surrogate's court litigation, real-estate litigation, real-estate practice, representation of foreign banks in the United States, securities law, securities litigation, sports law, tax department, tender offer strategy and litigation, trademark practice, white-collar criminal defense practice

Quarles and Brady

- *cyberspace:* quarles.com
- *earth place:* Milwaukee, WI
- *born on:* 18 May 1995 (middler)

Reed, Smith, Shaw & McClay

- *cyberspace:* rssm.com
- *earth place:* Pittsburgh, PA
- *born on:* 22 Feb 1995 (middler)
- *review:* From a content perspective, the Reed, Smith, Shaw & McClay site has several advantages over its counterparts: recent content is plentiful, detailed, and dated. Its recruiting information is detailed, and the site is updated often (within a week of this review).
- *practice areas:* bank regulatory, antitrust, marketing and trade regulation, consumer financial services, bankruptcy, restructur-

Mosaic
Barefoot wünderkind Marc Andreesen and others invented this program at the University of Illinois. Mosaic was the precursor to Netscape—the first widely available Web browser, distributed for free on the Internet. Andreesen would later graduate, get involved with a startup company in Mountain View, California, make a lot of money, and appear barefoot on the cover of *Time*.

ing and reorganization, corporate and securities, mergers and acquisitions, project finance, public finance securities, environmental, family business, asbestos litigation, construction, defamation, insurance coverage, product liability/torts, trade secret/restrictive covenant, financial institutions/transactions, matrimonial, international, white-collar crime, real estate, tax, tissue engineering, trusts and estates, utilities/energy, education, communications, employee benefits, export/import and customs, immigration, franchising, labor and employment, government contracts, government relations, health care, intellectual property, technology

Reid and Priest

- *cyberspace:* reidpriest.com
- *earth place:* New York, NY
- *born on:* 11 Feb 1997 (late adopter)

Reinhart, Boerner, et al.

- *cyberspace:* rbvdnr.com
- *earth place:* Milwaukee, WI
- *born on:* 14 Nov 1994 (early adopter)
- *review:* Designed and maintained in-house, this is an above-average site with excellent content. An impressive amount of time has gone into providing useful content—timely, informative publications that are sure to help clients. The additions do not seem to be as regular as they could be, and this shortcoming could very well limit repeat visits.
- *practice areas:* intellectual property, trusts and estates, litigation, health care, labor and employment, banking and bankruptcy, international, business organizations, tax, employee benefits, environmental, real estate

Riker, Danzig, Scherer, Hyland, and Perretti

- *cyberspace:* riker.com
- *earth place:* Morristown, NY
- *born on:* 06 Nov 1995 (middler)
- *review:* It is the "Legal Base" that is most impressive—a collection of more than 100 articles about each area of law in which the firm

practices (we'd like to see dates on the master list, though). The "Legal Base" is searchable by keyword, and also includes a good list of starting points for various areas of law. (Users looking for comprehensive lists would still be better served by going to FindLaw.) This site is well thought out, and is a great example of how to leverage content that the firm already has in electronic format.

- *practice areas:* bankruptcy and reorganization, labor and employment, closely held businesses, lending law, corporate, litigation, corporate trust, loan workout, eminent domain, project finance practice, environmental, public finance, family law, public utilities, financial services, real estate, governmental affairs, reinsurance, health-care practice, school law, insurance, solid waste, insurance intermediary disputes, tax practice, intellectual property, trusts and estates

Rivkin, Radler & Kremer

- *cyberspace:* rivkinradler.com
- *earth place:* Uniondale, NY
- *born on:* 07 Sep 1995 (middler)
- *review:* There is a goldmine behind "RR&K in Print"—the firm's virtual filing cabinet for well over fifty articles written in the past two years. The full text of each article is available, and most offer considerable depth on their particular topic. The lawyer biographies use the narrative style quite well.
- *practice areas:* appellate practice, administrative and government affairs, banking and insolvency, business litigation, corporate, environmental, science and technology, insurance coverage, litigation, medical malpractice, real estate, commercial finance

Robins, Kaplan, Miller & Ciresi

- *cyberspace:* robins.com
- *earth place:* Minneapolis, MN
- *born on:* 07 Jul 1994 (early adopter)

Robinson & Cole

- *cyberspace:* rc.com
- *earth place:* Hartford, CT
- *born on:* 26 Jan 1994 (early adopter)

- *review:* A good attempt is made by the firm to provide its clients with "Client Alerts" in electronic format to accompany the printed version. The Web site nevertheless falls short: The last "Client Alert" was six months old when we showed up. Either they aren't notifying their clients often enough, or someone isn't getting the content from the authors. Either way, the site fails to deliver on its goal of being an alternative means of distributing content. Lawyer biographies are useful, and "R&C Spotlight in the News" provided more timely information.

- *practice areas:* alternative dispute resolution, antitrust and trade regulation, asset planning and probate, bankruptcy and business workout, construction, corporate, labor, employment and benefits, entertainment, environmental, government relations, health care, immigration, institutional finance, insurance, intellectual property, international, land use, nonprofit, pro bono, product liability, professional liability, public finance, real estate, securities, tax, trial and appellate, utilities

Rogers & Wells

- *cyberspace:* rw.com
- *earth place:* New York, NY
- *born on:* 15 Sep 1995 (middler)

Ropes & Gray

- *cyberspace:* ropesgray.com
- *earth place:* Boston, MA
- *born on:* 12 Oct 1995 (middler)
- *review:* The lawyer listings are well done—you can find who you're looking for by name, by department, or by location. Law students looking for a job will find a wealth of information about the recruiting program, including compensation, living, and training information. For a firm of Ropes & Gray's size, it was shocking to see a complete absence of publications. There is literally no up-to-date information on the site.
- *practice areas:* corporate, creditors' rights, employee benefits and counseling, environmental, health law, labor and employment, litigation, real estate, taxation, trusts and estates

Rosenman & Colin

- *cyberspace:* rosenman.com
- *earth place:* New York, NY
- *born on:* 12 Dec 1994 (early adopter)
- *review:* The most recent articles on the site were from 1996. We continue to be puzzled by law firms that make the commitment to having a Web site, but then fail to support it by providing any content after the site goes live. Lawyer biographies are online, but the age of the "news" makes one wonder whether or not the biographies are up to date themselves.
- *practice areas:* corporate, employment, environmental, financial markets regulation, hotel/hospitality, insurance and reinsurance, litigation, real estate, tax/property tax, technology, trusts and estates, pro bono

Ross & Hardies

- *cyberspace:* rosshardies.com
- *earth place:* Chicago, IL
- *born on:* 26 Dec 1995 (middler)
- *review:* The content itself is decent, and the "What's New" section is organized thoughtfully by month—Ross & Hardies tells its visitors what has changed (and when!). Other firms should follow their lead. There were no lawyer biographies on the site at all, which is puzzling when one considers that this is one way to show off the talents of the people who make up the firm.
- *practice areas:* antitrust, bankruptcy, business litigation, corporate, securities and finance, employee benefits, environmental law, futures and commodities, government contracts, health care, institutional lending and financial services, insurance, intellectual property, international trade and customs, labor and employment relations, merg-

MovieLink (http://www.movielink.com/) Another zip-code driven Web site. This site will tell you what movies are showing in your area—you'll never have to call and get a busy signal again when trying to find out what's showing at the local theater. See also GistTV.

ers and acquisitions, municipal finance, real estate and land use, takeover advisory, telecommunications, tort, visa and immigration

Rudnick & Wolfe

- *cyberspace:* rudnickwolfe.com
- *earth place:* Chicago, IL
- *born on:* 14 Dec 1995 (middler)

Saul, Ewing, Remick & Saul

- *cyberspace:* saul.com
- *earth place:* Philadelphia, PA
- *born on:* 09 May 1995 (middler)
- *review:* Other than undated press releases about the firm, there is no original content on this site at all. Lawyer biographies are presented, though their layout makes them difficult to read.
- *practice areas:* bankruptcy and reorganization, business and tax, criminal defense, emerging business, environmental, estates and trusts, government relations, health care, insurance, labor and employee benefits, litigation, product liability, public finance, real estate, telecommunications, tort and insurance litigation

Schiff Hardin & Waite

- *cyberspace:* schiffhardin.com
- *earth place:* Chicago, IL
- *born on:* 05 Mar 1996 (late adopter)
- *review:* As for original content, a "Reference" section is provided, inviting users to browse the list of "Electronic Law Documents." These are not documents about "Electronic Law" but law documents that happen to be in an electronic format. In any event, after clicking through several screens, we were invited to register with the firm prior to gaining permission to download. And what a choice: There was exactly one document available for downloading ("A form for the debtor's adoption of symbol and authorization to file a financing statement by electronic means"). We guess there haven't been too many people who have bothered to ask for permission.
- *practice areas:* antitrust and trade regulation, bankruptcy, workouts and creditors' rights, commercial and corporate debt financing,

construction, employee benefits and executive compensation, energy, telecommunications and public utilities, environmental, estate planning and administration, financial institutions, general corporate and securities law, general litigation, insurance, intellectual property, international, investment companies and investment advisors, labor and employment, product liability, public law and finance, real estate, securities and futures market regulation, securities and futures litigation, taxation, white-collar criminal law

Schnader Harrison Segal & Lewis

- *cyberspace:* shsl.com

- *earth place:* Philadelphia, PA

- *born on:* 09 May 1994 (early adopter)

- *review:* Schnader Harrison received quite a bit of press last spring when it was the first law firm in the country to submit an amicus brief to the Supreme Court simultaneously on CD-ROM and on the Internet. A copy of that brief is at their Web site, and it remains one of the best and most persuasive arguments against the Communications Decency Act of 1996. Lawyer biographies are decent, including photographs of the lawyers, their e-mail addresses, and links to the more thorough Martindale-Hubbell biographies. "In the News" is a great collection of articles about the firm, and are even dated. Newsletters are published here, but are woefully out of date: the Intellectual Property's last (and only) entry is dated March 1995 (yes, 1995). "Nunc pro tunc" is a great section, taking a historical approach to the law, and, in some cases, Schnader Harrison's contribution to the law.

- *practice areas:* alternative dispute resolution, antitrust and

National Information Infrastructure

Accepting, for a moment, the "information superhighway" analogy, a network is analogous to a highway, which can be considered an infrastructure. Information is analogous to rest stops, national parks, and scenic lookouts, and libraries on the highway. But the National Information Infrastructure is a mixed metaphor. How can the rest stop *be* the highway? How can the end be the means? The National Information Infrastructure (NII) is a superset of the planned National Research and Education Network (NREN), which is part of the federal government's High Performance Computing initiative. The NII has not been funded and does not exist. The Internet exists and is privately funded. The two terms are often used interchangeably, but, if they are, then it should be "national information infrastructure" (small n, i, and i).

trade regulation, appellate and trial litigation, aviation, business and technology, business counseling and corporate law, communications, computer law, construction law, corporate finance and securities, creditors' rights, employee benefits, employment and labor law, environmental and solid waste management, family law, financial institutions practice, franchise and distribution, government contracts, health law, insurance regulatory, intellectual property, Internet and computer networking, international transactions, libel law, litigation and appellate practice, maritime law, product liability, railroad, real estate, securities and shareholder litigation, local, state, and federal taxation, trusts and estates, white-collar crime, and corporate compliance

Schulte, Roth and Zabel

- *cyberspace:* srz.com

- *earth place:* New York, NY

- *born on:* 11 Feb 1996 (late adopter)

- *review:* Profiles of the various practice areas are thorough and offer a fair amount of detail for interested readers. The "Publications" section contains a few recent articles, and a good sampling of more dated information. Schulte Roth & Zabel offers more recruiting information than any other site we've seen—definitely a plus if you're looking to change jobs.

- *practice areas:* corporate, environmental law group, individual client services, litigation, real estate, tax, employee benefits

Sedgwick, Detert, Moran & Arnold

- *cyberspace:* sdma.com

- *earth place:* San Francisco, CA

- *born on:* 28 Dec 1994 (early adopter)

Seyfarth, Shaw

- *cyberspace:* seyfarth.com

- *earth place:* Los Angeles, CA

- *born on:* 13 Nov 1995 (middler)

- *review:* Some good content can be found here under "Insights and Developments." Kudos to the Environmental Group, who appear to have contributed well over fifty articles (dating back to 1994) alone.

Other groups were less prolific, however. Lawyer biographies cover the basics, but fail to provide a visitor with any contact information.

- *practice areas:* business law, employee benefits, labor and employment, environmental, safety and health, government contracts, commercial litigation

Shaw, Pittman, Potts & Trowbridge

- *cyberspace:* shawpittman.com
- *earth place:* Washington, DC
- *born on:* 08 Nov 1995 (middler)
- *review:* The practice areas are well covered here, as are the law library's reference links. In the "Publications" section, many good newsletters are available in PDF format, but this area does not appear to be as up to date as it should be. Users looking for a particular lawyer better know whether that lawyer is a partner or an associate, because the list of lawyers is subdivided by this classification.
- *practice areas:* aviation, bankruptcy, workout, and reorganization, commercial finance, commercial space, construction, corporate finance and securities, Cuban project, distressed real estate, employee benefits and compensation, employment and labor law, energy, energy transactions, environmental, fair lending, federal appellate litigation, financial institutions, foreign bank tax, government contracts, government enforcement and internal investigations, government relations, health care, housing, immigration, intellectual property, international, international arbitration, litigation, alternative dispute resolution, international trade, Latin America, investment funds, litigation, natural gas—regulatory and transactions, offshore fund taxation, outsourcing, project finance, public-private partnerships, publishing, public securities, real

Net-Lawyers

Run by Arent Fox's Lew Rose, Net-Lawyers is a popular meeting place for practicing lawyers interested in the Internet. Traffic is manageable—a busy day will generate ten to twenty messages. The list is moderated, and posts tend to focus on Internet-related news of interest to lawyers, issues concerning legal Web sites, and legal developments affecting new technologies. To subscribe: Send e-mail to <listserv@peach.ease.lsoft.com>. In the body of the message, write: "subscribe net-lawyers [Your Name]" where [Your Name] is your name. Omit the quotes.

estate, structured finance/asset securitization, tax, technology, technology litigation, telecommunications, trademark, utility telecommunications

Shearman & Sterling

- *cyberspace:* shearman.com
- *earth place:* New York, NY
- *born on:* 15 Mar 1995 (middler)
- *review:* A good second-generation Web site, Shearman & Sterling's site has numerous newsletters and articles (and they're dated!) in their "Publications" section, though it had last been updated more than seven months prior to this writing. All publications make it easy to contact the author(s) of the article, though it would be even better to provide an e-mail address. Though the lawyer biographies are not available per se, we really like the approach Shearman takes: on each practice area page, photos of the lawyers are presented with a name and educational background. It's different, but it works.
- *practice areas:* corporate finance, tax, mergers and acquisitions, litigation, antitrust, property, project development and finance, compensation and benefits, individual clients, specialized finance and bankruptcy, leasing

Sheppard, Mullin, Richter & Hampton

- *cyberspace:* smrh.com
- *earth place:* Los Angeles, CA
- *born on:* 25 Sep 1995 (middler)
- *review:* A good attempt has been made to make some representative articles available; however, there aren't enough articles to convince someone that the visit is worthwhile. Most practice areas have just one or two articles available, and most are more than a year old. Law students looking for job hunting information will find plenty of good information about the firm under "Recruiting," and prospective clients will learn a lot about how the firm uses technology. Overall, a pretty good content strategy.
- *practice areas:* affordable housing practice, antitrust practice, banking and finance practice, construction litigation practice, corporate and securities practice, energy project practice, environmental law practice, governmental law practice, intellectual property and tech-

nology practice, international law practice, labor law practice, land use practice, litigation practice, pension practice, real-estate law practice, tax practice

Shook Hardy & Bacon

- *cyberspace:* shb.com
- *earth place:* Kansas City, MO
- *born on:* 10 Dec 1995 (middler)

Sidley & Austin

- *cyberspace:* sidley.com
- *earth place:* Chicago, IL
- *born on:* 26 Apr 1995 (middler)
- *review:* Other than the "Seminars" section being slightly out of date, there really isn't much wrong with this site. Bottom line: Sidley & Austin's Web site is one of the best professional Web sites (law firm or otherwise) currently online. Clients, law students, and prospective clients will all find something of value here—we did.
- *practice areas:* affordable housing practice, alternative dispute resolution, antitrust and trade regulation, appellate and constitutional litigation, association law practice, bankruptcy and corporate reorganization, certificate of need, class litigation, clean air practice, college and university practice, commercial contract litigation, commercial, financial and banking transactions, commodities and financial litigation, communications group, computer law, construction law, copyright and trademark litigation, corporate criminal defense and internal investigations practice, corporate control, securities and derivative suit litigation, corporate and securities, directors' and officers' liability litigation, distributor, franchise, and dealer termination litigation, electric utility practice, electromagnetic fields practice, electric utility environmental practice, employee benefits, employment and labor law, employment contract, restrictive covenant and trade-secret litigation, energy regulatory practice, entertainment, art, and sports law, entertainment finance, environmental management, environmental practice, executive compensation practice, federal, state, and local tax litigation, financial institutions regulatory practice, financial services transactions practice, food and drug law, government contracts and litigation, government regulation, land use and legislation, health care,

Illinois appellate practice, Illinois environmental practice, immigration services, injunctions, restraining orders and other emergency litigation, insurance coverage, insurance insolvency, intellectual property and marketing, international environmental legal consultancy, international practice, international trade regulation and counseling, investment company and investment adviser representation practice group, land use practice, Latin American and project finance practice, lender liability, licensing, sponsorship, marketing, and promotions practice, London practice, media and first amendment, media financing and restructuring, medical device practice, medical malpractice, municipal finance practice, not-for-profit organizations, OSHA practice, patent prosecution, licensing, counseling and litigation, personal and estate planning services, physician-hospital organizations and integrated delivery systems, privatization and related experience, pro bono, product liability, project finance, real estate and zoning litigation, real estate practice, regulated industries litigation and counseling, reinsurance practice, RICO and fraud practice, securitization and structured finance, state and local government practice, tax and employee benefits, Tokyo practice, transportation, women partners

Sills Cummis Zuckerman Radin Tischman & Gross

- *cyberspace:* sillscummis.com
- *earth place:* Newark, NJ
- *born on:* 26 Jan 1996 (late adopter)

Simpson Thacher & Bartlett

- *cyberspace:* stblaw.com
- *earth place:* New York, NY
- *born on:* 22 Oct 1996 (late adopter)

Skadden Arps Slate Meagher & Flom

- *cyberspace:* skadden.com
- *earth place:* New York, NY
- *born on:* 27 Oct 1995 (middler)
- *review:* It's disappointing to see so little content in a firm the size of Skadden Arps. The publications section presents an exhaustive list of articles, their authors, and the date of publication. Though this sounds good, that's all it is—a list. None of the articles is linked,

meaning that there's no way to actually read the content. Law students and lawyers looking to make a job change will find helpful information about Skadden Arps' hiring practices.

- *practice areas:* mergers and acquisitions, securities, corporate compliance, securities litigation, commercial contracts, antitrust, banking litigation, international litigation, products liability and toxic torts, government enforcement, intellectual property, alternative dispute resolution, finance, corporate, structured, banking and institutional investing, lease financing, project finance, public finance, derivative financial products, commodities and futures, investment companies, advisors and broker-dealers, private investment funds, international, privatizations, restructuring and bankruptcy reorganization, international trade, banking and financial institution regulation, international banking, financial institutions mergers and acquisitions, tax, legislative, political law, communications, energy, environment, gaming, health care, information technology, insurance, real estate, utilities, employee benefits and executive compensation, labor and employment law, trusts and estates, pro bono

Smith Helms Milluss & Moore, L.L.P.

- *cyberspace:* shmm.com
- *earth place:* Greensboro, NC
- *born on:* 23 Apr 1995 (middler)
- *review:* The designers of the Smith Helms site have done a good job presenting a wealth of information about the firm. It exists largely as a marketing vehicle—there is little to no original information other than the firm brochure. Lawyer biographies are well done, and e-mail addresses for every lawyer are listed.

network computer
Maybe we shouldn't be hauling our data around with us. Maybe we should be hauling (or perhaps palming) around a "thin client" NC, or "network computer." This is, by the way, the vision of Oracle's CEO Larry Ellison. Although it's a safe bet that CEO's of PC manufacturers share a different vision. You don't have to carry around an answering machine with you to retrieve voicemail. And some universal messaging services allow you to access e-mail, faxes, and voicemail via the telephone. Maybe client/server technology *is* right for the desktop! Imagine plugging a network laptop into a port in any hotel room and having access to your programs and data, which reside safely at some secure facility that is free of accident-prone Coke drinkers and magnet-toting toddlers. I'm not sure how much that service would cost today, but I'm guessing it would be more than the cost of my laptop. Then again, there's the cost of potentially lost data.

- *practice areas:* corporate, environmental and OSHA, health care, labor and employment, litigation, real estate

Snell & Wilmer, L.L.P.

- *cyberspace:* swlaw.com
- *earth place:* Phoenix, AZ
- *born on:* 20 Sep 1995 (middler)
- *review:* When we see a site with a "What's New" section, and their first several articles are more than a year old, we get concerned. Such is the case with Snell & Wilmer, an Arizona law firm that was, the home page proclaims, voted the best law firm in Arizona in 1993. That's right, 1993! Four years is a long time, and the general feeling one has after visiting this site is that little has changed in that time, at least with regard to the Web site. Snell & Wilmer has to find some content to put in the "What's New" page. Once that happens, the site will find some life.
- *practice areas:* alternative dispute resolution, appellate services, commercial litigation, construction services, employment litigation, environmental/natural resources litigation, health-care litigation, product liability litigation, securities, general litigation

Sonnenschein Nath & Rosenthal

- *cyberspace:* sonnenschein.com
- *earth place:* Chicago, IL
- *born on:* 13 Dec 1994 (early adopter)
- *review:* The "under construction" graphic hasn't changed in six months.

Southerland, Asbill & Brennan[4]

- *cyberspace:* sablaw.com
- *earth place:* Atlanta, GA
- *born on:* 28 Aug 1995 (middler)

---

4. The correct spelling of this firm's name is Sutherland, Asbill & Brennan, but to the Internet world they are known as Southerland, Asbill, & Brennan. When their information was submitted, the firm's name was misspelled. Obviously a problem if people are searching the InterNIC's database for you by the correct spelling of your name.

- *review:* From a content perspective, this site has a head start on its brethren: it has timely articles (some less than a month old), its structure invites simple navigation that is easy to figure out, and much of the information is presented succinctly.

- *practice areas:* corporate, corporate attorneys, energy and commodities, energy and commodities lawyers, insurance, insurance attorneys, litigation, litigation lawyers, real estate, real-estate lawyers, tax, tax lawyers

Squire, Sanders & Dempsey

- *cyberspace:* ssd.com

- *earth place:* Cleveland, OH

- *born on:* 31 Mar 1994 (early adopter)

- *review:* We liked the "You Make the Call" section—a nice departure from some staid presentations of other firms (though we confess to feeling a brief case of the chills, a reminder of law school exams from years past). Practice area profiles, such as their litigation section (claimed to be one of the oldest in the country), are decent, though the published articles could be more timely.

- *practice areas:* litigation, corporate, environmental, labor and employment, regulatory, tax

Steel Hector & Davis

- *cyberspace:* steelhector.com

- *earth place:* Miami, FL

- *born on:* 20 May 1996 (late adopter)

- *review:* Though the frames-based site is not 640x480 resolution friendly, the site itself is well done. Up-to-date content coupled with a good history of the firm and a "Meet the New Faces" section make this a great example of how to present your firm online. There may not be much to encourage people to come

News.Com (http://www.news.com/) Trying to keep up with the technology news junkies? Want to appear to know as much about the industry as Burgess Allison? C|Net's News.com site is your best bet—but Burgess will probably still know more than you.

phone numbers
See **555-1212.**

printer drivers
Software that must be hidden from office computer users.

back often, but those that stop by will leave with a good understanding of what the firm does—an accomplishment that too few of the NLJ 250 can claim.

- *practice areas:* general information, administrative law and government relation, admiralty/maritime, alternative dispute resolution, antitrust, banking and finance, civil rights class actions, construction, corporate and securities, distribution and franchising, eminent domain, employment and labor relations, energy and utilities law, environmental and land use, family law, financial services, general and commercial litigation, government contracts, health care, immigration and nationality, insurance, intellectual property, international, media and communication, mergers and acquisitions, product liability, project finance, real estate, securities litigation/arbitration, tax, trusts, estates and personal planning, white-collar criminal defense

Steptoe & Johnson

- *cyberspace:* steptoe.com
- *earth place:* Washington, DC
- *born on:* 10 Apr 1995 (middler)
- *review:* Were it not for Steptoe partner Stewart Baker (former General Counsel of the much-maligned National Security Agency), the "What's New" section would have little content at all. Thanks to Baker, there are a wealth of articles and links to Internet law resources—some of which we've seen, others we hadn't. Most useful is the fact that Steptoe places copies of the important documents on their server, which guarantees that information provided by a third party won't disappear. Under "Seminars," a plain-vanilla HTML page (no graphics, minimal formatting) has one link: to a seminar sponsored by Steptoe and Johnson that occurred more than one year ago.
- *practice areas:* alternative dispute resolution, antitrust, appellate, Commonwealth of Independent States (CIS) institutional, CIS/intellectual property, communications, corporate/securities, electric power, employee benefits, environmental, financial services, government contracts, immigration, insurance, intellectual property, international, labor, the Phoenix office, tax practice, technology, transportation, transportation (railroad)

Stoel Rives, L.L.P.

- *cyberspace:* stoel.com
- *earth place:* Portland, OR
- *born on:* 05 May 1995 (middler)
- *review:* Stoel Rives offers information about the firm, their lawyers, and their practice areas.
- *practice areas:* agriculture and agribusiness law, alternative dispute resolution, banking and financial institutions, bankruptcy and commercial law, construction and design law, corporate finance and securities, employee benefits, energy production and utilities law, environmental law, forest products, franchise law, government affairs, health and hospital law, immigration law, intellectual property law, international business, labor and employment law, land use planning, litigation, marketing and distribution law, mining, oil, and gas law, municipal law and finance, natural resources, product liability and toxic torts, professional liability, real-estate law, securities litigation, state and local tax law, taxation, technology law, tribal law, trusts and estate planning, water law, white-collar criminal law, workers' compensation law

Strasburger & Price, L.L.P.

- *cyberspace:* strasburger.com
- *earth place:* Dallas, TX
- *born on:* 15 Jun 1995 (middler)
- *review:* "Unfortunately we're presently constructing an all new Web Site. Production of the new site should be completed near the end of September, so please check back soon!" (Visited: November 11, 1997. Draw your own conclusions.)

Stroock & Stroock & Lavan

- *cyberspace:* stroock.com
- *earth place:* New York, NY
- *born on:* 27 Feb 1996 (late adopter)

Project Hermes

Long before judges were handing down decisions about nannies by e-mail, the U.S. Supreme Court had set up a nifty little system that ensured that anyone around the world who wanted a copy of the decision would have one. It works like this: After the Court publishes a decision, the clerk electronically transmits a copy to Carnegie-Mellon University, where the decisions are archived. Cornell's Legal Information Institute, in conjunction with Carnegie-Mellon, is notified that the decisions arrived, and proceeds to format the cases, and categorize them (intellectual property, constitutional law, etc.). They are then in Cornell's database of opinions, and are e-mailed to people who have requested decisions on that particular topic.

Sullivan & Cromwell

- *cyberspace:* sullcrom.com
- *earth place:* New York, NY
- *born on:* 04 Jun 1995 (middler)
- *review:* The best part of the site (from a content perspective, at least) is the "Working at S&C" section, which provides some of the most in-depth information about the firm's work environment, recruiting program, hiring practices, summer program, benefits, and so on—you get the idea. Lawyer biographies are simply their *Martindale-Hubbell* entries, residing locally on the Web server.
- *practice areas:* corporate and financial, securities, corporation law and counseling, asset-based finance, commodities, futures and derivatives, communications, corporate reorganization and bankruptcy, insurance, international trade and investment, investment companies, privatizations, mergers and acquisitions, commercial banking, commercial real estate, project finance, antitrust, European Community competition law, corporate and securities law, criminal defense and investigations, environmental, intellectual property, international commercial arbitration, labor and employment, product liability, estates and personal

Swidler & Berlin

- *cyberspace:* swidlaw.com
- *earth place:* Washington, DC
- *born on:* 21 Dec 1995 (middler)
- *review:* If you're looking for a recent picture of Swidler & Berlin's offices in Washington, DC, then this is the site for you. If you want to send e-mail to the firm, then you'll likely love the site content. With those two items, however, we've just identified the sum total of this firm's Web site. Couldn't they at least tell us that something's on the way? Surely this isn't their entire Web site. (As of this writing, the site hadn't been updated in four months.)

Taft, Stettinius & Hollister

- *cyberspace:* taftlaw.com
- *earth place:* Cincinnati, OH
- *born on:* 12 Sep 1995 (middler)

Testa, Hurwitz & Thibeault

- *cyberspace:* tht.com
- *earth place:* Boston, MA
- *born on:* 02 Feb 1995 (middler)
- *review:* Information about the practice areas is helpful, but the lawyer directory is very user unfriendly: all 200+ lawyers are listed on one page, with contact information and e-mail addresses. This page alone could be broken up into several separate pages to allow for quicker downloads and easier navigation.
- *practice areas:* banking, business and securities, creditors' rights, business restructurings and bankruptcy, employee benefits and ERISA, environmental, estate planning, trust and estate, federal and state taxation, labor and employment, litigation, mergers and acquisitions, new business formation and financing, patent and intellectual property, real estate, venture capital and private equity

Thacher, Proffitt & Wood

- *cyberspace:* thacherproffitt.com
- *earth place:* New York, NY
- *born on:* 17 Nov 1995 (middler)
- *review:* The "Firm History" is a lengthy narrative of the firm, and it spans more than 160 years. Touches like this lend a sense of familiarity to a firm that they might not otherwise have. Under "What's New," the firm does a good job of showcasing where they've been talked about, where they've published, and so on, but it needs to be updated more often. While we'd like to see the firm publish their newsletters online, they do seem to have an impressive catalog of back issues that might be of interest to visitors.
- *practice areas:* corporate, structured finance, banking, corporate finance, employment, compensation and benefits, intellectual property, real estate, litigation and dispute resolution, commercial litigation, admiralty, insurance, bankruptcy, tax, private client, international

Thelen, Marrin, Johnson & Bridges

- *cyberspace:* tmjb.com
- *earth place:* San Francisco, CA
- *born on:* 13 Jun 1995 (middler)

- *review:* Recent articles make a good impression, profiles of every practice area are thorough, and lawyer biographies are as comprehensive as any we've seen. Law students will appreciate the ability to search the lawyer directory by law school.

- *practice areas:* alternative dispute resolution, antitrust and trade regulation, banking litigation, bankruptcy and creditors' rights, business litigation, business transactions, commercial lending, construction, corporate and securities litigation, corporate, environmental litigation and counseling, ERISA/employee benefits, equipment leasing, insurance coverage, insurance regulatory, intellectual property litigation and counseling, international practice, labor and employment, maritime law, mining, product liability/toxic tort, project finance, real estate, tax, trusts and estates, technology law, trademarks, year 2000 issues

Thompson Coburn

- *cyberspace:* thompsoncoburn.com
- *earth place:* St. Louis, MO
- *born on:* 30 Aug 1996 (late adopter)
- *review:* "Access Forbidden." We think that's called "Marketing." Or is it "Client Services"?

Thompson Hine & Flory

- *cyberspace:* thf.com
- *earth place:* Cleveland, OH
- *born on:* 29 Jul 1995 (middler)
- *review:* Several practice areas, product quality newsletters, and current and past issues are archived online. Visitors are encouraged to view the newsletters in PDF format (the printouts certainly make a compelling argument for using Acrobat for this purpose), but someone in the firm took an extra few minutes so that you have the choice of viewing the files as HTML. Either way, the presentation is clean, and the content solid. Lawyer biographies are thorough and include photos of the lawyers. (A minor, but notable touch: Lawyer biographies are dated, letting you know when they were last updated.)
- *practice areas:* antitrust and trade regulation, government contracts, government practice, intellectual property, international, regulated industries, transportation law practice, banking and commercial fi-

nance, bankruptcy and workouts, closely held and emerging businesses, communications law, construction, corporate and securities, employee benefits, environmental, foundations and exempt organizations, health care, immigration and nationality law practice, labor, employment and workers' compensation, litigation, mediation, personal and succession planning, product liability, real estate, taxation

Thompson & Knight

- *cyberspace:* tklaw.com

- *earth place:* Dallas, TX

- *born on:* 14 May 1996 (late adopter)

- *review:* Under the "Newsletters" section, the firm publishes its most recent newsletter. This isn't a bad idea, because archives of dozens (if not hundreds) of articles can overwhelm a visitor. Thompson & Knight presented the newsletter as one file, however, which means that people reading it online must scroll through thirty screens of information to read everything. Probably not the best way to read a document online. Lawyer biographies could be better. Currently they consist of little more than birth date, undergraduate and law school, and bar memberships.

- *practice areas:* banking, corporate/securities, bankruptcy, energy, oil, and gas, environmental, health care, intellectual property, labor and employment law, real estate, tax, estate planning, international, trial

Troutman Sanders, L.L.P.

- *cyberspace:* troutmansanders.com

- *earth place:* Atlanta, GA

- *born on:* 29 Jul 1996 (late adopter)

Vedder, Price, Kaufman & Kammholz

- *cyberspace:* vedderprice.com

- *earth place:* Chicago, IL

- *born on:* 02 Dec 1995 (middler)

push technology

1. A technology foisted on Internet consumers by the likes of PointCast. In 1997, PointCast turned down an acquisition offer from News Corporation. What push proponents think they mean by "push" is the ability to send information out once and have millions of people receive it. (Think TV.) Instead, "push" today means millions of people set up their programs to request and receive information. (Think mail-order catalogs.) E-mail remains the dominant push technology in the Internet marketplace.

2. The ability to send information out once and have millions of people receive it. The next hot thing in the Internet marketplace. You heard it here first, push technology will rule the world!

Venable, Baetjer, Howard

- *cyberspace:* venable.com
- *earth place:* Washington, DC
- *born on:* 05 Mar 1994 (early adopter)
- *review:* The venerable venable.com site is starting to show its age. The home page is much too long and gives us little idea about the structure of the site. Sure there is lots of content, but it's unorganized. Many of the links on the home page are undated. Even the items marked "new" are undated. New since when? The content is strong, focusing on information law and intellectual property law. Links to *Martindale-Hubbell* lawyer profiles are included, and there is a primitive search engine. Venable was one of the first law firms to establish a Web site, but their site has not kept up with the times.
- *practice areas:* business, labor and litigation, government

Verner, Liipfert, Bernhard, McPherson, Hand

- *cyberspace:* verner.com
- *earth place:* Washington, DC
- *born on:* 13 Nov 1995 (middler)
- *review:* This firm has one of the nicest search engine interfaces that we've seen for lawyer profiles. The profiles themselves employ a very nice page layout and an effective narrative style. Unfortunately, only two publications (related to health law) were available.
- *practice areas:* antitrust, cogeneration and independent power, communications, corporate, securities and finance, employment and labor, energy, environmental, estate planning and probate, financial restructuring and bankruptcy, government procurement and dispute resolution, health care, international, internal investigations, legislative and federal affairs, litigation, white-collar criminal defense, privatization, development, the export/import bank, and the inter-American development bank, real estate, solid waste, water and wastewater facility development, state and local government, tax, technology, transportation

Vinson & Elkins, L.L.P.

- *cyberspace:* vinson-elkins.com
- *earth place:* Houston, TX
- *born on:* 27 May 1996 (late adopter)

Vorys, Sater, Seymour and Pease

- *cyberspace:* vssp.com
- *earth place:* Columbus, OH
- *born on:* 13 Jun 1995 (middler)

Wachtell, Lipton, Rosen & Katz

- *cyberspace:* wlrk.com
- *earth place:* New York, NY
- *born on:* 03 Oct 1995 (middler)

Warner Norcross & Judd

- *cyberspace:* wnj.com
- *earth place:* Grand Rapids, MI
- *born on:* 19 Apr 1995 (middler)
- *review:* Newsletters are subdivided by year, and though there aren't many online, the articles do a good job of at least outlining the firm's expertise. Lawyer biographies are listed by letter—all lawyers with a last name beginning with "S" are listed on the same page. This isn't the best way to do it, but at least it provides the necessary information for anyone trying to learn more about his or her lawyer.
- *practice areas:* banking and finance, bankruptcy and creditors' rights, closely held businesses, computers and technology, condominiums, corporate, employee benefits, environmental law, franchise law, health law, intellectual property, international, labor and employment, litigation, real estate, securities, tax-exempt organizations, tax planning and litigation, trusts and estates, workers' compensation

Weil, Gotshal & Manges

- *cyberspace:* weil.com
- *earth place:* New York, NY
- *born on:* 22 Feb 1995 (middler)

RFC
Request For Comments. The documents that specify the Internet's standards. Promulgated by the Internet Engineering Task Force, the volunteer Internet standards organization.

server
The publisher side of a client/server-based system. Servers make information available to clients.

SMTP
Simple Mail Transport Protocol. The protocol used by Internet e-mail software programs.

White & Case

- *cyberspace:* whitecase.com
- *earth place:* New York, NY
- *born on:* 06 Aug 1995 (middler)
- *review:* In our opinion, White & Case ought to brag a little more about their newsletters. Going beyond the traditional summaries found in most publications that pass for content on law firm Web sites, the articles that White & Case have published are remarkable for their depth. The information contained in these articles is timely, and is bound both to convince prospective clients of White & Case's expertise in European and financial services law and to help law students who need to write a paper for classes in those subjects. The recruiting information is also helpful for any law students looking for a job. Interestingly, White & Case also provides a lot of information for legal assistants—many of whom are bound to have Internet access.
- *practice areas:* antitrust, arbitration and alternative dispute resolution, banking and financial institutions, bankruptcy and reorganization, capital markets, construction and engineering, corporate, employee benefits, environmental law, equipment and facility finance, European Union, fiduciary, intellectual property, international trade, labor and employment, Latin America, legislative/law reform, litigation, mergers and acquisitions, private clients, privatization, project finance, public international law, public finance, real estate, sovereign, tax, telecommunications

White Williams

- *cyberspace:* whitewms.com
- *earth place:* Philadelphia, PA
- *born on:* 05 Aug 1997 (late adopter)
- *review:* Password protected. It may not happen to you, but it happened to us: More than once, when searching for this firm, we ended up at the firm Williams & White (williamsandwhite.com).

Whitman, Breed, Abbott & Morgan

- *cyberspace:* financelaw.com
- *earth place:* Essex, CT
- *born on:* 11 Jan 1996 (late adopter)

Wildman, Harrold, Allen & Dixon

- *cyberspace:* whad.com
- *earth place:* Chicago, IL
- *born on:* 17 Nov 1995 (middler)
- *review:* Wildman, Harrold, Allen & Dixon's site is sparse on content. Over the past few months, they've actually taken away the "Newsletters" link altogether. The recruiting information, however, is top-notch, and is bound to provide interested law students with as much information as they want. We were particularly interested in this statistic: "Number of 1996 Summer Associates who fell in love with each other and became engaged: 2."
- *practice areas:* accreditation, alternative dispute resolution, antitrust, appellate, banking, bankruptcy, business organizations, closely held corporations, commercial litigation, commercial and residential development, creditors' rights, criminal, employment, employee benefits and executive compensation, environmental, environmental enforcement litigation, environment liabilities in property and asset transfer, environmental regulatory compliance, estate planning, estate and trust litigation, family law, financial services, governmental practices, health care, insurance antitrust, insurance business, insurance coverage, insurance company organization, intellectual property, labor, land use regulation, local government litigation and extraordinary remedies, mergers and acquisitions, municipal bonds, probate administration, product liability, professional liability, recurrent litigation, real-estate joint ventures and syndications, real-estate leasing, real-estate lending, real-estate municipal affairs, real-estate purchases and sales, securities and corporate finance, superfund, tax, toxic tort, trade associations, workout

Wiley, Rein & Fielding

- *cyberspace:* wrf.com
- *earth place:* Washington, DC
- *born on:* 23 Apr 1994 (early adopter)
- *review:* Current articles cover many of the primary practice areas that Wiley, Rein & Fielding list on their

software
See **Computer ESP.**

spam
Sending many copies of the same message to places it doesn't belong and to people who don't want it. See **Canter & Siegel.**

site. In some cases, the articles are as detailed as what you'd find in a law review, making them helpful not just to prospective clients, but to other lawyers and law students. By putting them on their Web site, the firm shows off a bit, and manages to contribute to the general public as well.

- *practice areas:* advertising, antitrust, appellate, communications, corporate, cyberspace, election law and government ethics, employment and labor, energy, environmental, food and drug, franchise law, government affairs, government contracts, health-care fraud, insurance, intellectual property, international, litigation, postal, transportation and aviation, white-collar defense

William A. Fenwick

- *cyberspace:* fenwick.com
- *earth place:* Palo Alto, CA
- *born on:* 09 Jul 1995 (middler)
- *review:* Fenwick & West is a leading Silicon Valley law firm that has represented hundreds of growth-oriented companies from inception. Their impressive "Client List" page makes you wonder why other firms don't offer a similar page. Recent publications (which are all dated) are bound to be useful for current clients and prospective clients alike.
- *practice areas:* intellectual property, corporate, litigation, tax

Willkie Farr & Gallagher

- *cyberspace:* willkie.com
- *earth place:* New York, NY
- *born on:* 30 Jul 1995 (middler)

Wilmer, Cutler & Pickering

- *cyberspace:* wilmer.com
- *earth place:* Washington, DC
- *born on:* 09 Feb 1993 (early adopter)

Wilson, Elser, Moskowitz, Edelman & Dicker c/o MDY Advanced Technologies

- *cyberspace:* wemed.com
- *earth place:* Fair Lawn, NJ

- *born on:* 22 Nov 1995 (middler)

- *review:* The "Publications" section contains only descriptions of various firm publications, not their full text, so there is little reason to return to this section (unless you want to sign up to receive copies of something you've never seen).

- *practice areas:* accident, life and health, accountants, agents and brokers, alternate dispute resolution, appellate practice, architects and engineers, asbestos, aviation, banking, casualty liability, construction, corporate and commercial, creditors' rights and bankruptcy, defamation, directors and officers, employment, entertainment, environmental, ERISA/medical insurance, fidelity, general liability, governmental affairs/lobbying, health-care law, insurance, corporate and regulatory, international law, labor law, lead liability, legal malpractice, manufacturing, marine, medical malpractice, municipal liability, pharmaceutical, political risk, premises security, product liability, professional liability, real estate law, securities/broker/dealer, sexual harassment, trucking, transportation and cargo, trusts and estates

Wilson, Sonsini, Goodrich & Rosati

- *cyberspace:* wsgr.com

- *earth place:* Palo Alto, CA

- *born on:* 31 Mar 1992 (visionary)

- *review:* A lot of new content was recently added to the site, making the Wilson Sonsini site an example of how to provide substantive information that manages to make you look good and (hopefully) convince people to hire you. While many of the articles lack dates (making their value dubious at best—does the article about hiring practices reflect recent caselaw, or is it from 1995?), the content is nevertheless top-notch. At the very least, they demonstrate that the firm knows what it's talking about.

- *practice areas:* corporate securities, litigation, technology and intellectual property, life sciences, tax, real estate and environmental, employee benefits and compensation, estate planning and probate

Winstead, Sechrest & Minick

- *cyberspace:* winstead.com

- *earth place:* Austin, TX

- *born on:* 25 Nov 1994 (early adopter)

- *review:* This recently developed site has learned by observing what other firms have done (and done wrong). Not only are the full text of newsletters published, they are provided in a browser-friendly manner (in other words, not presenting a thirty-screen file for browsing). Coupled with the practice area profiles, visitors to the site will learn a lot about the firm, which is exactly why developing a Web site makes sense.

- *practice areas:* asset securitization, aviation and product liability, bankruptcy, cable and communications, construction and surety, corporate, securities, energy, environmental, environmental litigation, ERISA, employee benefits, financial institutions, government relations, health care, insurance, intellectual property, international, labor and employment, litigation, public finance, real estate, sports, entertainment, taxation, trust/estate planning, zoning and local government

Winston & Strawn

- *cyberspace:* winston.com

- *earth place:* Chicago, IL

- *born on:* 12 Oct 1993 (early adopter)

- *review:* The section "News & Events" doesn't really contain any original content—just press releases and snippets of announcements made by the firm in recent months. After spending a few minutes at the site, however, we discovered that the real content (all 100+ articles!) is under "Resource Library," which is not the most obvious place, but once you find it, you could spend hours wading through all the information. Running off of a Lotus Notes server, Winston & Strawn has provided an enormous number of articles. It's encouraging to see firms make this kind of commitment. (And because sites like this are dynamically generated, the upkeep is minimal.) Lawyer biographies use the bulleted format to provide basic biographical information, but go into little detail.

- *practice areas:* antitrust and trade regulation, arbitration, insolvency, bankruptcy, and business reorganization, corporate, banking, and securities, employee benefits, employment and labor relations, energy, environmental law, government contracts, governmental relations and regulatory affairs, health care, intellectual property, international, international trade regulation, litigation, maritime, real estate, taxation, transportation, trusts and estates

Winthrop, Stimson

- *cyberspace:* winstim.com
- *earth place:* New York, NY
- *born on:* 16 Sep 1995 (middler)
- *review:* Sometimes you have to give site designers points for honesty. When we clicked on "Publications," an impossible-to-miss graphic popped up telling us "This link is not currently active." Oh well. The firm's brochure—under "Firm Overview"—provides two- to three-sentence descriptions of each practice area. This is helpful if you want a quick overview, but it won't give prospective clients the information they'll need when deciding whether or not to hire your firm. Lawyer biographies were not on the site. A link called "Client Communications" was also "not currently active." (Which begs the question: Why put it there in the first place?)
- *practice areas:* administrative, antitrust, Asian practice, aviation, banking and finance, bankruptcy and workouts, business fraud investigation, protection and litigation, commercial contracting and technology transfer, communications, media and space, employee benefits, environmental, European practice, health care, individual client services, labor, legislative and regulatory, litigation, mergers and acquisitions, not-for-profit, project finance, real estate, securities, tax, trade, utilities, venture capital, vessel finance

Wolf, Block, Schorr & Solis-Cohen

- *cyberspace:* wolfblock.com
- *earth place:* Philadelphia, PA
- *born on:* 20 Nov 1995 (middler)
- *review:* Lawyer biographies are clean, but it appears that much of the rest of the site is under construction. Two areas that promise content in the near future

television
See **GIST TV Listings.**

telnet
A program that allows a user on one computer to log in to another computer for general use. A telnet connection is a virtual circuit, much like a telephone connection.

are "Seminars/Speeches" and "Publications," but both produced "Coming Soon" when clicked.

- *practice areas:* bankruptcy, corporate, domestic relations, employee benefits, environmental, trusts and estates, financial services, health law, intellectual property, labor, litigation, real estate, surety, fidelity and liability, tax, government assistance and affordable housing

Womble Carlyle Sandridge and Rice

- *cyberspace:* wcsr.com
- *earth place:* Winston-Salem, NC
- *born on:* 15 Apr 1995 (middler)
- *review:* Forgive us if we didn't exactly feel lucky when this site told us "Congratulations! You are visitor 5014 to our site." (After all, there's nothing more gratifying than being given a number.) The "Breaking News" section was undated. Lawyer profiles are on the short side, and newsletters covering such topics as product liability and employment law are available, but are organized mostly chronologically. We suspect that users will leave the site with a negative impression of its form (mainly because of the overuse of frames) rather than a positive impression of the content (which is good if you can find it).
- *practice areas:* technology, finance, manufacturing, health care, communications

Wyatt, Tarrant & Combs

- *cyberspace:* wyattfirm.com
- *earth place:* Louisville, KY
- *born on:* 03 Dec 1995 (middler)
- *review:* Lawyer phone numbers, but not profiles, are provided. Newsletters are available, but the layout of those pages is poor: they're not 640x480 resolution friendly, and the navigation frame takes a lot of space. A search engine would be helpful here.
- *practice areas:* general business, financial institutions, real estate and lending, real estate transactions, lending, taxation, estate planning, employee benefits, public finance, health care, entertainment law, sports, intellectual property and technology licensing, opinions and standards, antitrust, securities litigation, commercial liti-

gation, governmental law, construction litigation, mineral and energy, environmental, regulatory compliance, communications practice, labor and employment practice, tort and insurance defense, bankruptcy/creditors' rights

---

THE BEST OF THE REST

Robert L. Sommers c/o Attorneys at Law

- *cyberspace:* taxprophet.com
- *earth place:* San Francisco, CA
- *born on:* 21 Sep 1994 (early adopter)
- *review:* Whether you're a practicing lawyer looking for substantive material relating to tax issues, or you're a layperson in need of a tax lawyer, **taxprophet.com** is a great starting point. By publishing numerous articles, authoring several FAQs relating to tax law, and providing a search engine to browse through the volumes of information on this site, lawyer Robert Sommers has given the rest of the field an example of how a content-rich site can steer traffic (and business) to your firm.
- *practice areas:* tax

Brian T. Cullen

- *cyberspace:* nowlan.com
- *earth place:* Chicago, IL
- *born on:* 31 May 1996 (late adopter)
- *review:* When your firm isn't one of the largest in the country, odds are that you don't publish as many articles or newsletters as the big guys. You also practice fewer specialties, instead preferring to focus on those areas that you know you can do well. Nowlan & Mouat, based in Janesville, Wisconsin, demonstrate that their site,

The Legal List
From 1992 to 1995, Erik wrote seven editions of his book *The Legal List: Law-Related Resources on the Internet and Elsewhere.* The last two editions were published by Lawyers Cooperative Publishing, and all seven editions were available for free in electronic format. *The Legal List* was an early attempt to catalog law-related resources on the Internet and to write a book with a really long title.

though modest in comparison with some of the behemoths we've reviewed, stands up very well on its own. By relying on text, Nowlan & Mouat ensures that anyone who searches on terms relating to litigation in Wisconsin will find them. And that's exactly what you want. The best part of the site is the Southern Wisconsin Relocation Law Site—now that's what we call a niche. Nevertheless, everything you'd want as a business owner is here, and that makes Nowlan & Mouat's site a good example of how to leverage what you know to a larger market.

- *practice areas:* Wisconsin, litigation

Glass McCullough Sherrill & H.[5]

- *cyberspace:* gmshlaw.com

- *earth place:* Atlanta, GA

- *born on:* 07 Oct 1996 (late adopter)

- *review:* This office of fifty lawyers has developed a site that demonstrates how integral technology can be to a non-intellectual-property law firm. An entire section of the site is dedicated to "How We Use Technology," and ends up providing a good tutorial on how many law firms should use technology (but don't). Lawyer biographies display most of the relevant information a visitor would want, and FAQs about areas of the law in which the firm practices (environmental, product liability, and so on) demonstrate that the firm is willing to show off what they know.

- *practice areas:* environmental, product liability

Jeff Kuester

- *cyberspace:* kuesterlaw.com

- *earth place:* Atlanta, GA

- *born on:* 02 Mar 1995 (middler)

- *review:* Anyone looking for technology law resources ought to start here. Atlanta lawyer Jeff Kuester's Web site was a staple of early Internet research in 1995. More than two years later, it is still vital to practitioners and students alike, which demonstrates that an early commitment to a simple goal can yield tremendous results. Though by no means exhaustive, Kuester's list of "Tech Attorneys" is never-

---

5. The firm that designed this site, Inherent.Com, is our prior employer.

theless a great networking opportunity for those involved—and a small example of a community that becomes reason enough for frequenting the site. The links to numerous articles, cases, and Web sites make Kuester's site a vital bookmark for any intellectual property attorney.

- *practice areas:* technology law, intellectual property, patents, copyrights, trademarks, trade secrets

Martin Howard Patrick, P.A.

- *cyberspace:* dirtlaw.com
- *earth place:* Bay Harbor Island, FL
- *born on:* 19 Apr 1995 (middler)
- *review:* Not so much one of the best, but certainly notable. Once users are registered with "dirtlaw.com," they have the ability to request property title searches just by filling out a form on the Web site. Users are charged a small fee for this service, but considering that people from geographically remote areas may need this kind of assistance, this is the kind of thing that more small and mid-sized firms ought to do—leverage their local presence on behalf of an international market.

Miller, Griffin & Marks, P.S.C.

- *cyberspace:* horselaw.com
- *earth place:* Lexington, KY
- *born on:* 16 Sep 1996 (late adopter)
- *review:* Horselaw.com and Kentuckylaw.com are both produced by the same firm, but they demonstrate how one site can feed off the other. Horselaw.com is the primary site for the firm, which specializes in legal issues involving horses. Not only is the domain name guessable if you're looking for this kind of help, but the information is truly helpful—caselaw and articles relating to the issue are found on this site. From a content strategy perspective, this site ensures that you will get the right crowd over time. For small firms who have similar expertise, the example set by firms like Miller, Griffin & Marks is that you need to leverage your strength. Show it off, boast about it, and let the clients qualify you instead of the other way around.

- *practice areas:* equine law, horse law

Miller, Griffin & Marks, P.S.C.

- *cyberspace:* kentuckylaw.com
- *earth place:* Lexington, KY
- *born on:* 13 Nov 1996 (late adopter)
- *review:* See horselaw.com.

Moye Giles

- *cyberspace:* mgovg.com
- *earth place:* Denver, CO
- *born on:* 22 Oct 1995 (middler)
- *review:* This content strategy is one of those times when a sense of humor can go a long way to giving you a feel for how the law firm views itself. Instead of lawyer jokes (see Anderson Kill), the Webmaster at Moye, Giles, O'Keefe, Vermeire & Forrell starts out by proclaiming on the home page: "Moye, Giles, O'Keefe, Vermeire & Forrell: Really Good Lawyers." Continue through the site and you'll see links to legal humor—such as an actual decision written in verse by the judge. On the serious side, there's a tremendous amount of original content that ensures plenty of new visitors each week, not to mention those visitors who will return periodically to find out what's new. Users can download the electronic versions of popular publications by the firm, but they can also view the document as a series of Web pages: it may not be as pretty, but it's much quicker.

Muchmore & Wallwork, P.C.

- *cyberspace:* mmww.com
- *earth place:* Phoenix, AZ
- *born on:* 05 Jan 1995 (middler)
- *review:* Clearly a professionally designed site, Muchmore & Wallwork's site stresses simplicity over bells and whistles. We like the articles (though HTML versions of the PDF files would've been a nice gesture). After reading a few articles, visitors know that they're dealing with an Internet-savvy firm that is eager to use proven technology for their clients' benefit. Lawyer biographies are well laid out, and give visitors the information they'd want about each lawyer.

Oppedahl & Larson

- *cyberspace:* patents.com
- *earth place:* Yorktown Heights, NY

- *born on:* 21 Jun 1994 (early adopter)

- *review:* Not too many law firms can claim to be both a useful Web site and a litigant in a landmark case about the use of the Web. For reasons that aren't altogether clear, several Web sites embedded the name of this firm in their "meta" tags (those tags that aren't displayed by a Web browser but are "read" by search engines). Oppedahl & Larson sued, and the lawsuit is ongoing.[6]

  The patents.com site, as you may have guessed, has to do with patents. This is an intellectual property firm, however, so much of the content on the site deals with other issues, such as domain names, trademark law, and copyright on the Internet. A marvelous content strategy makes this a useful site for anyone in the Internet community, because an hour here will acquaint one with many of the important issues facing the growing law of the Internet.

- *practice areas:* technology law, intellectual property, patents, copyrights, trademarks, trade secrets

Sharon Sooho, Esq., c/o Steven L. Fuchs

- *cyberspace:* sooho.com

- *earth place:* Newton, MA

- *born on:* 31 Jul 1996 (late adopter)

- *review:* It's refreshing to see one good idea generate others. Such is the case with Newton, MA-based lawyer Sharon Sooho, whose sole-practitioner Web site created a virtual community focused on family law. Along with two other colleagues, Sharon helped develop DivorceNet, a nationwide community for people interested in finding representation on divorce matters. A clean design complements a wealth of information—from instructions on how to file for divorce to how to find representation—and makes this a first-rate site. Visitors can subscribe to Ms. Sooho's newsletter, Family Law Advisor (sent out by e-mail), and can view articles (separated by topic) going back to 1995.

- *practice areas:* family law

Siskind and Susser, Attorneys at Law

- *cyberspace:* visalaw.com

- *earth place:* Nashville, TN

---

6. For a humorous take on this situation, see **http://www.geocities .com/CapitolHill/ Lobby/6620/index.htm.**

- *born on:* 04 May 1995 (middler)

- *review:* One of the original "proof of concept" Web sites, VisaLaw was a Web site almost before the law firm existed. Originally a collaboration of Greg Siskind & Lynn Susser, this site grew to become one of the most visited sites of its kind. There is so much here that's done right—a focus on original content, a form to fill out so visitors can receive the firm newsletter by e-mail (a great way to remind people of your services), the display of contact information at all times—that it's no wonder that people often cite VisaLaw as one of the early examples of how a firm can exploit the Web.

  note: Note that another lawyer has registered **visa-law.com.**

- *practice areas:* immigration

The Law Office of David Loundy

- *cyberspace:* loundy.com

- *earth place:* Highland Park, IL

- *born on:* 09 Sep 1995 (middler)

- *review:* Along with Jeff Kuester, Chicago lawyer David Loundy sets the standard by which personal pages dedicated to a particular topic of law are judged. David's page, which contains his own articles written for the *Chicago Daily Law Bulletin,* among other things—is a great collection of links relating to what he calls "E-Law," or electronic law. If you're looking for something relating to the Internet and the law, and you can't find it here or at **Kuesterlaw.com,** then it probably doesn't exist. Both end up being great examples of how to establish yourself early and build on that name recognition for projects and opportunities down the road.

- *practice areas:* technology law

CHAPTER **SIX**

Full-text Law Journals

Overview

Looking through our relatively short list of journals, readers will no doubt ask why there aren't more listed. After all, lists at FindLaw (**http://www .findlaw.com/lawreviews**) and the USC Law Library (**http://www.usc.edu/dept/ law-lib/legal/journals.html**) are much longer. The short answer for why our list is shorter: editorial discretion.

There is a little more to it. In writing this chapter (and, in a larger sense, this book), we needed to decide how readers would use it. Since the purpose of the book is to provide a snapshot of where the legal profession is on the Internet, it seemed counterproductive to provide entries for any-one that wasn't really *on* the Internet. This seems to be a problem with many books that try to categorize information—they tend to err on the side of including too much information.

So rather than give you an exhaustive list of every law journal that has a home page, we decided that the only ones that were truly of interest were those that are publishing online. In other words, if a law review has a home page that lists their e-mail contact information and displays ab-stracts of every issue they've published, we've excluded them. We limited this chapter to law journals and law reviews that publish online the full content of each issue. In addition, we eliminated those whose content was more than a year old. (In these cases, we presume that the journal has stopped publishing altogether, or is not actively generating content. In either case, it is not reliable as a source of secondary information.)

There are really two classes of law journals—those that publish exclu-sively online, and those that are print publications that publish their con-tent simultaneously online. We have not distinguished between them—

we assume that either is acceptable. There are a few issues to contend with, though. Is it possible to cite to the online version of the article? If it is a print publication, you will need page numbers (which are irrelevant in an online environment) or paragraph numbers. The truly useful online articles will make citation simple (ideally by numbering paragraphs), will hyperlink to relevant materials (like provisions of the U.S. Code, other online law review articles, text of Supreme Court decisions, and so on), and will even update information when there are developments in the law after the original article was published.

Why should a print journal publish online? There are a few reasons. First of all, the purpose of a law journal is to contribute to the general body of knowledge on a particular subject. Traditionally, law journals' readership is limited to law libraries and firms that subscribe. By publishing on the Internet, law journals have a markedly larger audience—well beyond the narrow scope of law library visitors.

Another reason is cost: the additional cost to publish data that already exists digitally (almost all law journals today publish with desktop publishing tools) is minimal. With some help from the university's information technology division, the content will be up in no time. And millions more will have the ability to read the articles.

Where is this headed? The grail for those of us in the legal profession is to have low-cost access to quality information. Once more journals publish online, articles that cite to other articles can be hyperlinked to each other. From the practitioner's perspective, this produces a comprehensive look at a particular subject of law. A good example of this is an article published in the *Richmond Journal of Law & Technology* by Professor Greg Sergienko (**http://www.richmond.edu/~jolt/v2i1/sergienko.html**). The article, dealing with constitutional implications of cryptography, cites often to an article by University of Miami professor Michael Froomkin. Professor Froomkin's article was (and still is) available online at an archive at the Massachusetts Institute of Technology (M.I.T.). When Professor Sergienko's article was published in the *Richmond Journal of Law & Technology*, many of the footnotes contained direct links to Professor Froomkin's article at M.I.T.

Some have asked if this won't render services like LEXIS-NEXIS and WESTLAW obsolete. Hardly. While getting the information to "know" about the other related publications is a first step, the most valuable service provided by LEXIS-NEXIS and WESTLAW is their ability to search documents. By making the front-end to all materials (caselaw, legislation, law journals, newspapers, and so on) common, searches by researchers will yield far more accurate results. But combining the search interface of

LEXIS-NEXIS with the flexibility of hyperlinked documents around the Internet is what we want.

Best Meta Sites

FindLaw: Law Journals (**http://www.findlaw.com/lawreviews/**). When looking for a law journal on the Web, your search should start with FindLaw. In addition to providing links to most law reviews, you can search the full text of many law reviews—thanks to a cooperative project sponsored by FindLaw and used by many law school publications.

USC Law Library Law Journals List (**http://www.usc.edu/dept/law-lib/ legal/journals.html**). This is by far the most complete list of law journals on the Internet. It makes no distinction between those that publish online and those that don't, so you might follow a link just to find that the publications lists names and e-mail addresses of the editorial board.

LAW JOURNALS

Across Borders

- *cyberspace:* http://law.gonzaga.edu/borders/borders.html
- *earth place:* WA
- *review: Across Borders* is a practice-oriented international law journal, student-edited by law review standards, and created specifically for World Wide Web publishing. Its goal is to serve as a forum for academics, lawyers, business people, and government officials with an interest in international matters.
- *practice areas:* international, government, corporate, trade

Akron Law Review

- *cyberspace:* http://www.uakron.edu/lawrev/alr.html
- *earth place:* OH
- *review:* The *Akron Law Review* is a student organization of the University of Akron School of Law. Its board of student editors publishes four printed issues per year.

American University Law Review, The

- *cyberspace:* http://www.wcl.american.edu/pub/journals/lawrev/ aulrhome.htm

- *earth place:* DC

- *review:* The *American University Law Review* is both the oldest and the largest journal at the Washington College of Law at American University. In recent years, articles in *The Law Review* have addressed a broad range of topics, including health-care issues, environmental law, land rights in Israel, voting rights in North Carolina, securities law, habeas corpus cases, and many others. Also, *The Law Review* is the only journal in the nation to publish annually an issue dedicated to decisions of the Federal Circuit Court of Appeals regarding patent law, international trade, government contracts, and Native American law.

Berkeley Technology Law Journal

- *cyberspace:* http://server.berkeley.edu/BTLJ/

- *earth place:* CA

- *review:* The *Berkeley Technology Law Journal,* a continuation of the *High Technology Law Journal* effective with volume 11, is edited and published twice each year by the students of Boalt Hall School of Law, University of California at Berkeley.

- *practice areas:* communications, high technology, intellectual property, Internet

Computer Law Review and Technology Journal

- *cyberspace:* http://www.smu.edu/~csr/smuscr.htm

- *earth place:* TX

- *review:* The *Computer Law Review and Technology Journal* is published quarterly at the Southern Methodist School of Law, in cooperation with the Computer Section of the State Bar of Texas.

- *practice areas:* communications, high technology, intellectual property, Internet

Emory University Law Review

- *cyberspace:* http://www.law.emory.edu/EILR/eilrhome.htm

- *earth place:* GA

Federal Communications Law Journal

- *cyberspace:* http://www.law.indiana.edu/fclj/fclj.html

- *earth place:* IN

- *review:* Published by the Indiana University School of Law–Bloomington and the Federal Communications Bar Association.

- *practice areas:* communications, government, high technology

Florida State University Law Review

- *cyberspace:* http://www.law.fsu.edu/lawreview/

- *earth place:* FL

- *review:* The *Florida State University Law Review* first appeared online in June 1995, making the FSU *Law Review* the oldest continuously published print-based general law review online.

Human Rights Brief

- *cyberspace:* http://www.wcl.american.edu/pub/humright/brief/index.htm

- *earth place:* DC

- *review:* The *Human Rights Brief* is an official publication of the Center for Human Rights and Humanitarian Law at Washington College of Law at American University. Its purpose is to report on contemporary human rights and humanitarian law issues and on the various activities of the Center and the WCL community.

- *practice areas:* constitutional, immigration, international

Intellectual Property and Technology Forum

- *cyberspace:* http://infoeagle.bc.edu/bc_org/avp/law/st_org/ipg/iptf/

- *earth place:* MA

- *review:* The *Intellectual Property and Technology Forum* at Boston College Law School is a legal publication dedicated to providing readers with rigorous, innovative scholarship, timely reporting, and ongoing discussion from the legal community concerning technology law and intellectual property.

- *practice areas:* high technology, intellectual property

TheList.Com
An early example of how the Internet could empower consumers. (A much more visible example would come a few years later when Intel tried to deny the rumors of a Pentium bug.) TheList's raison d'etre is pretty simple: Catalog all the ISPs in the country so that when someone needs Internet access, they go to TheList, enter their area code, and get a list of who provides service in that area. For a while, the purveyors of TheList allowed users to rate their ISP—until they realized that competitors were simply telling everyone else how bad their competition was. TheList is now a service of MecklerMedia, the same folks who publish *Internet World.*

Journal of Technology Law & Policy

- *cyberspace:* http://grove.ufl.edu/~techlaw/
- *earth place:* FL
- *review:* The *Journal of Technology Law & Policy* was founded in the spring of 1995 at the University of Florida College of Law. The *Journal* publishes articles concerning legal issues in technology as well as policy.
- *practice areas:* communications, high technology, intellectual property, Internet

Mercer Law Review

- *cyberspace:* http://review.law.mercer.edu
- *earth place:* GA
- *review:* The *Mercer Law Review* is edited and published by the students of the Walter F. George School of Law of Mercer University. *Mercer Law Review* was founded in 1949 and is the oldest continually published law review in Georgia.

Michigan Telecommunications & Technology Law Review

- *cyberspace:* http://www.law.umich.edu/mttlr/
- *earth place:* MI
- *review:* The *Michigan Telecommunications & Technology Law Review* is a scholarly journal published jointly by The University of Michigan Law School and The University of Michigan Business School.
- *practice areas:* communications, high technology

National Journal of Sexual Orientation Law

- *cyberspace:* http://sunsite.unc.edu/gaylaw/
- *earth place:* NC
- *review:* The *Journal's* primary purpose is to disseminate information and ideas about law and sexual orientation in an efficient and timely manner. The *Journal* specializes in reports and studies germane to gay and lesbian legal issues, transcriptions of proceedings, panels and programs, briefs filed by litigators around the country in key cases, and essays, student work, and other forms of traditional law review scholarship.
- *practice areas:* constitutional, government

On-line Journal of Ethics, The

- *cyberspace:* http://depaul.edu/ethics/ethg1.html

- *earth place:* IL

- *review:* The *On-line Journal of Ethics* explores both theoretical and applied ethical issues involved in the practice of business and the professions. The journal publishes papers that address pressing ethical issues in a more topical fashion.

- *practice areas:* ethics and professional responsibility

Richmond Journal of Law & Technology

- *cyberspace:* http://www.richmond.edu/~jolt/

- *earth place:* VA

- *review:* The *Richmond Journal of Law & Technology* is the oldest United States law review to be published exclusively online. First published on April 10, 1995, the *Journal* focuses on the impact that computer-related and emerging technologies have on the law.

- *practice areas:* communications, high technology, intellectual property, Internet

Stanford Technology Law Review

- *cyberspace:* http://stlr.stanford.edu

- *earth place:* CA

- *review:* Founded in 1997, the *Stanford Technology Law Review* is an innovative forum for intellectual discourse on critical issues at the intersection of law, science, technology, and public policy.

- *practice areas:* communications, high technology, intellectual property, Internet

UCLA Bulletin of Law & Technology

- *cyberspace:* http://www.law.ucla.edu/Student/Organizations/BLT/

- *earth place:* CA

- *review:* The *Bulletin of Law & Technology* is an online journal dedicated to publishing timely and relevant materials addressing the law's attempts to keep pace with the ever-expanding horizon of technological innovation. These materials include traditional scholarly articles and comments, practical advice and "heads-ups" from lawyers broaching the cutting edge, and links to other sites on the World Wide Web that are tackling similar issues.

- *practice areas:* high technology, communications, intellectual property, Internet

Villanova Environmental Law Journal

- *cyberspace:* http://vls.law.vill.edu/students/orgs/elj/
- *earth place:* PA
- *review:* The *Villanova Environmental Law Journal* seeks to publish material representing meritorious viewpoints on subjects of interest to the legal community.
- *practice areas:* environmental

Virginia Journal of Law and Technology

- *cyberspace:* http://scs.student.virginia.edu/~vjolt/
- *earth place:* VA
- *practice areas:* communications, high technology, Internet, intellectual property

West Virginia Journal of Law and Technology

- *cyberspace:* http://www.wvjolt.wvu.edu
- *earth place:* WV
- *practice areas:* communications, government, high technology, intellectual property, Internet

CHAPTER**SEVEN**

ABA-Approved Law Schools

Overview

There are 178 law schools listed below. For this list, we relied on the American Bar Association's list of Accredited Law Schools at **http:// www.abanet.org/legaled/approved.html**. In almost all cases, the law schools have a domain name (or, more accurately, the university to which the law school belongs has a domain name). There is no standard for law school URLs, though we would like to see one. For example, above all, URLs should be memorable. And how memorable can **http://www.school.edu/ depts/grad/law/law.html** really be? A simple solution to this would be to give the law school a machine name—like **law.school.edu**. Not only does this make finding the law school's Web site incredibly easy, but it also gives the law school system administrator an easy way to administer law school-only e-mail. (Instead of **email@school.edu**, students can now have addresses **email@law.school.edu**—a better solution.)

Reviews of most of the schools are not included here, primarily because they aren't necessary. While we wanted to know if the schools have a Web presence (or, in rare cases, their own domain name), the content of these sites is less important. Most schools are only interested in telling interested applicants about the school, and in some cases, in providing biographical information about the faculty. Some schools are top-tier information providers (Cornell, Emory, Villanova), and we've included reviews about their sites. While we'd like to see more schools follow the lead of these early adopters, we don't expect law schools to lead the profession forward in using the Internet.

For those schools that don't have access to the kind of original material that Cornell et al. have, there are at least a few basics that ought to be found on the Web site. First, give interested students contact information. Let them send you e-mail if they want more information. Give them a phone number if they want to request a catalog (why not let them apply online?). Perhaps visitors are looking for a friend who's enrolled at the law school; a directory of students would be helpful so that people can browse for the friend's e-mail addresses. The course catalog should be online so applicants can see what classes are available, and faculty biographies should be easily accessible.

Best Meta Sites

ABA-Approved Law Schools (http://www.abanet.org/legaled/approved.html) lists every law school that is accredited by the American Bar Association Accreditation Committee. Lists are prepared alphabetically, by region, state, and type (public or private).

FindLaw List of Law Schools (http://www.findlaw.com/02lawschools/) provides a full list of law schools (including those not accredited by the ABA), as well as links to the *U.S. News & World Report* Top 25 law schools, international law schools, and other rankings of law schools.

Yahoo Law Schools (http://www.yahoo.com/Government/Law/Law_Schools/) lists 236 law schools (fifty-six more than the ABA) as of this writing.

Visionaries

Akron, University of (uakron.edu)
Alabama, University of (ua.edu)
American University (american.edu)
Arizona State University (asu.edu)
Arizona, University of (arizona.edu)
Arkansas, Fayetteville, University of (uark.edu)
Arkansas, Little Rock, The University of (ualr.edu)
Baylor University (baylor.edu)
Boston College (bc.edu)
Boston University (bu.edu)
Brigham Young University (byu.edu)
California, Berkeley, University of (berkeley.edu)
California, Davis, University of (ucdavis.edu)
California, Los Angeles, University of (ucla.edu)
Campbell University (campbell.edu)
Capital University (capital.edu)
Case Western Reserve University (cwru.edu)

Catholic University of America, The (cua.edu)
Chicago, University of (uchicago.edu)
Chicago-Kent College of Law (kentlaw.edu)
Cincinnati, University of (uc.edu)
City University of New York (cuny.edu)
Cleveland State University (csuohio.edu)
Colorado, University of (colorado.edu)
Columbia University (columbia.edu)
Connecticut, University of (uconn.edu)
Cornell University (cornell.edu)
Creighton University (creighton.edu)
Dayton, University of (udayton.edu)
Denver, University of (du.edu)
DePaul University (depaul.edu)
Drake University (drake.edu)
Duke University (duke.edu)
Duquesne University (duq.edu)
Emory University (emory.edu)
Florida State University (fsu.edu)
Florida, University of (ufl.edu)
Fordham University (fordham.edu)
George Mason University (gmu.edu)
George Washington University
    (gwu.edu)
Georgetown University
    (georgetown.edu)
Georgia State University (gsu.edu)
Georgia, University of (uga.edu)
Gonzaga University (gonzaga.edu)
Hamline University (hamline.edu)
Harvard University (harvard.edu)
Hawaii, University of (hawaii.edu)
Hofstra University (hofstra.edu)
Houston, University of (uh.edu)
Howard University (howard.edu)
Idaho, University of (uidaho.edu)
Illinois, Urbana–Champaign,
    University of (uiuc.edu)
Indiana University (indiana.edu)
Indiana University–Purdue University
    at Indianapolis (iupui.edu)
Iowa, University of (uiowa.edu)

▼▼▼▼▼

thesaurus
Suppose you don't need to know what a word means, but you're looking for an alternate word to use. What's another word for thesaurus? How about WordNet (http://www .cogsci.princeton.edu/~wn/), a thesaurus-like research tool from Princeton University. Because it's interactive, it does more than a thesaurus, and the algorithm was designed to give you synonyms for related concepts and for related words. The database is nearly 20 megabytes, which is much larger than your everyday thesaurus. WordNet also runs as a stand-alone program and is available in various flavors (UNIX, Windows, MacOS). For more information, see ftp://clarity.princeton.edu/pub/ wordnet/README or send e-mail to wordnet @princeton.edu. An older, and a bit more clunky, interface to a thesaurus is also available from the National Institute of Health (gopher:// odie.niaid.nih.gov/77/.thesaurus/index).

thin client
See **network computer.**

John Marshall Law School, The (jmls.edu)
Kansas, University of (ukans.edu)
Kentucky, University of (uky.edu)
Lewis & Clark College (lclark.edu)
Louisiana State University (lsu.edu)
Louisville, University of (louisville.edu)
Loyola Marymount University (lmu.edu)
Loyola University (loyno.edu)
Loyola University Chicago (luc.edu)
Maine, University of (maine.edu)
Marquette University (mu.edu)
Maryland, University of (umd.edu)
Miami, University of (miami.edu)
Michigan, ITD, University of (umich.edu)
Minnesota, University of (umn.edu)
Mississippi, University of (olemiss.edu)
Missouri, Columbia, University of (missouri.edu)
Missouri, Kansas City, University of (umkc.edu)
Montana, University of (umt.edu)
Nebraska, Lincoln, University of (unl.edu)
New Mexico, University of (unm.edu)
New York University (nyu.edu)
North Carolina Central University (nccu.edu)
North Carolina, Chapel Hill, University of (unc.edu)
North Dakota, University of (nodak.edu)
Northeastern University (northeastern.edu)
Northern Illinois University (niu.edu)
Northwestern University (nwu.edu)
Notre Dame, University of (nd.edu)
Nova Southeastern University (nova.edu)
Ohio Northern University (onu.edu)
Ohio State University (ohio-state.edu)
Oklahoma, The University of (uoknor.edu)
Oregon, University of (uoregon.edu)
Pace University (pace.edu)
Pacific, University of the (uop.edu)
Pennsylvania, University of (upenn.edu)
Pepperdine University (pepperdine.edu)
Pittsburgh, University of (pitt.edu)
Puerto Rico, University of (cun.edu)
Richmond, University of (urich.edu)

Rutgers University (rutgers.edu)
Rutgers University, Newark (rutgers.edu)
San Diego, University of (acusd.edu)
San Francisco, University of (usfca.edu)
Santa Clara University (scu.edu)
Seattle University (seattleu.edu)
Seton Hall University (shu.edu)
South Carolina, University of (scarolina.edu)
South Dakota, University of (usd.edu)
Southern California, University of (usc.edu)
Southern Illinois University (siu.edu)
Southern Methodist University (smu.edu)
Southern University (subr.edu)
St. John's University (stjohns.edu)
St. Louis University (slu.edu)
St. Mary's University (stmarytx.edu)
Stanford University (stanford.edu)
Syracuse University (syr.edu)
Temple University (temple.edu)
Tennessee, University of (utk.edu)
Texas, Austin, University of (utexas.edu)
Texas Tech University School of Law (ttu.edu)
Toledo, University of (utoledo.edu)
Tulane University (tulane.edu)
Tulsa, University of (utulsa.edu)
Utah, University of (utah.edu)
Valparaiso University (valpo.edu)
Vanderbilt University (vanderbilt.edu)
Villanova University (vill.edu)
Virginia, University of (virginia.edu)
Wake Forest University (wfu.edu)
Washington & Lee University (wlu.edu)
Washington University (wustl.edu)
Washington, University of (washington.edu)
Wayne State University (wayne.edu)
West Virginia University (wvu.edu)
Widener University (widener.edu)
Willamette University (willamette.edu)
William & Mary, The College of (wm.edu)
Wisconsin, University of (wisc.edu)
Wyoming, University of (uwyo.edu)

Yale University (yale.edu)
Yeshiva University c/o Albert Einstein College of Medicine (yu.edu)

Early Adopters
Baltimore, University of (ubalt.edu)
Brooklyn Law School (brooklaw.edu)
California Western School of Law (cwsl.edu)
Detroit College of Law (dcl.edu)
Detroit–Mercy, University of (udmercy.edu)
Dickinson School of Law, The (dsl.edu)
Franklin Pierce Law Center (fplc.edu)
Golden Gate University (ggu.edu)
Hastings College of the Law, University of California (uchastings.edu)
Inter American University of Puerto Rico (inter.edu)
Memphis, The University of (memphis.edu)
Mississippi College (mc.edu)
New England School of Law (nesl.edu)
Northern Kentucky University (nku.edu)
Oklahoma City University (okcu.edu)
Quinnipiac College (quinnipiac.edu)
Regent University (regent.edu)
Samford University (samford.edu)
South Texas College of Law (stcl.edu)
St. Thomas University (stthom.edu)
Stetson University (stetson.edu)
Vermont Law School (vermontlaw.edu)
Western New England College (wnec.edu)
Whittier College (whittier.edu)
William Mitchell College of Law (wmitchell.edu)

Middlers
Albany Law School of Union University (als.edu)
Mercer University (mercer.edu)
New York at Buffalo, State University of (buffalo.edu)
Suffolk University (suffolk.edu)
Texas Southern University Law School (tsulaw.edu)
Thomas Cooley Law School, The (cooley.edu)
Touro Law Center (tourolaw.edu)

Late Adopters
New York Law School (nyls.edu)
Pontificia Universidad Catolica de Puerto Rico (pucpr.edu)

Southwestern University School of Law (**swlaw.edu**)
Texas Wesleyan University (**txwesleyan.edu**)
Thomas Jefferson School of Law (**jeffersonlaw.edu**)
Washburn University School of Law (**washlaw.edu**)

LAW SCHOOLS

Akron, University of
- *cyberspace:* uakron.edu
- *earth place:* Akron, OH
- *born on:* 01 Oct 1988 (visionary)

Alabama, University of
- *cyberspace:* ua.edu
- *earth place:* Tuscaloosa, AL
- *born on:* 12 May 1988 (visionary)

Albany Law School of Union University
- *cyberspace:* als.edu
- *earth place:* Albany, NY
- *born on:* 24 Aug 1995 (middler)

American University
- *cyberspace:* american.edu
- *earth place:* Washington, DC
- *born on:* 03 Jun 1991 (visionary)

Arizona State University
- *cyberspace:* asu.edu
- *earth place:* Tempe, AZ
- *born on:* 27 Jul 1987 (visionary)

Arizona, University of
- *cyberspace:* arizona.edu
- *earth place:* Tucson, AZ
- *born on:* 23 Jan 1986 (visionary)

unified messaging
The concept of having one inbox for all of your incoming messages—not just e-mail, fax, and voice, but video, pager messages, and anything else you can think of—is called universal messaging, and it is starting to catch on. And the inbox doesn't have to be an e-mail inbox. Truly universal messaging also has a voicemail interface.

Arkansas, Fayetteville, University of

- *cyberspace:* uark.edu
- *earth place:* Fayetteville, AR
- *born on:* 31 Aug 1989 (visionary)

Arkansas, Little Rock, The University of

- *cyberspace:* ualr.edu
- *earth place:* Little Rock, AR
- *born on:* 05 Jun 1991 (visionary)

Baltimore, University of

- *cyberspace:* ubalt.edu
- *earth place:* Baltimore, MD
- *born on:* 16 Sep 1993 (early adopter)

Baylor University

- *cyberspace:* baylor.edu
- *earth place:* Waco, TX
- *born on:* 18 May 1989 (visionary)

Boston College

- *cyberspace:* bc.edu
- *earth place:* Chestnut Hill, MA
- *born on:* 01 Feb 1991 (visionary)

Boston University

- *cyberspace:* bu.edu
- *earth place:* Boston, MA
- *born on:* 25 Mar 1986 (visionary)

Brigham Young University

- *cyberspace:* byu.edu
- *earth place:* Provo, UT
- *born on:* 19 Jan 1987 (visionary)

Brooklyn Law School

- *cyberspace:* brooklaw.edu
- *earth place:* Brooklyn, NY
- *born on:* 20 Jun 1994 (early adopter)

California, Berkeley, University of

- *cyberspace:* berkeley.edu
- *earth place:* Berkeley, CA
- *born on:* 24 Apr 1985 (visionary)

California, Davis, University of

- *cyberspace:* ucdavis.edu
- *earth place:* Davis, CA
- *born on:* 19 Mar 1986 (visionary)

California, Los Angeles, University of

- *cyberspace:* ucla.edu
- *earth place:* Los Angeles, CA
- *born on:* 24 Apr 1985 (visionary)

California Western School of Law

- *cyberspace:* cwsl.edu
- *earth place:* San Diego, CA
- *born on:* 22 Aug 1994 (early adopter)

Campbell University

- *cyberspace:* campbell.edu
- *earth place:* Buie's Creek, NC
- *born on:* 17 Jan 1992 (visionary)

Capital University

- *cyberspace:* capital.edu
- *earth place:* Columbus, OH
- *born on:* 21 Sep 1992 (visionary)

Case Western Reserve University

- *cyberspace:* cwru.edu
- *earth place:* Cleveland, OH
- *born on:* 21 Mar 1988 (visionary)

Catholic University of America, The

- *cyberspace:* cua.edu
- *earth place:* Washington, DC
- *born on:* 04 May 1988 (visionary)

Chicago, University of

- *cyberspace:* uchicago.edu
- *earth place:* Chicago, IL
- *born on:* 22 Nov 1991 (visionary)

Chicago-Kent College of Law

- *cyberspace:* kentlaw.edu
- *earth place:* Chicago, IL
- *born on:* 24 Mar 1992 (visionary)
- *review:* The Legal Domain Network alone (searchable archives of law-related listserv lists and Usenet newsgroups) is worth the price of admission! Also contains opinions from the United States Court of Appeals for the Seventh Circuit.

Cincinnati, University of

- *cyberspace:* uc.edu
- *earth place:* Cincinnati, OH
- *born on:* 16 Nov 1987 (visionary)

City University of New York

- *cyberspace:* cuny.edu
- *earth place:* New York, NY
- *born on:* 22 Apr 1987 (visionary)

Cleveland State University

- *cyberspace:* csuohio.edu
- *earth place:* Cleveland, OH
- *born on:* 08 Dec 1989 (visionary)

Colorado, University of

- *cyberspace:* colorado.edu
- *earth place:* Boulder, CO
- *born on:* 02 Jun 1986 (visionary)

Columbia University

- *cyberspace:* columbia.edu
- *earth place:* New York, NY
- *born on:* 05 Jul 1985 (visionary)

Connecticut, University of

- *cyberspace:* uconn.edu
- *earth place:* Storrs, CT
- *born on:* 18 Aug 1987 (visionary)

Cornell University

- *cyberspace:* cornell.edu
- *earth place:* Ithaca, NY
- *born on:* 15 Jul 1985 (visionary)
- *review:* According to AltaVista, Cornell Law School's Legal Information Institute is linked to by over 33,000 other Web pages and sites! This makes it the king of not only law school Web sites, but all law-related Web sites. Why? Because this site has a wealth of value-added content, most notably U.S. Supreme Court decisions. Like a sock drawer, this site is not particularly well organized, but once you get used to it, you can find what you're looking for.

Creighton University

- *cyberspace:* creighton.edu
- *earth place:* Omaha, NE
- *born on:* 26 Mar 1991 (visionary)

Dayton, University of

- *cyberspace:* udayton.edu
- *earth place:* Dayton, OH
- *born on:* 25 Apr 1989 (visionary)

▼▼▼▼▼

URL
Uniform Resource Locator. The shorthand used to describe various Internet services. URLs are used by Web browsers. The format of a URL is method://machine.domain/directory/file. The URL http://www.abanet.org/lpm/magazine/nbn/home.html means use the HTTP protocol to connect to the Web server in the abanet.org domain (and then download the file home.html from the /lpm/magazine/nbn/ directory).

Denver, University of

- *cyberspace:* du.edu
- *earth place:* Denver, CO
- *born on:* 25 Feb 1988 (visionary)

DePaul University

- *cyberspace:* depaul.edu
- *earth place:* Chicago, IL
- *born on:* 02 Sep 1986 (visionary)

Detroit College of Law

- *cyberspace:* dcl.edu
- *earth place:* Detroit, MI
- *born on:* 30 Jul 1994 (early adopter)

Detroit–Mercy, University of

- *cyberspace:* udmercy.edu
- *earth place:* Detroit, MI
- *born on:* 12 Jan 1993 (early adopter)

Dickinson School of Law, The

- *cyberspace:* dsl.edu
- *earth place:* Carlisle, PA
- *born on:* 26 Oct 1994 (early adopter)

Drake University

- *cyberspace:* drake.edu
- *earth place:* Des Moines, IA
- *born on:* 15 Oct 1990 (visionary)

Duke University

- *cyberspace:* duke.edu
- *earth place:* Durham, NC
- *born on:* 02 Jun 1986 (visionary)

Duquesne University

- *cyberspace:* duq.edu
- *earth place:* Pittsburgh, PA
- *born on:* 06 Mar 1991 (visionary)

Emory University

- *cyberspace:* emory.edu
- *earth place:* Atlanta, GA
- *born on:* 02 Jun 1986 (visionary)
- *review:* The presentation of this Web site (that is, the integration of text and graphic elements) is by far the best of the ten reviewed sites. While you are there, be sure to check out the Electronic Reference Desk and the U.S. Federal Courts Finder (complete with a clickable map of the United States).

Florida State University

- *cyberspace:* fsu.edu
- *earth place:* Tallahassee, FL
- *born on:* 24 Nov 1987 (visionary)
- *review:* This site's online catalog is a great example of how the Web can be used to help people find what they are looking for quickly and easily. The site is very well organized, and most resources can be accessed directly from the home page.

Florida, University of

- *cyberspace:* ufl.edu
- *earth place:* Gainesville, FL
- *born on:* 25 Mar 1986 (visionary)

Fordham University

- *cyberspace:* fordham.edu
- *earth place:* New York, NY
- *born on:* 05 Jun 1991 (visionary)

Franklin Pierce Law Center

- *cyberspace:* fplc.edu
- *earth place:* Concord, NH
- *born on:* 06 Dec 1994 (early adopter)

George Mason University

- *cyberspace:* gmu.edu
- *earth place:* Fairfax, VA
- *born on:* 14 Oct 1987 (visionary)

George Washington University

- *cyberspace:* gwu.edu
- *earth place:* Washington, DC
- *born on:* 23 Dec 1987 (visionary)

Georgetown University

- *cyberspace:* georgetown.edu
- *earth place:* Washington, DC
- *born on:* 05 Nov 1986 (visionary)

Georgia State University

- *cyberspace:* gsu.edu
- *earth place:* Atlanta, GA
- *born on:* 25 Jun 1990 (visionary)

Georgia, University of

- *cyberspace:* uga.edu
- *earth place:* Athens, GA
- *born on:* 14 Mar 1988 (visionary)

Golden Gate University

- *cyberspace:* ggu.edu
- *earth place:* San Francisco, CA
- *born on:* 05 May 1994 (early adopter)

Gonzaga University

- *cyberspace:* gonzaga.edu
- *earth place:* Spokane, WA
- *born on:* 22 May 1992 (visionary)

Hamline University

- *cyberspace:* hamline.edu
- *earth place:* St. Paul, MN
- *born on:* 01 Dec 1989 (visionary)

Harvard University

- *cyberspace:* harvard.edu
- *earth place:* Cambridge, MA
- *born on:* 27 Jun 1985 (visionary)

Hastings College of the Law, University of California

- *cyberspace:* uchastings.edu
- *earth place:* San Francisco, CA
- *born on:* 22 Jan 1993 (early adopter)

Hawaii, University of

- *cyberspace:* hawaii.edu
- *earth place:* Honolulu, HI
- *born on:* 27 Oct 1986 (visionary)

Hofstra University

- *cyberspace:* hofstra.edu
- *earth place:* Hempstead, NY
- *born on:* 20 Mar 1991 (visionary)

Houston, University of

- *cyberspace:* uh.edu
- *earth place:* Houston, TX
- *born on:* 21 Oct 1987 (visionary)

Howard University

- *cyberspace:* howard.edu
- *earth place:* Washington, DC
- *born on:* 06 Jul 1990 (visionary)

Idaho, University of

- *cyberspace:* uidaho.edu
- *earth place:* Moscow, ID
- *born on:* 12 Jun 1988 (visionary)

▼▼▼▼▼

URL Minder (http://www.netmind.com/)
Here's a service destined to simplify your web browsing. Type in a URL that you visit often, and URL Minder will send you an e-mail when the site is changed in any way. Now you don't need to stop by repeatedly and be disappointed by the same page you saw last week. URL Minder will just tell you when you need to visit.

Illinois, Urbana–Champaign, University of

- *cyberspace:* uiuc.edu
- *earth place:* Urbana, IL
- *born on:* 18 Jul 1985 (visionary)

Indiana University

- *cyberspace:* indiana.edu
- *earth place:* Bloomington, IN
- *born on:* 03 Mar 1986 (visionary)

Indiana University–Purdue University at Indianapolis

- *cyberspace:* iupui.edu
- *earth place:* Indianapolis, IN
- *born on:* 22 Jun 1989 (visionary)

Inter American University of Puerto Rico

- *cyberspace:* inter.edu
- *earth place:* San Juan, PR
- *born on:* 30 Sep 1994 (early adopter)

Iowa, University of

- *cyberspace:* uiowa.edu
- *earth place:* Iowa City, IA
- *born on:* 30 Mar 1988 (visionary)

John Marshall Law School, The

- *cyberspace:* jmls.edu
- *earth place:* Chicago, IL
- *born on:* 27 Aug 1992 (visionary)

Kansas, University of

- *cyberspace:* ukans.edu
- *earth place:* Lawrence, KS
- *born on:* 17 Jun 1986 (visionary)

Kentucky, University of

- *cyberspace:* uky.edu
- *earth place:* Lexington, KY
- *born on:* 27 May 1987 (visionary)

Lewis & Clark College

- *cyberspace:* lclark.edu
- *earth place:* Portland, OR
- *born on:* 13 Jun 1991 (visionary)

Louisiana State University

- *cyberspace:* lsu.edu
- *earth place:* Baton Rouge, LA
- *born on:* 19 Jan 1987 (visionary)

Louisville, University of

- *cyberspace:* louisville.edu
- *earth place:* Louisville, KY
- *born on:* 11 Sep 1989 (visionary)

Loyola Marymount University

- *cyberspace:* lmu.edu
- *earth place:* Los Angeles, CA
- *born on:* 23 Nov 1992 (visionary)

Loyola University

- *cyberspace:* loyno.edu
- *earth place:* New Orleans, LA
- *born on:* 18 Sep 1990 (visionary)

Loyola University Chicago

- *cyberspace:* luc.edu
- *earth place:* Chicago, IL
- *born on:* 22 Jul 1991 (visionary)

Maine, University of

- *cyberspace:* maine.edu
- *earth place:* Orono, ME
- *born on:* 02 Dec 1988 (visionary)

Marquette University

- *cyberspace:* mu.edu
- *earth place:* Milwaukee, WI
- *born on:* 04 Mar 1987 (visionary)

Maryland, University of

- *cyberspace:* umd.edu
- *earth place:* College Park, MD
- *born on:* 31 Jul 1985 (visionary)

Memphis, The University of

- *cyberspace:* memphis.edu
- *earth place:* Memphis, TN
- *born on:* 09 Mar 1994 (early adopter)

Mercer University

- *cyberspace:* mercer.edu
- *earth place:* Macon, GA
- *born on:* 06 Feb 1995 (middler)

Miami, University of

- *cyberspace:* miami.edu
- *earth place:* Miami, FL
- *born on:* 23 Jul 1987 (visionary)

Michigan, ITD, University of

- *cyberspace:* umich.edu
- *earth place:* Ann Arbor, MI
- *born on:* 07 Oct 1985 (visionary)

Minnesota, University of

- *cyberspace:* umn.edu
- *earth place:* Minneapolis, MN
- *born on:* 21 Jan 1987 (visionary)

Mississippi College

- *cyberspace:* mc.edu
- *earth place:* Clinton, MS
- *born on:* 21 Jul 1993 (early adopter)

Mississippi, University of

- *cyberspace:* olemiss.edu
- *earth place:* University, MS
- *born on:* 19 Oct 1988 (visionary)

Missouri, Columbia, University of

- *cyberspace:* missouri.edu
- *earth place:* Columbia, MO
- *born on:* 22 Dec 1987 (visionary)

Missouri, Kansas City, University of

- *cyberspace:* umkc.edu
- *earth place:* Kansas City, MO
- *born on:* 11 Sep 1989 (visionary)

Montana, University of

- *cyberspace:* umt.edu
- *earth place:* Missoula, MT
- *born on:* 19 Sep 1990 (visionary)

Nebraska, Lincoln, University of

- *cyberspace:* unl.edu
- *earth place:* Lincoln, NE
- *born on:* 28 Jul 1987 (visionary)

▼▼▼▼▼

Usenet

A waste of time. Back when there weren't millions (billions, according to Jupiter Communications) of Internet users, Usenet worked as a concept. The idea is to have a hierarchical division of topics for anyone to post questions or answers. Long ago, people actually read messages posted on Usenet as if they were e-mail messages. Today, you could get every citizen in New York reading them and you'd never keep up. Thanks to services like DejaNews, Usenet is marginally useful, as you can now search archives of all Usenet posts for your question. See **misc.legal.moderated.**

New England School of Law

- *cyberspace:* nesl.edu
- *earth place:* Boston, MA
- *born on:* 24 Aug 1994 (early adopter)

New Mexico, University of

- *cyberspace:* unm.edu
- *earth place:* Albuquerque, NM
- *born on:* 27 Aug 1986 (visionary)

New York at Buffalo, State University of

- *cyberspace:* buffalo.edu
- *earth place:* Buffalo, NY
- *born on:* 15 Jun 1995 (middler)

New York Law School

- *cyberspace:* nyls.edu
- *earth place:* New York, NY
- *born on:* 19 Jun 1996 (late adopter)

New York University

- *cyberspace:* nyu.edu
- *earth place:* New York, NY
- *born on:* 08 Oct 1986 (visionary)

North Carolina Central University

- *cyberspace:* nccu.edu
- *earth place:* Durham, NC
- *born on:* 18 May 1990 (visionary)

North Carolina, Chapel Hill, University of

- *cyberspace:* unc.edu
- *earth place:* Chapel Hill, NC
- *born on:* 17 Jun 1986 (visionary)

North Dakota, University of

- *cyberspace:* nodak.edu
- *earth place:* Fargo, ND
- *born on:* 15 Jul 1988 (visionary)

Northeastern University

- *cyberspace:* northeastern.edu
- *earth place:* Boston, MA
- *born on:* 25 Mar 1986 (visionary)

Northern Illinois University

- *cyberspace:* niu.edu
- *earth place:* DeKalb, IL
- *born on:* 08 Dec 1988 (visionary)

Northern Kentucky University

- *cyberspace:* nku.edu
- *earth place:* Highland Heights, KY
- *born on:* 12 Jul 1994 (early adopter)

Northwestern University

- *cyberspace:* nwu.edu
- *earth place:* Evanston, IL
- *born on:* 22 Jan 1987 (visionary)

Notre Dame, University of

- *cyberspace:* nd.edu
- *earth place:* Notre Dame, IN
- *born on:* 07 Jul 1988 (visionary)

Nova Southeastern University

- *cyberspace:* nova.edu
- *earth place:* Fort Lauderdale, FL
- *born on:* 19 Mar 1990 (visionary)

Ohio Northern University

- *cyberspace:* onu.edu
- *earth place:* Ada, OH
- *born on:* 14 Jun 1990 (visionary)
- *review:* This site's conservative use of graphics and simple design make it a pleasure to navigate.

Ohio State University

- *cyberspace:* ohio-state.edu
- *earth place:* Columbus, OH
- *born on:* 18 Aug 1987 (visionary)

Oklahoma City University

- *cyberspace:* okcu.edu
- *earth place:* Oklahoma City, OK
- *born on:* 29 Jul 1993 (early adopter)

Oklahoma, The University of

- *cyberspace:* uoknor.edu
- *earth place:* Norman, OK
- *born on:* 14 Dec 1987 (visionary)

Oregon, University of

- *cyberspace:* uoregon.edu
- *earth place:* Eugene, OR
- *born on:* 23 Feb 1988 (visionary)

Pace University

- *cyberspace:* pace.edu
- *earth place:* Pleasantville, NY
- *born on:* 22 Oct 1992 (visionary)

Pacific, University of the

- *cyberspace:* uop.edu
- *earth place:* Stockton, CA
- *born on:* 03 Sep 1987 (visionary)

Pennsylvania, University of

- *cyberspace:* upenn.edu
- *earth place:* Philadelphia, PA
- *born on:* 02 Jun 1986 (visionary)

Pepperdine University

- *cyberspace:* pepperdine.edu
- *earth place:* Malibu, CA
- *born on:* 17 Jan 1989 (visionary)

Pittsburgh, University of

- *cyberspace:* pitt.edu
- *earth place:* Pittsburgh, PA
- *born on:* 21 Jun 1989 (visionary)

Pontificia Universidad Catolica de Puerto Rico

- *cyberspace:* pucpr.edu
- *earth place:* Ponce, PR
- *born on:* 07 Sep 1996 (late adopter)

Puerto Rico, University of

- *cyberspace:* cun.edu
- *earth place:* San Juan, PR
- *born on:* 25 Aug 1988 (visionary)

Quinnipiac College

- *cyberspace:* quinnipiac.edu
- *earth place:* Hamden, CT
- *born on:* 17 Dec 1994 (early adopter)

Regent University

- *cyberspace:* regent.edu
- *earth place:* Virginia Beach, VA
- *born on:* 23 Jun 1993 (early adopter)

▼▼▼▼▼

USPS Zip Code Finder
(http://www.usps.gov/ncsc/)
You may not realize how often you need to find a zip code until you start using this site. By entering in a street address, the city, and state, this Web site will give you the nine-digit zip code.

Richmond, University of

- *cyberspace:* urich.edu
- *earth place:* Richmond, VA
- *born on:* 05 Jan 1989 (visionary)

Rutgers University

- *cyberspace:* rutgers.edu
- *earth place:* Piscataway, NJ
- *born on:* 25 Apr 1985 (visionary)

Rutgers University, Newark

- *cyberspace:* rutgers.edu
- *earth place:* Newark, NJ
- *born on:* 25 Apr 1985 (visionary)

Samford University

- *cyberspace:* samford.edu
- *earth place:* Birmingham, AL
- *born on:* 05 Dec 1993 (early adopter)

San Diego, University of

- *cyberspace:* acusd.edu
- *earth place:* San Diego, CA
- *born on:* 12 Jul 1989 (visionary)

San Francisco, University of

- *cyberspace:* usfca.edu
- *earth place:* San Francisco, CA
- *born on:* 02 Nov 1990 (visionary)

Santa Clara University

- *cyberspace:* scu.edu
- *earth place:* Santa Clara, CA
- *born on:* 19 Feb 1989 (visionary)

Seattle University

- *cyberspace:* seattleu.edu
- *earth place:* Seattle, WA
- *born on:* 19 Jul 1990 (visionary)

Seton Hall University

- *cyberspace:* shu.edu
- *earth place:* South Orange, NJ
- *born on:* 02 May 1991 (visionary)

South Carolina, University of

- *cyberspace:* scarolina.edu
- *earth place:* Columbia, SC
- *born on:* 27 Oct 1986 (visionary)

South Dakota, University of

- *cyberspace:* usd.edu
- *earth place:* Vermillion, SD
- *born on:* 10 Jul 1986 (visionary)

South Texas College of Law

- *cyberspace:* stcl.edu
- *earth place:* Houston, TX
- *born on:* 15 Aug 1994 (early adopter)

Southern California, University of

- *cyberspace:* usc.edu
- *earth place:* Los Angeles, CA
- *born on:* 20 Aug 1985 (visionary)
- *review:* This site is very well organized and has everything from law student Web pages to links to legal resources on the Internet. Its simple and functional design makes it easy to find what you're looking for.

Southern Illinois University

- *cyberspace:* siu.edu
- *earth place:* Carbondale, IL
- *born on:* 27 Jan 1989 (visionary)

Southern Methodist University

- *cyberspace:* smu.edu
- *earth place:* Dallas, TX
- *born on:* 31 Aug 1987 (visionary)

Southern University

- *cyberspace:* subr.edu
- *earth place:* Baton Rouge, LA
- *born on:* 06 Aug 1992 (visionary)

Southwestern University School of Law

- *cyberspace:* swlaw.edu
- *earth place:* Los Angeles, CA
- *born on:* 19 Apr 1996 (late adopter)

St. John's University

- *cyberspace:* stjohns.edu
- *earth place:* Jamaica, NY
- *born on:* 23 Sep 1991 (visionary)

St. Louis University

- *cyberspace:* slu.edu
- *earth place:* St. Louis, MO
- *born on:* 13 Apr 1989 (visionary)
- *review:* Jim Milles's list of recommended law-related Internet resources ("Law on the Web") is an excellent starting point. Be sure to browse the compilation of Internet training materials (under "SLU Law Internet Resources").

St. Mary's University

- *cyberspace:* stmarytx.edu
- *earth place:* San Antonio, TX
- *born on:* 16 Oct 1990 (visionary)

St. Thomas University

- *cyberspace:* stthom.edu
- *earth place:* Houston, TX
- *born on:* 25 May 1994 (early adopter)

Stanford University

- *cyberspace:* stanford.edu
- *earth place:* Stanford, CA
- *born on:* 04 Oct 1985 (visionary)

Stetson University

- *cyberspace:* stetson.edu
- *earth place:* DeLand, FL
- *born on:* 13 Jul 1993 (early adopter)

Suffolk University

- *cyberspace:* suffolk.edu
- *earth place:* Boston, MA
- *born on:* 01 Aug 1995 (middler)

Syracuse University

- *cyberspace:* syr.edu
- *earth place:* Syracuse, NY
- *born on:* 02 Sep 1986 (visionary)

Temple University

- *cyberspace:* temple.edu
- *earth place:* Philadelphia, PA
- *born on:* 27 May 1987 (visionary)

Tennessee, University of

- *cyberspace:* utk.edu
- *earth place:* Knoxville, TN
- *born on:* 04 Jun 1987 (visionary)

Texas, Austin, University of

- *cyberspace:* utexas.edu
- *earth place:* Austin, TX
- *born on:* 13 Aug 1985 (visionary)

Texas Southern University Law School

- *cyberspace:* tsulaw.edu
- *earth place:* Houston, TX
- *born on:* 30 Jun 1995 (middler)

Texas Tech University School of Law

- *cyberspace:* ttu.edu
- *earth place:* Lubbock, TX
- *born on:* 16 Sep 1988 (visionary)

▼▼▼▼▼

WAIS

Pronounced "ways," it stands for Wide Area Information Servers. WAIS is a networked full-text information retrieval system developed by Thinking Machines, Apple Computer, and Dow Jones. WAIS was designed to be a high-tech solution to distributed information retrieval. WAIS-enthusiasts originally disliked the Web (and many purists still do), where competing standards (for example, HTML) abound. But the Web is also *the* distributed information tool of choice on the Net today. So while WAIS clients and servers still exist, WAIS has been relegated to a lesser role: indexing the full text of local Web sites. As such, WAIS became the first of the Internet search engines. Other commercial search engines now compete with WAIS for this market, including Excite for Web Servers, Verity Topic Server, and Infoseek. For more information on WAIS, see the Web site of Thinking Machines Corporation (http://www.think.com/).

Texas Wesleyan University

- *cyberspace:* txwesleyan.edu
- *earth place:* Fort Worth, TX
- *born on:* 02 Jul 1996 (late adopter)

Thomas Cooley Law School, The

- *cyberspace:* cooley.edu
- *earth place:* Lansing, MI
- *born on:* 28 Dec 1995 (middler)
- *review:* Not to be confused with Cooley Godward, L.L.P. (**cooley.edu**).

Thomas Jefferson School Of Law

- *cyberspace:* jeffersonlaw.edu
- *earth place:* San Diego, CA
- *born on:* 17 Oct 1996 (late adopter)

Toledo, University of

- *cyberspace:* utoledo.edu
- *earth place:* Toledo, OH
- *born on:* 14 Dec 1988 (visionary)

Touro Law Center

- *cyberspace:* tourolaw.edu
- *earth place:* Huntington, NY
- *born on:* 15 Aug 1995 (middler)

Tulane University

- *cyberspace:* tulane.edu
- *earth place:* New Orleans, LA
- *born on:* 14 Apr 1987 (visionary)

Tulsa, University of

- *cyberspace:* utulsa.edu
- *earth place:* Tulsa, OK
- *born on:* 22 Apr 1988 (visionary)

Utah, University of

- *cyberspace:* utah.edu
- *earth place:* Salt Lake City, UT
- *born on:* 16 Dec 1986 (visionary)

Valparaiso University

- *cyberspace:* valpo.edu
- *earth place:* Valparaiso, IN
- *born on:* 17 Jun 1992 (visionary)

Vanderbilt University

- *cyberspace:* vanderbilt.edu
- *earth place:* Nashville, TN
- *born on:* 27 Jul 1987 (visionary)

Vermont Law School

- *cyberspace:* vermontlaw.edu
- *earth place:* South Royalton, VT
- *born on:* 01 Nov 1994 (early adopter)

Villanova University

- *cyberspace:* vill.edu
- *earth place:* Villanova, PA
- *born on:* 24 Jul 1990 (visionary)
- *review:* A National Center for Automated Information Research (NCAIR) sponsored institute, the Villanova Center for Information Law and Policy at Villanova Law School contains several key law-related indices, including The Federal Court Locator and The State Court Locator. This site also contains novel projects of interest to the legal/Internet community, such as the Virtual Magistrate project (online dispute resolution).

Virginia, University of

- *cyberspace:* virginia.edu
- *earth place:* Charlottesville, VA
- *born on:* 19 Mar 1986 (visionary)

Wake Forest University

- *cyberspace:* wfu.edu
- *earth place:* Winston-Salem, NC
- *born on:* 03 Mar 1986 (visionary)

Washburn University School of Law

- *cyberspace:* washlaw.edu
- *earth place:* Topeka, KS
- *born on:* 13 Sep 1996 (late adopter)
- *review:* Web-based chat rooms and CU-SeeMe video conferencing are two of the applications available on this Web site. Washburn is also well known in the legal/Internet community for hosting many law-related listserv lists.

Washington & Lee University

- *cyberspace:* wlu.edu
- *earth place:* Lexington, VA
- *born on:* 21 Nov 1989 (visionary)

Washington University

- *cyberspace:* wustl.edu
- *earth place:* St. Louis, MO
- *born on:* 07 Dec 1987 (visionary)
- *review:* Perhaps the most novel application on this site is its online admissions application, which allows prospective students to apply for admission via the Web!

Washington, University of

- *cyberspace:* washington.edu
- *earth place:* Seattle, WA
- *born on:* 04 Sep 1986 (visionary)

Wayne State University

- *cyberspace:* wayne.edu
- *earth place:* Detroit, MI
- *born on:* 29 Jan 1988 (visionary)

West Virginia University

- *cyberspace:* wvu.edu
- *earth place:* Morgantown, WV
- *born on:* 28 May 1992 (visionary)

Western New England College

- *cyberspace:* wnec.edu
- *earth place:* Springfield, MA
- *born on:* 20 Jan 1994 (early adopter)

Whittier College

- *cyberspace:* whittier.edu
- *earth place:* Whittier, CA
- *born on:* 19 Aug 1993 (early adopter)

Widener University

- *cyberspace:* widener.edu
- *earth place:* Chester, PA
- *born on:* 24 Jul 1990 (visionary)

Willamette University

- *cyberspace:* willamette.edu
- *earth place:* Salem, OR
- *born on:* 03 Jun 1991 (visionary)

William & Mary, The College of

- *cyberspace:* wm.edu
- *earth place:* Williamsburg, VA
- *born on:* 19 Oct 1988 (visionary)

William Mitchell College of Law

- *cyberspace:* wmitchell.edu
- *earth place:* St. Paul, MN
- *born on:* 08 Jun 1993 (early adopter)

wire fraud

We don't know what it is, but we know what it's not. Recall the 1994 case against David LaMacchia (http://www-swiss.ai.mit.edu/dldf/dismiss-order.html). LaMacchia was indicted for conspiracy to commit wire fraud in violation of a federal statute, despite the fact that he had not profited from his activities. The federal wire fraud statute was enacted in 1952 to combat wire fraud—the use of the telephone to defraud unsuspecting individuals. LaMacchia was accused of running a computer bulletin board used for uploading (copying to) and downloading (copying from) copyrighted commercial software. LaMacchia apparently was aware that the copying was going on, although he was not accused of any illegal copying. While the federal government had a very good case for saying that Mr. LaMacchia had done some things that are not very nice, it did not have a wire fraud case at all. LaMacchia's motion to dismiss was granted, but he should never have been charged in the first place.

Wisconsin, University of

- *cyberspace:* wisc.edu
- *earth place:* Madison, WI
- *born on:* 30 Sep 1985 (visionary)

Wyoming, University of

- *cyberspace:* uwyo.edu
- *earth place:* Laramie, WY
- *born on:* 21 Jun 1988 (visionary)

Yale University

- *cyberspace:* yale.edu
- *earth place:* New Haven, CT
- *born on:* 17 Mar 1987 (visionary)

Yeshiva University c/o Albert Einstein College of Medicine

- *cyberspace:* yu.edu
- *earth place:* Bronx, NY
- *born on:* 04 Apr 1987 (visionary)

*CHAPTER*EIGHT

State Law Stuff

Overview
All fifty states are listed below, along with the primary domain name for each state. Note that the ".gov" domain is now reserved for the exclusive use of the United States federal government. It didn't always used to be this way. And a few states managed to get their own domain names in the ".gov" hierarchy before the rules were changed.

Best Meta Sites
FindLaw: State Law Resources (http://www.findlaw.com/11stategov/). Each state has their own page here, and the results are a mixed bag. Some states have made a strong push to take advantage of the Web, while others still view it with skepticism. At the very least, FindLaw makes it easy to identify which states are using the Net and which aren't.

Yahoo State Law Resources (http://www.yahoo.com/Government/Law/U_S_States/). We're pretty sure that there are fifty states, but Yahoo has just twenty-six listed here. It's doubtful that this will have much that FindLaw doesn't, but it's not a bad idea to double-check.

States in the ".gov" Domain (and They're All Visionaries)[1]
California (ca.gov)
Hawaii (hawaii.gov)
Montana (mt.gov)
Ohio (ohio.gov)
Texas (texas.gov)

---

1. These states registered ".gov" domain names before the ".gov" top-level domain was reserved for the exclusive use of the U.S. federal government.

STATES

Alabama

- *cyberspace:* state.al.us
- *earth place:* AL
- *review:* Official sources of law that are linked to from this site include ALALINC (http://www.alalinc.net/).
- *practice areas:* Alabama

Alaska

- *cyberspace:* state.ak.us
- *earth place:* AK
- *review:* Includes legislative information. Other sources include Touch N' Go Systems, Inc. (http://www.touchngo.com/sp/spindex.htm), and the Alaska State Court Law Library (http://www.alaska.net/~akctlib/).
- *practice areas:* Alaska

Arizona

- *cyberspace:* state.az.us
- *earth place:* AZ
- *review:* Includes legislative information and Arizona Court of Appeals decisions.
- *practice areas:* Arizona

Arkansas

- *cyberspace:* state.ar.us
- *earth place:* AR
- *review:* Includes legislative information and Arkansas Supreme Court opinions.
- *practice areas:* Arkansas

California

- *cyberspace:* ca.gov
- *earth place:* Sacramento, CA
- *born on:* 12 Oct 1989 (visionary)

- *review:* Quick and easy access to California laws and codes. Other sources include CalLaw (http://www.callaw.com/), JuriSearch (http://www.unilegal.com/), and Netlaw Libraries, Inc. (http://www.netlawlibraries.com/).

- *practice areas:* California

Colorado

- *cyberspace:* state.co.us
- *earth place:* CO
- *review:* Includes legislative information and Colorado court cases.
- *practice areas:* Colorado

Connecticut

- *cyberspace:* state.ct.us
- *earth place:* CT
- *review:* What we like about this site is that the major areas of the site are defined and briefly described—in short, easy-to-read paragraphs—on the home page. This helps eliminate guess work from your browsing.
- *practice areas:* Connecticut

Delaware

- *cyberspace:* state.de.us
- *earth place:* DE
- *review:* Includes legislative information.
- *practice areas:* Delaware

Florida

- *cyberspace:* state.fl.us
- *earth place:* FL
- *review:* This site, the Florida Communities Network (FCN), has won lots of awards, and it

WWW

World Wide Web. A hypertext software program that allows users on one computer (the Web client/browser) to connect to another computer (the Web server) for the purpose of viewing files or connecting to other Web servers. The Web is easier to demonstrate than to describe. By allowing one Web server to connect to another, the Web allows users to look at files from Web servers all over the world—so once you have connected to one Web server, you can (theoretically) connect to them all. The main difference between Gopher and the Web is that Gopher uses text-based menus while the Web uses text and graphics-based hypertext pages. The Web is used to describe both the software programs (Web clients, called browsers; and Web servers) and the virtual information space that they create. The Web is only one of the many programs that run on the Internet, but lately "The World Wide Web" or simply "The Web" has been used interchangeable with "The Internet."

does have good useful content. But we spent a long time trying to figure out exactly what the FCN is—and who runs it. Is this the official site of the state of Florida? Every site should answer the basic reporter questions (who, what, where, when, how) up front.

- *practice areas:* Florida

Georgia

- *cyberspace:* state.ga.us
- *earth place:* GA
- *review:* Includes legislative info and Georgia Supreme Court cases.
- *practice areas:* Georgia

Hawaii

- *cyberspace:* hawaii.gov
- *earth place:* HI
- *born on:* 27 Jan 1989 (visionary)
- *practice areas:* Hawaii

Idaho

- *cyberspace:* state.id.us
- *earth place:* ID
- *review:* Includes legislative information and Idaho court opinions.
- *practice areas:* Idaho

Illinois

- *cyberspace:* state.il.us
- *earth place:* IL
- *review:* Includes Illinois court cases (http://www.state.il.us/court/), but the URL does not appear on the home page!
- *practice areas:* Illinois

Indiana

- *cyberspace:* state.in.us
- *earth place:* IN
- *review:* Includes legislative information and Indiana court cases.
- *practice areas:* Indiana

Iowa

- *cyberspace:* state.ia.us
- *earth place:* IA
- *review:* Includes legislative information.
- *practice areas:* Iowa

Kansas

- *cyberspace:* state.ks.us
- *earth place:* KS
- *review:* Includes legislative information and Kansas court cases.
- *practice areas:* Kansas

Kentucky

- *cyberspace:* state.ky.us
- *earth place:* KY
- *practice areas:* Kentucky

Louisiana

- *cyberspace:* state.la.us
- *earth place:* LA
- *review:* Includes legislative information and Louisiana court opinions.
- *practice areas:* Louisiana

Maine

- *cyberspace:* state.me.us
- *earth place:* ME
- *review:* Includes legislative information and Maine court cases.
- *practice areas:* Maine

Maryland

- *cyberspace:* state.md.us
- *earth place:* MD

Yahoo Maps
(http://maps.yahoo.com/yahoo/)
Ever wanted to know how to get from point A to point B? Or maybe you need to know how many miles away a particular site is. In either case, use Yahoo Maps, a private-label service from Vicinity Corp. Enter in two cities, or for more precise info, two street addresses, and Yahoo will tell you how to get from one to the other. Beware: Sometimes recent construction and road diversions are not included!

- *review:* Includes legislative information.
- *practice areas:* Maryland

Massachusetts

- *cyberspace:* state.ma.us
- *earth place:* MA
- *review:* Includes legislative information. Other sources include the Social Law Library (http://www.socialaw.com/).
- *practice areas:* Massachusetts

Michigan

- *cyberspace:* state.mi.us
- *earth place:* MI
- *practice areas:* Michigan

Minnesota

- *cyberspace:* state.mn.us
- *earth place:* MN
- *review:* Includes legislative information and Minnesota court cases. Other sources include Finance and Commerce (http://www .finance-commerce.com/).
- *practice areas:* Minnesota

Mississippi

- *cyberspace:* state.ms.us
- *earth place:* MS
- *review:* Includes legislative information and Mississippi court cases with a very mature search interface.
- *practice areas:* Mississippi

Missouri

- *cyberspace:* state.mo.us
- *earth place:* MO
- *review:* Includes legislative information and Missouri court cases.
- *practice areas:* Missouri

Montana

- *cyberspace:* mt.gov
- *earth place:* Helena, MT
- *born on:* 02 Jun 1992 (visionary)
- *review:* Includes legislative information.
- *practice areas:* Montana

Nebraska

- *cyberspace:* state.ne.us
- *earth place:* NE
- *review:* Includes legislative information. Other sources include Nebrask@ Online (**http://www.nol.org/**).
- *practice areas:* Nebraska

Nevada

- *cyberspace:* state.nv.us
- *earth place:* NV
- *review:* Includes legislative information.
- *practice areas:* Nevada

New Hampshire

- *cyberspace:* state.nh.us
- *earth place:* NH
- *review:* Here is a prime example of how state Web sites cater to different audiences. The home page contains links to the state lottery and liquor commission. Can you say "live free or die"?
- *practice areas:* New Hampshire

New Jersey

- *cyberspace:* state.nj.us
- *earth place:* NJ
- *practice areas:* New Jersey

New Mexico

- *cyberspace:* state.nm.us
- *earth place:* NM

- *review:* Includes legislative information.
- *practice areas:* New Mexico

New York

- *cyberspace:* state.ny.us
- *earth place:* NY
- *review:* There is also a state government page that is very poorly organized, but with a little work (and the simple "find" feature built into most browsers) you can find what you're looking for. Other sources include the New York State Unified Court System (http://ucs.ljx.com/).
- *practice areas:* New York

North Carolina

- *cyberspace:* state.nc.us
- *earth place:* NC
- *practice areas:* North Carolina

North Dakota

- *cyberspace:* state.nd.us
- *earth place:* ND
- *practice areas:* North Dakota

Ohio

- *cyberspace:* ohio.gov
- *earth place:* Columbus, OH
- *born on:* 05 Apr 1991 (visionary)
- *practice areas:* Ohio

Oklahoma

- *cyberspace:* state.ok.us
- *earth place:* OK
- *practice areas:* Oklahoma

Oregon

- *cyberspace:* state.or.us
- *earth place:* OR

- *review:* One click on "Government" and we immediately found the Oregon Revised Statutes. This site is organized simply and functionally. And the home page graphics are beautiful.
- *practice areas:* Oregon

Pennsylvania
- *cyberspace:* state.pa.us
- *earth place:* PA
- *practice areas:* Pennsylvania

Rhode Island
- *cyberspace:* state.ri.us
- *earth place:* RI
- *practice areas:* Rhode Island

South Carolina
- *cyberspace:* state.sc.us
- *earth place:* SC
- *practice areas:* South Carolina

South Dakota
- *cyberspace:* state.sd.us
- *earth place:* SD
- *practice areas:* South Dakota

Tennessee
- *cyberspace:* state.tn.us
- *earth place:* TN
- *practice areas:* Tennessee

Texas
- *cyberspace:* texas.gov
- *earth place:* TX
- *born on:* 23 May 1990 (visionary)

yellow pages
BigBook's Web site (http://www.bigbook
.com/) is a business directory based on the yellow pages model. More precisely, BigBook is yellow pages with an attitude. Their Web site says, for example, "We're not too fond of monopolies. That's how consumers end up with just one Yellow Pages directory." You can include your business in BigBook for free; their Web site is 100-percent advertiser supported. Future BigBook innovations may make you forget that the Yellow Pages were ever paper-based.

zip codes
See **USPS Zip Code Finder.**

- *review:* Texas takes a different approach from most, putting lots of links to subdirectories on the site's home page. The approach is similar to Connecticut's and works just as well. Includes legislative information.
- *practice areas:* Texas

Utah

- *cyberspace:* state.ut.us
- *earth place:* UT
- *review:* Utah obviously takes the design of its Web site very seriously. The design from the opening graphics to the interface is professionally produced with the user in mind. The feedback page, for example, is not merely a form; it guides the user through the process. On the home page, users immediately learn that the Utah law (http://www.utcourts.gov/) is online. And we love the name of their search engine: YeeHaw!
- *practice areas:* Utah

Vermont

- *cyberspace:* state.vt.us
- *earth place:* VT
- *practice areas:* Vermont

Virginia

- *cyberspace:* state.va.us
- *earth place:* VA
- *review:* The home page employs an eye-catching postcard-like motif. And the "quick index" is a useful site navigation tool.
- *practice areas:* Virginia

Washington

- *cyberspace:* state.wa.us
- *earth place:* WA
- *practice areas:* Washington

West Virginia

- *cyberspace:* state.wv.us
- *earth place:* WV
- *practice areas:* West Virginia

Wisconsin

- *cyberspace:* state.wi.us
- *earth place:* WI
- *practice areas:* Wisconsin

Wyoming

- *cyberspace:* state.wy.us
- *earth place:* WY
- *practice areas:* Wyoming

Index by Chapter

Federal Law Organizations

Law Firms

Law Journals

Law Schools

State Law Organizations

Index by Practice Area

Selected Books From . . .
THE LAW PRACTICE MANAGEMENT SECTION

ABA Guide to Lawyer Trust Accounts. This book deals with how lawyers should manage trust accounts to comply with ethical & statutory requirements.

ABA Guide to Professional Managers in the Law Office. This book shows how professional management can and does work. It shows lawyers how to practice more efficiently by delegating management tasks to professional managers.

Billing Innovations. This book examines how innovative fee arrangements and your approach toward billing can deeply affect the attorney-client relationship. It also explains how billing and pricing are absolutely intertwined with strategic planning, maintaining quality of services, marketing, instituting a compensation system, and firm governance.

Changing Jobs, 2nd Ed. A handbook designed to help lawyers make changes in their professional careers. Includes career planning advice from nearly 50 experts.

Compensation Plans for Law Firms, 2nd Ed. This second edition discusses the basics for a fair and simple compensation system for partners, of counsel, associates, paralegals, and staff.

Computer-Assisted Legal Research: A Guide to Successful Online Searching. Covers the fundamentals of LEXIS®-NEXIS® and WESTLAW®, including practical information such as: logging on and off; formulating your search; reviewing results; modifying a query; using special features; downloading documents.

Connecting with Your Client. Written by a psychologist, therapist, and legal consultant, this book presents communications techniques that will help ensure client cooperation and satisfaction.

Do-It-Yourself Public Relations. A hands-on guide for lawyers with public relations ideas, sample letters and forms. The book includes a diskette that includes model letters to the press that have paid off in news stories and media attention.

Finding the Right Lawyer. This guide answers the questions people should ask when searching for legal counsel. It includes a glossary of legal specialties and the ten questions you should ask a lawyer before hiring.

Flying Solo: A Survival Guide for the Solo Lawyer, 2nd ed. An updated and expanded guide to the problems and issues unique to the solo practitioner.

How to Draft Bills Clients Rush to Pay. A collection of techniques for drafting bills that project honesty, competence, fairness and value.

How to Start and Build a Law Practice, 3rd ed. Jay Foonberg's classic guide has been updated and expanded. Included are more than 10 new chapters on marketing, financing, automation, practicing from home, ethics and professional responsibility.

Visit our Web site:
http//www.abanet.org/lpm/catalog

To order: Call Toll-Free 1-800-285-2221

Law Office Policy and Procedures Manual, 3rd Ed. Provides a model for law office policies and procedures. It covers law office organization, management, personnel policies, financial management, technology, and communications systems. Includes diskette.

The Lawyer's Guide to Creating Web Pages. A practical guide that clearly explains HTML, covers how to design a Web site, and introduces Web-authoring tools.

The Lawyer's Guide to the Internet. A guide to what the Internet is (and isn't), how it applies to the legal profession, and the different ways it can -- and should -- be used.

The Lawyer's Guide to Marketing on the Internet. This book talks about the pluses and minuses of marketing on the Internet, as well as how to develop an Internet marketing plan.

The Lawyer's Quick Guide to Microsoft® Internet Explorer; The Lawyer's Quick Guide to Netscape® Navigator. These two guides offer special introductory instructions on the most popular Internet browsers. Four quick and easy lessons including: Basic Navigation, Setting a Bookmark, Browsing with a Purpose, Keeping What You Find.

The Lawyer's Quick Guide to WordPerfect® 7.0/8.0 for Windows®. This easy-to-use guide offers lessons on multitasking, entering and editing text, formatting letters, creating briefs, and more. Perfect for training, this book includes a diskette with practice exercises and word templates.

Leaders' Digest: A Review of the Best Books on Leadership. This book will help you find the best books on leadership to help you achieve extraordinary and exceptional leadership skills.

Living with the Law: Strategies to Avoid Burnout and Create Balance. This multi-author book is intended to help lawyers manage stress, make the practice of law more satisfying, and improve client service.

Practicing Law Without Clients: Making a Living as a Freelance Lawyer. This book describes the freelance legal researching, writing, and consulting opportunities that are available to lawyers.

Running a Law Practice on a Shoestring. Targeted to the solo or small firm lawyer, this book offers a crash course in successful entrepreneurship. Features money-saving tips on office space, computer equipment, travel, furniture, staffing, and more.

Survival Guide for Road Warriors. A guide to using a notebook computer and combinations of equipment and technology so lawyers can be effective in their office, on the road, in the courtroom or at home.

Through the Client's Eyes. Includes an overview of client relations and sample letters, surveys, and self-assessment questions to gauge your client relations acumen.

Women Rainmakers' 101+ Best Marketing Tips. A collection of over 130 marketing tips suggested by women rainmakers throughout the country. Includes tips on image, networking, public relations, and advertising.

Order Form

Qty	Title	LPM Price	Regular Price	Total
_____	ABA Guide to Lawyer Trust Accounts (5110374)	$ 69.95	$ 79.95	$_____
_____	ABA Guide to Prof. Managers in the Law Office (5110373)	69.95	79.95	$_____
_____	Billing Innovations (5110366)	124.95	144.95	$_____
_____	Changing Jobs, 2nd Ed. (5110334)	49.95	59.95	$_____
_____	Compensation Plans for Lawyers, 2nd Ed. (5110353)	69.95	79.95	$_____
_____	Computer-Assisted Legal Research (5110388)	69.95	79.95	$_____
_____	Connecting with Your Client (5110378)	54.95	64.95	$_____
_____	Do-It-Yourself Public Relations (5110352)	69.95	79.95	$_____
_____	Finding the Right Lawyer (5110339)	19.95	19.95	$_____
_____	Flying Solo, 2nd Ed. (5110328)	59.95	69.95	$_____
_____	How to Draft Bills Clients Rush to Pay (5110344)	39.95	49.95	$_____
_____	How to Start & Build a Law Practice, 3rd Ed. (5110293)	32.95	39.95	$_____
_____	Law Office Policy & Procedures Manual (5110375)	99.95	109.95	$_____
_____	Lawyer's Guide to Creating Web Pages (5110383)	54.95	64.95	$_____
_____	Lawyer's Guide to the Internet (5110343)	24.95	29.95	$_____
_____	Lawyer's Guide to Marketing on the Internet (5110371)	54.95	64.95	$_____
_____	Lawyer's Quick Guide to Microsoft Internet® Explorer (5110392)	24.95	29.95	$_____
_____	Lawyer's Quick Guide to Netscape® Navigator (5110384)	24.95	29.95	$_____
_____	Lawyer's Quick Guide to WordPerfect® 7.0/8.0 (5110395)	34.95	39.95	$_____
_____	Leaders' Digest (5110356)	49.95	59.95	$_____
_____	Living with the Law (5110379)	59.95	69.95	$_____
_____	Practicing Law Without Clients (5110376)	49.95	59.95	$_____
_____	Running a Law Practice on a Shoestring (5110387)	39.95	49.95	$_____
_____	Survival Guide for Road Warriors (5110362)	24.95	29.95	$_____
_____	Through the Client's Eyes (5110337)	69.95	79.95	$_____
_____	Women Rainmakers' 101+ Best Marketing Tips (5110336)	14.95	19.95	$_____

*HANDLING	**TAX		
$10.00-$24.99 ... $3.95	DC residents add 5.75%	SUBTOTAL:	$_____
$25.00-$49.99 ... $4.95	IL residents add 8.75%	*HANDLING:	$_____
$50.00+ $5.95	MD residents add 5%	**TAX:	$_____
		TOTAL:	$_____

PAYMENT

☐ Check enclosed (to the ABA)   ☐ Bill Me

☐ Visa   ☐ MasterCard   ☐ American Express   Account Number:_____

Exp. Date:_____ Signature_____

Name_____

Firm_____

Address_____

City_____ State_____ ZIP_____

Phone number_____

Mail to: ABA Publication Orders   **Phone:**   (800) 285-2221   **Fax:** (312) 988-5568
P.O. Box 10892
Chicago, IL 60610-0892   **World Wide Web:** http//www.abanet.org/lpm/catalog
Email: abasvcctr@abanet.org

THE SECTION OF
LAW PRACTICE
MANAGEMENT

CUSTOMER COMMENT FORM

Title of Book: _____

We've tried to make this publication as useful, accurate, and readable as possible. Please take 5 minutes to tell us if we succeeded. Your comments and suggestions will help us improve our publications. Thank you!

1. How did you acquire this publication:

☐ by mail order   ☐ at a meeting/convention   ☐ as a gift

☐ by phone order   ☐ at a bookstore   ☐ don't know

☐ other: (describe) _____

Please rate this publication as follows:

	Excellent	Good	Fair	Poor	Not Applicable
Readability: Was the book easy to read and understand?	☐	☐	☐	☐	☐
Examples/Cases: Were they helpful, practical? Were there enough?	☐	☐	☐	☐	☐
Content: Did the book meet your expectations? Did it cover the subject adequately?	☐	☐	☐	☐	☐
Organization and clarity: Was the sequence of text logical? Was it easy to find what you wanted to know?	☐	☐	☐	☐	☐
Illustrations/forms/checklists: Were they clear and useful? Were there enough?	☐	☐	☐	☐	☐
Physical attractiveness: What did you think of the appearance of the publication (typesetting, printing, etc.)?	☐	☐	☐	☐	☐

Would you recommend this book to another attorney/administrator? ☐ Yes ☐ No

How could this publication be improved? What else would you like to see in it?

_____

_____

_____

Do you have other comments or suggestions? _____

_____

_____

Name _____

Firm/Company _____

Address _____

City/State/Zip _____

Phone _____

Firm Size: _____ Area of specialization: _____

We appreciate your time and help.

Fold

BUSINESS REPLY MAIL

FIRST CLASS   PERMIT NO. 16471   CHICAGO, ILLINOIS

POSTAGE WILL BE PAID BY ADDRESSEE

AMERICAN BAR ASSOCIATION
PPM, 8th FLOOR
750 N. LAKE SHORE DRIVE
CHICAGO, ILLINOIS 60611–9851

Fold

AMERICAN BAR ASSOCIATION

Membership Application

 Law Practice Management Section

Access to all these information resources and discounts – for just $3.33 a month!

Membership dues are just $40 a year – just $3.33 a month.
You probably spend more on your general business magazines and newspapers.
But they can't help you succeed in building and managing your practice
like a membership in the ABA Law Practice Management Section.
Make a small investment in success. Join today!

☑ **Yes!** I want to join the ABA Section of Law Practice Management Section and gain access to information helping me add more clients, retain and expand business with current clients, and run my law practice more efficiently and competitively!

Check the dues that apply to you:

❑ $40 for ABA members   ❑ $5 for ABA Law Student Division members

Choose your method of payment:

❑ Check enclosed (make payable to American Bar Association)
❑ Bill me
❑ Charge to my: ❑ VISA®   ❑ MASTERCARD®   ❑ AMEX®

Card No.: _____   Exp. Date: _____

Signature: _____   Date: _____

ABA I.D.*: _____
　　　　　(* *Please note: Membership in ABA is a prerequisite to enroll in ABA Sections.*)

Name: _____

Firm/Organization: _____

Address: _____

City/State/ZIP: _____

Telephone No.: _____   Fax No.: _____

Primary Email Address: _____

Get Ahead. 🏃

 AMERICAN BAR ASSOCIATION Law Practice Management Section

Save time by Faxing or Phoning!

▶ Fax your application to: (312) 988-5820
▶ Join by phone if using a credit card: (800) 285-2221 (ABA1)
▶ Email us for more information at: lpm@abanet.org
▶ Check us out on the Internet: http://www.abanet.org/lpm

750 N. LAKE SHORE DRIVE
CHICAGO, IL 60611
PHONE: (312) 988-5619
FAX: (312) 988-5820
Email: lpm@abanet.org

I understand that Section dues include a $24 basic subscription to Law Practice Management; this subscription charge is not deductible from the dues and additional subscriptions are not available at this rate. Membership dues in the American Bar Association are not deductible as charitable contributions for income tax purposes. However, such dues may be deductible as a business expense.